'This book does "what it says on the tin": it introduces students to the fundamentals of British politics. It does so without compromising on historical context or failing to mention the key debates in each topic. I recommend it to any student looking for a short but wide-ranging book to give them a thorough grounding in British politics.' - *Professor Daniel Stevens, University of Exeter, UK*

'Bill Jones has produced another clear and concise introductory text on British politics. Whilst condensed, this text provides a coherent foundation of knowledge of the discipline and, as such, promises to be a popular choice amongst undergraduate students in particular.' - *Dr Oliver Harrison, Nottingham Trent University, UK*

BRITISH POLITICS

THE BASICS

Over the last two decades British politics has undergone a remarkable transformation. While some components of the system have been eroded, such as voter turnout and membership of the big parties, other parts have flourished, such as nationalist parties, the insurgent UKIP, as well as the new media.

British Politics: The Basics analyses these changes and places them within the context of the evolution of British society from absolute monarchy to representative democracy. It considers each of the major components of British politics, such as the monarchy and the House of Lords, the Commons, voting behaviour, parties and pressure groups, the prime minister and cabinet, devolution, local government, and foreign policy. Its contents include coverage of recent events such as the Scottish Referendum and the 2015 General Election.

This readable and comprehensive introduction will be of key interest to A-level students, undergraduates and those new to the study of British politics.

Bill Jones was formerly Director of Extra-Mural Studies at Manchester University 1986–91, Professor of Politics and History at Liverpool Hope University, UK, and is now Senior Honorary Research Fellow at the same university.

THE BASICS

BRITISH POLITICS

THE BASICS

BILL JONES

Routledge
Taylor & Francis Group

LONDON AND NEW YORK

First published 2016
by Routledge
2 Park Square, Milton Park, Abingdon, Oxon OX14 4RN

and by Routledge
711 Third Avenue, New York, NY 10017

Routledge is an imprint of the Taylor & Francis Group, an informa business

British Library Cataloguing in Publication Data
A catalogue record for this book is available from the British Library

Library of Congress Cataloging in Publication Data
Names: Jones, Bill, 1946- author.
Title: British politics: the basics / Bill Jones.
Description: New York, NY: Routledge, 2016. | Series: The basics
Identifiers: LCCN 2015025878 | ISBN 9780415835695 (hbk) | ISBN
    9780415835718 (pbk.) | ISBN 9781315651316 (ebook)
Subjects: LCSH: Great Britain—Politics and government—21st century.
Classification: LCC JN238. J66 2016 | DDC 320.441—dc23
LC record available at http://lccn.loc.gov/2015025878

ISBN: 978-0-415-83569-5 (hbk)
ISBN: 978-0-415-83571-8 (pbk)
ISBN: 978-1-315-65131-6 (ebk)

Typeset in Bembo
by Swales & Willis Ltd, Exeter, Devon, UK

To Carolyn and former students at Liverpool Hope University.

CONTENTS

PREFACE AND ACKNOWLEDGEMENTS

Over the last two decades British politics has undergone an amazing transformation. While some parts of the system have atrophied – turnout at elections, membership of the big parties – other parts have flourished: nationalist parties and the insurgent UKIP, plus the new media.

This book aims to analyse these changes within the context of British society and the British economy, sketching in the extraordinary millennium-long evolution of its polity, from absolute monarchy to representative democracy: a template for the world.

It considers the system's major components: the unwritten constitution, the monarchy and House of Lords, voting behaviour, the Commons, political ideas, parties and pressure groups, prime minister and cabinet, ministers and departments, devolution, the mass media, local government and British relations with the rest of the world.

The book began its life, to some extent, with an earlier publisher, Manchester University Press, in 2010. In 2013 a transfer of the project took place to Routledge when it was decided to 'customise' it for the popular Basics Series. This process resembled the pouring of two pints into a pint pot, as the original book was considerably longer. Naturally enough, it has been substantially updated to take account of the many political changes which have occurred over the past five years.

I hope it now, in its present form, represents a useful addition to the series and an effective introduction to the social context, underlying ideas, institutions and processes of British politics. It is based on a first-year course I wrote for my undergraduates at Liverpool Hope University but is also intended for students at A-level and for those – media or social worker students for example – who require an understanding of politics for part of their studies.

Part of the slimming-down process for this Basics volume has entailed covering the separate areas of the British political system in a new format, comprising six parts:

1. Introduction, with a first chapter providing an overview of the system and another then outlining its historical evolution
2. The political context, with three chapters, on political culture, the social and economic context and the unwritten constitution
3. Mediating agencies – political parties, pressure groups and the mass media
4. The legislature – the monarchy, the House of Lords, voting behaviour and the House of Commons
5. The executive – prime minister and cabinet, ministers and civil servants and policy-making
6. Sub-national government – devolution, local government, the judiciary.

I have tried to embody all the recent developments in British politics, including the Scottish independence referendum of 2014, the rise and rise of UKIP, the 2015 general election, Tory problems with its Euro-sceptical wing and Labour's problematic leadership, including the election of Jeremy Corbyn in September 2015. A short glossary is provided at the end of the book, which includes some key terms that are not necessarily fully explained elsewhere in the text. Each chapter ends with a few questions for discussion and a short reading list. A comprehensive bibliography is given at the back of the book.

Warm thanks are due to Tony Mason at Manchester University Press for allowing me to draw on content from the original work. Also to Andrew Taylor at Routledge, who has nursed this project along with skill, judgement and considerable care. As at MUP, I was fortunate to have the services of a first-class copy-editor, Ralph Footring; my warmest thanks to him for contributions, as usual, well beyond the mere call of duty. I would also like to thank successive years of my students at Liverpool Hope University 2007–14. I hope this little book provides a good comprehensive yet accessible summary and that it will help inform another younger generation of voters. Finally, I must thank my wife, Carolyn, for the help and support in writing this book which she unstintingly gives in all aspects of my life.

Bill Jones
Beverley, 2016

1

INTRODUCTION

THE EVOLUTION OF THE BRITISH POLITICAL SYSTEM

The British political system is the product of an extraordinary evolution, from Anglo-Saxon times to the twentieth century, when our present structure essentially emerged. From absolute monarchy to representative democracy in a millennium and a half would not be too bad an approximation of the transition involved. The history and ancient nature of this process tell us the British are a conservative people, slow to change and keen to hang on, even with a degree of nostalgia, to outdated symbols of our monarchical past, like the annual opening of Parliament and the ceremony attending the Queen's Speech.

THE WITAN

The story begins with the Anglo-Saxon Witangemot – or Witan – itself probably related to the German assemblies or *folkmoots* from whence our islands' then immigrant inhabitants originated. This King's Council, comprising the most powerful people in the kingdom, including senior clergy, was very much the creature of the monarch. He decided on its composition; it was summoned at his command, he presided over its proceedings and it was dismissed by him as well. It also has to be realised that in a disunited land, there was more than one Witan.

But the Witans did accrete to themselves certain important functions. While the Witan usually had little influence on royal succession, it did issue a formal approval of a new monarch. In 1013 Aethelread was called back from exile by the Witan and re-established as monarch after the death of the Danish King, Sweyn Forkbeard. The Witan also proffered advice to the King and the King was expected to listen respectfully to its views on taxation and what laws should be passed. But this tradition of seeking the Witan's advice on revenue and the law, as well as *legitimation* of the succession, was the crucible of what later matured into democratic parliamentary government.

CURIA REGIS

The Normans' eleventh-century invasion destroyed much of the Anglo-Saxon heritage but their own 'King's Council', the *Curia Regis*, effectively continued the tradition of the Witan and, indeed, strengthened it, coming to deal with all the functions of government, whether law-making (*legislative*), policy implementation (*executive*) or interpretation and enforcement of the law (*judicial*). Crucially it took on two incarnations: a large assembly of all the King's landholders plus his officers, which met when summoned; and a smaller version in permanent session, which included his chief officers of the state, or, if we prefer, his *ministers*. This smaller curia, was in effect the King's *court*, which was not static but moved around the kingdom with him. So here we see the embryo of the King's *government* or executive and, in its wider form, of *parliament*.

LORDS AND COMMONS MEET SEPARATELY

At the time of Magna Carta, when the nobles forced King John to moderate his rule, he agreed to expand his council to include more ordinary people or *commoners*, though in practice they were drawn from the landed gentry, business people and lawyers. Representatives were drawn from the shires and the centres of population, and eventually this entailed some form of election. During the fourteenth century this speaking assembly, or 'parliament', began to meet separately: the nobility in what became known as the *House Lords* and the commoners in the *House of Commons*. King John had also been obliged to submit his proposals for taxation to this parliament and, over time, it became the lower house which acquired precedence in this respect. This ability to control the source and extent of the nation's finances was the crucial lever used by parliament to extract recognised rights regarding its powers and functions.

PARLIAMENT'S AUTHORITY INCREASES

The Hundred Year War was substantially funded by grants from parliament and its authority grew in consequence. Its power increased still more when Henry VIII used it to legitimise his break from Rome, his establishment of a separate church and his looting of the monasteries. Henry was still, however, in the sixteenth century, the very image of the absolute monarch, able to oversee and command every aspect of his 1000-strong court, served by brilliant commoners like Thomas Wolsey (father a butcher) and Thomas Cromwell (father a blacksmith); and he was able to pick and choose wives from his court (even when they were already married) as well as frame them and others who had lost his favour (like the afore-mentioned Cromwell) in order to execute them. However, after the reign of Elizabeth I the power of the monarch began to wane. Charles I, denied much-needed funds by parliament, tried to rule without it, resulting in the so-called Long Parliament, when he refused to convene it after 1640 (it finally came to an end long after the Civil War – in 1660).

CIVIL WAR, 1640–49

It now seems remarkable that it happened, but a parliament with a powerful sense of grievance, and led by the extraordinary Oliver Cromwell, rose up against Charles, raised and trained its own army and defeated the serried ranks of royal cavaliers and their professional troops. Some aristocrats sided with parliament, though most stayed true to their class and supported the King against what has been described as a kind of middle-class revolution. Having been defeated in the first Civil War (1642–45), the King escaped to lead another charge at parliament's forces (1648–49); after a second defeat he was tried for treason and beheaded January 1649.

IDEAS AND CIVIL WAR, 1642–49

Political ideas about government seemed to polarise during the Civil War. Charles sought to adduce the merits of 'absolute monarchy' on the grounds that the King was appointed by God and therefore was beyond criticism or any judgement by mere parliamentary mortals. For their part, the multifaceted forces arrayed against him allowed their thoughts to embrace a wide range of alternative forms of government and society at the 1647 *Putney Debates*. The *Levellers* movement, for instance, sought: popular sovereignty, one man one vote, equality before the law and tolerance of differing religious beliefs. Cromwell and his army supporters balked at such radicalism and suppressed these flights of fancy, yet it is possible to discern the first emergence at this time of the ideas which later created the representative democracy which has governed Britain since the early twentieth century.

GLORIOUS REVOLUTION, 1688–89

The restored monarchy discovered it was very much *not* business as usual. The monarchy had been bested by a body with some claim to represent the country and from now on monarchs ignored public sentiment at their peril. Consequently, the attempts of James II to introduce Catholicism to what was now, largely, a Protestant nation repelled the political class in his own country. William of Orange was approached by seven leading politicians – Whig and Tory – and invited to overthrow his father-in-law. This was an astonishing act of treason from one point of view, but it is always the victors who write the history and, in 1689, William proceeded to become such a person, and with the minimum of bloodshed. On 11 April 1689, William and his wife, Mary, were crowned King and Queen, but they had accepted the Declaration of Rights, subsequently embodied in the Bill of Rights, which effectively gave parliament the final say in making the law of the land. The historic importance of this 'Glorious' revolution is that it opened the door to genuine democratic government through a generally – though imperfect – representative parliamentary assembly.

THE HANOVERIAN DYNASTY

As Queen Anne had no heir, a great-grandson of William I was invited – a second imported monarch – to rule Britain, in addition to his native Hanover. While he preferred his homeland to these damp shores and never really learnt the language, his dynasty dominated the century, with his son and grandson becoming George II and George III, respectively. George I was happy to leave governing to his ministers, all of whom were Members of Parliament.

THE FIRST PRIME MINISTER

George I communicated with his committee of ministers, or cabinet, as it had come to be called, via the most senior finance minister. For a long time this key intermediary was the First Lord of the Treasury, Robert Walpole: initially called the first 'prime minister', with an irony destined soon to disappear as Walpole came to dominate the mid-eighteenth-century government of the country. He was followed by a number of exceptional talents, especially Pitt the Elder and his son, Pitt the Younger, who became prime minister in 1783 at the astonishingly early age of twenty-four.

POLITICAL PARTIES

Inevitably, if a large number of people in an assembly hold substantial power, they will seek to group together the better to win votes. In the eighteenth century, the two main groupings were the Whigs and the Tories.

THE WHIGS

This group was formed in the late seventeenth century, when it resisted the Catholicism of James II, but became associated thereupon with Nonconformity, the industrial interest and reform. They dominated during the century via the so-called Whig 'junto', which lasted until the Tories took the lead under Pitt the Younger. The Whigs went on to form the basis of the Liberal Party in the nineteenth century.

THE TORIES

This group supported James II after 1680. Although they accepted the Glorious Revolution, they then supported the 'Jacobite' 'Pretenders' to the throne; as a result, they stayed out of power until the reign of George III.

PATRONAGE

This was a crucial means of controlling power in the eighteenth century; it was used by the aristocracy and the monarch to control personnel in the Commons and to reward supporters from all walks of life. The monarch owned over 100 offices, as well as many sinecures, pensions and contracts – monarchs could therefore deploy their largesse in such a way as to advance their own policies. The large landowners used their power of appointment to help determine who sat in the Commons via the 'rotten boroughs' and 'pocket boroughs' that were in their gift.

THE ENLIGHTENMENT

The twentieth-century philosopher and historian Bertrand Russell argued that Descartes initiated this intellectual movement in Europe in the seventeenth century with his individualistic assertion that 'I think, therefore I am': a tacit rebuttal of the religious and feudal ideas of his age. The ferment of ideas called the Enlightenment which swept through Europe in the eighteenth century arguably began in the late seventeenth century in Britain with the advance of science: Isaac

Newton and thinkers like Thomas Hobbes. Essentially, Enlightenment thinkers applied the tests of reason and humanity to existing social, economic and political conditions and came up with answers fundamentally challenging traditional assumptions about religion, the role of the individual and relationships between state and citizen.

In France, Voltaire flayed the *ancien régime* with his wit and rational critiques; his works and those of similar writers affected the intellectual atmosphere in which all political activity took place. Freedom of speech and movement, tolerance of differing views and beliefs, the sanctity of the individual and the reality of people's basic rights plus the obligations of the state to the citizen were all ideas picked up and applied in Britain by the likes of John Locke, Adam Smith, David Hume and Tom Paine. Baron Montesquieu, the French Enlightenment thinker, contributed the idea of the 'separation of powers': the idea that the three functions of government – legislative, judicial and executive (making laws, interpreting laws and implementing them, respectively) – should be embodied in separate institutions, thus balancing each other's power and preventing tyranny by any single centre.

Meanwhile, across the Atlantic the framers of the US constitution produced their classic Enlightenment document – the American constitution built around the same notion of the separation of powers. All this ferment of ideas and activity created a sense in which the British form of government, already praised for its emphasis on liberty, was ripe for further reform.

THE INFLUENCE OF THE FRENCH REVOLUTION, 1789

Events in France had a huge impact on encouraging reform and a movement for democracy throughout Europe.

Bliss it was . . . to be alive,
But to be young was very Heaven.

So wrote the young poet William Wordsworth (*The Prelude*, 1805) of the French Revolution, which began in 1789. While the course of the Revolution took much of the passion out of the reform movement, 'liberty, equality and fraternity' were ideas which, thanks to the likes of Tom Paine, crossed the Channel. Such thinkers helped to advance the idea that individual citizens had the right to help determine how they were governed, rather than by a hereditary monarchy or by religious ideas. In the aftermath of the French Revolution, dissatisfaction grew at the need for constitutional reform in Britain. Henry 'Orator' Hunt was just one of the radical voices causing a stir among the working classes in the aftermath of the Napoleonic Wars. In August 1819 he headed up to Manchester to give a speech now immortalised in history.

THE PETERLOO MASSACRE

This famous event occurred when Hunt addressed 60,000 people assembled to support the idea that the new industrial towns should be granted representation by MPs. As Martin Wainwright wrote in *The Guardian* on the 188th anniversary of the event (13 August 2007):

> Less than 2% of the population had the vote at the time, and resentment was sharpened by 'rotten boroughs' such as the moribund Wiltshire village of Old Sarum which had 11 voters and two MPs. Manchester, Leeds and Liverpool had none. Plans to elect a 'shadow parliament' put the wind up the Tory government which was also frightened that the power of Henry 'Orator' Hunt, the main speaker at Peterloo, might turn the Manchester crowd into a mob. The local volunteer yeomanry, described as 'younger members of the Tory party in arms', was ordered to disperse the meeting, with fatal results.

However, the 11 deaths were not in vain, as the indignation generated by the massacre led directly to the formation of the Chartists and fed into the movement for the Great Reform Act.

GREAT REFORM ACT 1832

The government of Lord Liverpool (1812–27) was widely seen as reactionary, seeking to douse possible flames of revolution in

Britain. There were widespread signs of unrest – in Spa Fields and the Peterloo Massacre, for example – and repressive legislation like the so-called 'Six Acts'. George Canning, who became prime minister in 1827, was a more liberal Tory but was followed by the Duke of Wellington, who considered the British constitution to be 'perfect' and not in need of reform. It was finally Lord Grey's Whig government that passed the Great Reform Act in 1832. Amid threats to create new peers to overcome passionate resistance in the Lords and much popular agitation, the bill was passed, inaugurating the age of democratic government in Britain. The Act did not expand the electorate to much more than half a million out of a population of 14 million – but that was double what it was before – and it did abolish anomalies like 'rotten boroughs' and constituencies, which had virtually no voters but still returned an MP. The system was placed on a new basis and a beginning was made on the road to democracy. The Great Reform Act was followed by further Acts, of 1867, 1884 and 1885, which expanded the electorate to some 5 million voters and achieved a rough correspondence between population and representation throughout the country. Now it was elections that determined the colour of government and not the will of the monarch or the aristocracy. Queen Victoria was not without influence, but the role of the monarch had been reduced effectively to one of ceremonials and symbolism.

POLITICAL PARTIES FROM THE MID NINETEENTH TO THE LATE TWENTIETH CENTURY

CONSERVATIVE PARTY

This emerged from the Tory Party, a name which is still interchangeable with its modern nomenclature. In the wake of the 1832 Act, Robert Peel was active in establishing the basis of the modern party, registering members and drawing up a programme in 1834 – the Tamworth Manifesto. Conservative associations formed at that time are still to be found all over the country. The party represented and advanced the interests of the landed gentry but increasingly came to represent those of industry, commerce and property in general. In the twentieth century, the Tories seemed to be the 'natural party of government', in that they were in office two-thirds of the time, to Labour's one-third. Churchill more or less accepted Labour's changes in the 1950s but when the economy began to decline in the 1960s the Conservatives urged a return to a more 'free market' economy. Edward Heath, Prime Minister 1970–74, did not really deliver such an outcome but he did succeed in negotiating the UK's entry into the European Community, a historic and still controversial decision. By the end of the decade, Margaret Thatcher had become leader and after 1979 she pursued a robust policy of making the British economy competitive again. This entailed allowing traditional and inefficient industries to go bankrupt, confronting and subduing the trade unions and imposing her formidable personality upon her party. By 1990, it had had enough and John Major took over, until his political capital was exhausted as the 1997 election approached.

LIBERAL PARTY

This emerged in the 1860s from an amalgam of the Whigs, the Manchester Radicals and disenchanted Conservatives – often followers of Robert Peel. Its outposts in the country can still be seen in the form of the many 'Reform' and Liberal clubs in towns, cities and countryside. The party tended to speak for the 'newly' rich entrepreneurs, advocating 'classical' free market economics and opposing aggressive foreign policies in favour of encouraging world trade. After periods of power led by the 'Grand Old Man', William Gladstone, the Liberals won a huge landslide victory in 1906. They thereupon enacted historic legislation reforming parliament and laying the foundations of the welfare state.

When World War I broke out, however, Herbert Asquith was found not to be equal to the task and his hugely talented junior, David Lloyd George, the 'Welsh Wizard', took over, going on to become a great war leader. However, Asquith was not happy to be usurped by the younger man and the feud between them caused the party to rupture in the 1920s into two factions, both of which gradually lost support until, by 1950, it had only 12 seats.

LABOUR PARTY

At the end of the nineteenth century, trade unions realised that they could better advance the cause of their members by organising to get representatives directly elected to parliament. In 1900, an embryonic body was established which won seats in the 1906 election and later played a role in government during World War I. By 1924, the party had tasted government via the short minority premiership of Ramsay MacDonald, the illegitimate son of a Scottish crofter. It experienced a second period of government in 1929–31, but then suffered a long period of opposition until its leaders shared power with Winston Churchill in his coalition government during World War II. In 1945, it won a surprise landslide under its leader Clement Attlee, who led the historic post-war government that introduced nationalisation of the key utilities, as well as the welfare state. Labour also ruled in 1964–70 and 1974–79 (under Harold Wilson and James Callaghan), but suffered a long period in opposition until 1997, when Tony Blair won a landslide victory.

LORDS–COMMONS CONFLICT RESOLVED

With the Commons controlling financial decisions and coming to dominate the major debates of the day, it became increasingly difficult for a prime minister to sit in the Lords. The Conservatives, moreover, controlled the majority in that chamber by virtue of the hereditary peers. The conflict was brought to a climax by the Liberal government of 1906, when Lloyd George's challenge to 'Mr Balfour's Poodle' (the Lords) lit the blue touch paper to a massive constitutional battle, which the Lords eventually lost in 1911, when its powers were reduced to that of delay of a bill by 24 months. From now on, no prime minister could sit in the Lords and the number of ministers who could do the same effectively became limited as well. In 1949 the period of delay of a bill was reduced to a single year.

FURTHER LORDS REFORMS

In 1958 life peerages were introduced – serving to revive the energy of a chamber some said was fast becoming moribund – and in 1963 the Peerage Act enabled peers, should they wish, to renounce their titles. In 1999 hereditary peers were banned from sitting in the Lords, apart from a compromise 92 who still remain at the time of writing, as does a comprehensive reform of the second chamber.

PARLIAMENTARY TERMS

In 1715 the Septennial Act was passed, extending the maximum term a parliament could run from three to seven years and, indeed, most of them did run for approximately that period in the eighteenth century. During the nineteenth century, however, the average was four years and the 1911 Parliament Act reduced the maximum to five years. However, prime ministers still wielded the power to call an election when the polls and the economy suggested they might win. In 2011 the Conservative–Liberal Democrat coalition government passed the Fixed Term Parliament Act, which obliges MPs to face re-election every five years on the first Thursday in May of the fifth year after the previous general election; the next election is due in 2020.

VOTES FOR WOMEN

Mary Wollstonecraft wrote a pamphlet in support of women's rights as early as 1792 and John Stuart Mill urged votes for women around the middle of the nineteenth century. But the cause did not progress and it took the militant grouping called the 'suffragettes', under the Pankhursts, to add momentum to the campaign. During World War I, women worked in the war effort and the movement won votes for women aged over 30 in 1918. In 1928, full voting rights were accorded to women.

DEVOLUTION

These major decentralising reforms were made in response to the growth of nationalist movements in Wales and Scotland.

IRELAND

This 'part' of Britain, which the British government had long ruled badly, was partitioned, with six of its north-east counties forming the province of Northern Ireland. It thus effectively received devolution, with a legislative assembly, via the Government of Ireland Act 1920. But the nationalist minority within the province continued the struggle for unification with the Irish Republic and blighted British politics with three decades of 'the Troubles' between Catholics and Protestant communities from the end of the 1960s. Eventually the Good Friday Agreement of 1998 established the basis for the formation of a power-sharing government, which, somewhat belatedly, came into being in 2007.

WALES AND SCOTLAND

In 1998 the Blair government set up the Scottish Parliament and the Welsh Assembly.

EPILOGUE

From being an absolute monarchy at the close of the Dark Ages, British government saw the evolution of an advisory council into a bicameral legislature that assumed much of the monarch's power but paradoxically chose to vest it in the leader of the biggest party elected to the lower house of the legislature. Instead of an 'absolute' monarch, we now arguably have a secular 'president' in the form of the prime minister – certainly when the office was in the hands of Thatcher and Blair. Something which has transformed the way politics is conducted since the inception of democracy is the media, which now permeate and ventilate – for good and ill – every aspect of the system, from elections to appointed quangos.

FURTHER READING

The major textbooks deal with this historical perspective: Jones *et al.* (2013), Kingdom (2013: variously in the first four chapters) and Leach *et al.* (2006: ch. 3).

Black, J. (2000) *Modern British History Since 1900*, Macmillan.
Jones, B. (2004) *The Dictionary of British Politics*, Manchester University Press.
Jones, B., *et al.* (2013) *Politics UK* (8th edition), Pearson (chapter 2).

Kingdom, J. (2013) *Government and Politics in Britain: An Introduction* (3rd edition), Polity.

Leach, R., *et al.* (2006) *British Politics*, Palgrave.

Schama, S. (2002) *A History of Britain, Vol. III*, BBC Publications.

WEBSITES

British Government and Politics on the Internet, from the School of Politics, International Relations and Philosophy, Keele University: http://www.keele.ac.uk/depts/por/ukbase.htm.

European Consortium for Political Research: http://www.essex.ac.uk/ecpr.

UKPOL: http://www.ukpol.co.uk.

2

INTRODUCTORY OVERVIEW OF THE BRITISH POLITICAL SYSTEM

This chapter seeks to set the scene of the British political system by explaining briefly how its major elements – voting, parties, the media and so forth – interact with each other. This provides an over-arching introduction to the more detailed explanations which follow in subsequent chapters.

THE UNDERLYING IDEAS

It is important to appreciate, as the previous chapter explained, that British democracy was never planned; rather, it evolved out of a completely different original *autocratic* system. Few countries enjoy the luxury of the United States in the late eighteenth century, whose founding fathers, presented with a 'blank page', were able to plan something close to their idea of an ideal *democratic* political system. It took a millennium for the present British system to evolve, but it is possible to identify the key ideas which enable it to work.

Britain is a *representative democracy*: citizens vote for representatives, who formulate the laws of the land and also serve to form its government. But governments in such a system cannot assume they have an indefinite lease on power: elections make governments answerable to voters; regular elections ensure that any government which has not earned the confidence of voters can be removed by them. At election time the government has to defend its record and offer a new *manifesto*, or set of proposals, for the forthcoming session. Meanwhile, those parties opposing the government use every opportunity, especially during the 'official' four-week campaign (the unofficial campaign can be months or even years long) which precedes an election, to criticise and offer alternative programmes. Elections make governments *accountable* or *responsible* to voters.

VOTING AND PARTY GOVERNMENT

In a country of 62.4 million people (2011 figure), any kind of *direct democracy* substantially involving every citizen is not possible. So representatives are elected to a national parliament, where the issues of the day are discussed and new laws are debated before being passed into law. Across the UK, 650 MPs (Members of Parliament) are elected by 46.1 million registered voters from *constituencies*, each containing around 60,000 voters. While MPs are elected individually, it would be very difficult for so many people to agree on detailed courses of action, so, since the middle of the nineteenth century, activists have combined with like-minded people to form and run modern political parties. These provide the vehicles which enable democracy to function.

These organisations seek membership from voters and seek to create policies likely to attract votes not just from their own members and supporters but from the totality of voters. They also, through their networks of local branches, seek to win electoral contests at constituency level by campaigning via leaflets, meetings and door-to-door *canvassing*. After polling on election day, the party with the most elected MPs forms the government, its party leader becoming prime minister, who, according to the ritual, is invited to do so by the person who used to run governments before democratic times: the Queen.

The second largest party of MPs becomes the official *opposition*, which provides a 'shadow' government, critically monitoring government actions and, with the next election in mind, seeking to assemble its case for being the 'government in waiting'. During the two world wars of the twentieth century, *coalition* governments were formed to prosecute the conflict more effectively. In peace-time, British elections, using the simple majority system ('first past the post'), have tended to produce one-party governments but in May 2010 a *hung parliament* was returned – one with no overall majority – resulting in a coalition between the biggest party, the Conservatives, and the third largest, the Liberal Democrats. Labour became the opposition. In 2015, to the great surprise of almost every-one, including the party leadership, the Conservatives won an overall majority, albeit small.

THE MAJOR PARTIES

The Conservatives (alternatively 'Tories') have been the major party of government in the democratic era: in power for two-thirds of the twentieth century and doing pretty well in the twenty-first. The party represents the core interests of business, property owners and the middle classes, though it argues, as do all political parties, that its remedies are the best ones for all citizens in all classes. Ideologically it has traditionally been pragmatic, though Margaret Thatcher's period of leadership witnessed an injection of ideological zeal which still flourishes on the party's right wing.

Labour began life in 1900 as the party of the workers, typically members of trade unions. Traditionally it has condemned free enter-prise capitalism in favour of 'high tax and high spend' economic and social policies, seeking to detach some of the wealth from the rich to assist the plight of the less well-off. However, the party has never commanded the confidence of all working-class voters and during the 1980s Thatcher was able to attract a large segment of the work-ing class through a mix of policies, combined with disillusion with Labour. After 18 years in opposition in the latter part of the twen-tieth century, Labour moved towards acceptance of *capitalism*, with 'New Labour' policies which married this support to that of well funded free public services like health and education. Labour used to have an ideologically oriented 'left wing', but the experience of the early 1980s, when the party was viewed as extreme and impracti-cal, seems to have dissuaded such a faction from forming in recent years. However, the election of Jeremy Corbyn as Labour leader in September 2015 perhaps revealed a reservoir of support, quiescent for over a decade but awakened by the May 2015 Conservative victory and the intensification of its 'austerity' policies.

The Liberal Democrats (Lib Dems) were born out of the merging of the small Liberal Party with the break-away Social Democratic Party in 1988. Its *centrist* message – capitalism plus generous welfare services – was essentially adopted by Tony Blair's New Labour during the 1990s. However, under the leadership of Paddy Ashdown and Charles Kennedy, it increased its number of MPs to 62 in 2005. Then, in 2010, under Nick Clegg, it eschewed alliance with Labour, to support instead a coalition with the Conservatives; in consequence, in 2015 it suffered a disastrous meltdown of support, ending up with only eight MPs.

Nationalist parties are those favouring independence for their respective countries. They are active in the 'Celtic fringe' and seek devolved governments for Scotland and Wales. The Scottish National Party (SNP) won a thumping majority – 69 seats of the Scottish Parliament's 129 – in the 2011 elections and came close to winning its independence referendum in September 2014. In Wales, in 2011, Plaid Cymru won 11 out of the 60 available seats. In the Northern Ireland Assembly elections of 2011, Sinn Fein won 29 out of the 108 seats available. Sinn Fein won four seats in the 2015 general election but, as in previous elections, refused to take up its seats.

The United Kingdom Independence Party (UKIP) emerged in the 1990s to appeal to a fast growing *Euro-sceptic* constituency, threatening Conservative *marginals* and making its influence felt in areas where immigration was perceived as a problem demanding a radical solution. By 2014 its leader, Nigel Farage, had established himself as a national political figure, winning two television debates on British membership of the European Union (EU) with Deputy Prime Minister Nick Clegg in April 2014 and gaining its first two MPs when Douglas Carswell and Mark Reckless defected from the Conservatives and won their resultant *by-elections*.

On the far right, the British National Party (BNP) emerged in 1982 from an amalgam of smaller far-right groupings. It has enjoyed some success at local council level and it won two seats in the European Parliament in 2009. In the 2010 general election it gained 1.9% of the vote without winning any seats. Like many fringe parties it has tended to suffer from factional disputes.

LEGISLATURE: HOUSE OF COMMONS AND HOUSE OF LORDS

The *legislature* is the body which makes the laws and is the platform on which the affairs of the nation are conducted. The Commons is the elected chamber and, since the Parliament Act of 1911, is dominant over the unelected Lords. Legislative proposals or *bills* can be initiated in either house and a complex process of readings and debates takes place, involving both Houses, until the Queen's signature passes a measure formally into law. The Commons provides the foundation and platform of major political careers – the prime minister has not sat in the Lords for over a century – and the Lords' power only of delay makes its benches repositories for mostly retired senior politicians and others distinguished in their professions.

However, the Lords performs a useful function in revising and amending bills as they pass through, often in dire need of such attentions. Reform of parliament, especially of the antiquated Lords, whose members are appointed and not elected, has been a recurring theme in British politics for well over a century but the Lords remains stubbornly unreformed, despite several attempts following Tony Blair's abolition of the hereditary principle in 1998.

THE EXECUTIVE

PRIME MINISTER (PM) AND CABINET

These politicians provide the pinnacle of the nation's *executive* arm of government, in charge of the day-to-day running of the country. This comprises the nation's political leadership at any one time and the nerve centre of the most important decisions. The PM chooses a senior ministerial team, which comprises the *cabinet*, and while it is the PM's leadership which is crucial, senior ministers help him or her to formulate policies, deliver them into practice and gather and sustain support within the majority party in parliament as well as the country as a whole. If PMs have the full support of their parties, they can usually rely on passing whatever measures they think fit.

The prime minister nominates a cabinet of some 20–23 members to fill the main offices of state, plus a clutch of junior ministers, all of whom have to belong to one of the two Houses of Parliament (Commons or Lords). They, the ministers, are 'our' (voters') representatives in the centre of government, representing the party we have elected and implementing the policies we have endorsed in the winning manifesto. The extent of their control and their success defines the degree of democracy we have – just how *much* control we have is a subject of much debate.

CIVIL SERVICE

Civil servants staff the departments of state in Whitehall and elsewhere. Senior officials advise ministers and often their skill (senior civil servants are highly educated and able) plus experience (they are permanent professionals, unlike the transient ministers nominally in charge) enable them to become the real authors of departmental policy.

REFORM

Under Thatcher, routine functions of the big departments were hived off to become *executive agencies*. The British civil service is non-partisan and permanent: it still tends to be led by arts graduates from elite universities.

PRESSURE GROUPS

These are groups which seek to influence policy; unlike political parties, they do not seek to take control of government. There are two basic types: 'sectional' groups representing different groups in society, like workers or business; and 'cause' groups, championing ideas or ideals like protecting the environment, animals or abused children. Each policy area attracts an almost permanent cluster of groups determined to advance their particular interest through influencing the decision-making process. 'Insider groups' tend to be at the centre of the process, while 'outsider' groups are more removed and often use loud public demonstrations to exert influence.

LOCAL GOVERNMENT

Local government employs hundreds of thousands of people and performs essential functions like collecting and disposing of rubbish, street cleaning, planning and promoting the economic interests of local areas. Local government developed enormously during the early twentieth century but after 1945 it was extensively reformed and entered a decline. It lost functions to other bodies and became controversial during the 1980s when Thatcher passed measures to reduce its powers and replace its functions with other bodies, such as the so-called 'arms-length' *quasi-autonomous non-governmental organisations (quangos)*.

EUROPEAN UNION (EU)

The EU is a major 'player' in British politics by virtue of the fact that, as a member of the Brussels-based body, Britain is obliged to recognise that EU law is superior to domestic law, thus threatening the very British notion of *parliamentary sovereignty*. The EU became a major factor in British politics, especially the party political debate, once 'Euro-scepticism' became a force to be reckoned with. This view maintained that membership of the EU impaired the independence of the country through loss of *sovereignty* and loss of identity as the EU was nudged by its unelected personnel towards some vision of a united Europe. This perspective emerged within the Tory Party initially, during the 1980s, and was then encouraged by Margaret Thatcher's sympathetic conversion to the view. But soon a significant section of country as a whole, often concerned at the rapid inflow of immigrants in the early years of the twenty-first century, began to feel that the advantages of being a member of the EU were slight or even non-existent.

THE MEDIA

The media perform a crucial role, as they are the mediating agent, interpreting messages between the government and people, not to mention the different elements of the political system, as well as influencing both the context in which decisions are taken and those decisions themselves. Good relations with and effective use of the media are central to the successful conduct of politics. A major criticism of New Labour under Blair was that it focused too much on media presentation.

But arguably any government these days is driven by the 24–7 media coverage: the constant pressure which focuses on key politicians and the need to feed the 'feral beast' (as Blair called the media). Given the appointment of *spin doctors*, however, to manage party–media relations, it must be admitted that much of the obsession with the media derives from the desire to win points over the 'enemy' parties.

QUESTIONS

1. Explain the terms 'legislative' and 'executive'.
2. Explain the roles of: local government; House of Commons and Lords; and the media.

FURTHER READING

All the major textbooks contain introductory sections from which students new to British politics will benefit. Jones and Norton (2013) was first published in 1990 and remains, excuse my partisanship, the best source for both A-level and undergraduate students. It provides in-depth analyses of political ideas, political institutions and major policy areas like economic and foreign policy. A much shorter text is King (2015). For a critical analysis of the British system see the excellent Jones (2014).

Crick, B. (2000) *In Defence of Politics*, Continuum. (Classic analysis of politics as a process of negotiation and compromise.)

Jones, B. and Norton, P. (2013) *Politics UK* (8th edition), Routledge.

Jones, O. (2014) *The Establishment*, Allen Lane.

King, A. (2015) *Who Governs Britain?* Penguin.

Lasswell, H. (1936) *Who Gets What, Where, When and How?* McGraw-Hill. (Another classic text defining the essence of political activity.)

Paxman, J. (2002) *The Political Animal*, Michael Joseph. (Fascinating analysis of the kind of people who enter politics and rise to wield power.)

Tansey, S. D. and Jackson, N. (2008) *Politics: The Basics* (4th edition), Routledge. (Best-selling concise analysis of the world of politics in the modern age.)

WEBSITES

The internet is a valuable source for facts and ideas about British politics, though has to be used with care.

British Government and Politics on the Internet, from the School of Politics, International European Consortium for Political Research: http://www.essex.ac.uk/ecpr.

Relations and Philosophy, Keele University: http://www.keele.ac.uk/depts/por/ukbase.htm (an excellent resource)

Political Education Forum: http://www.politicaleducationforum.com/site/content_home.php (useful for students intending to study politics at university).

UKPOL: http://www.ukpol.co.uk.

II

THE POLITICAL CONTEXT

All political systems reflect the traditions and nature of the society it purports to rule: the political context. For the purposes of this volume, three elements are identified as constituting such a context: political culture, the social and economic context, and the constitution.

3

POLITICAL CULTURE

This rather vague concept is nevertheless crucial when trying to understand any democratic system of government. One useful definition is that provided by Maclean (1996) in his Dictionary of Politics (p. 379): political culture is 'the attitudes, beliefs, and values which underpin the operation of a particular political system'. These will include, he writes: 'knowledge and skills'; positive and negative emotional feelings' towards the system of government; and evaluative judgements about it.

How important is political culture? Often overlooked by students of politics, perhaps because the idea lacks clarity, the political culture of a country is vital in determining its stability and its degree of political success. Political culture is one of the key factors which mediate demands made upon political systems and often determines outcomes. People often wonder why characteristics persist in a country over long periods or why attempts to import new systems fail.

For example, Russian history shows a marked *authoritarian* tendency: the tsars were succeeded by a man sometimes described as the Red Tsar, Joseph Stalin. Following the implosion of his creation, the Soviet Union, there were hopes democracy would emerge and expunge the authoritarian tendency. But Vladimir Putin's career suggests otherwise, as he has come to express this same tendency and, what is more, win popularity for doing so. From a different viewpoint, George Bush was intent on introducing democracy into Iraq after Saddam Hussein, but it proved a frail enough plant and, arguably, after Nouri al-Maliki's period in power, up to September 2014, proved even more fragile.

KEY HISTORICAL FACTORS IN THE EVOLUTION OF BRITISH POLITICAL CULTURE

Firstly, unlike many European countries, Britain met pivotal challenges sequentially and not at the same time. In the sixteenth century, a settlement was reached between church and state; in the seventeenth century, conflict between monarch and parliament was resolved through the limitation of the monarch's powers; while in the nineteenth century social unrest was mitigated by the gradual extension of the *franchise* to include all classes of voters by the middle of the twentieth century. So when a problem arose, there tended to be a focus of energy mobilised to solve it and, the Civil War notwithstanding, mostly without bloodshed. Other countries were not so fortunate.

Secondly, the centuries-long growth of the British Empire proved hugely popular with British citizens, who were proud of the worldwide reach their tiny island had established. Thousands flocked to live in the new colonies and enjoy a standard of living far higher than back home. This national confidence provided the 'feel good' element which politicians relish and which helps maintain stability. The downside of such exuberant nationalistic confidence could often be expressed in the form of a sense of superiority towards other countries, together with more openly *racist* attitudes.

ECONOMIC INFLUENCES

The means by which wealth is created in a society are of great importance in determining its political culture. Britain's role as the first industrialised country meant its social divisions were accentuated. This created conflict between the 'haves' and 'have-nots' but rarely anything approaching the kind of revolution Karl Marx predicted was inevitable. Why? There are two main reasons. Firstly, working people opted to hang on to what little they had, rather than risk all on a potentially bloody revolution. Secondly, the British ruling class, while frequently happy to resist calls for reform, were sufficiently wise to recognise changed political reality and make concessions to head off crises and avoid threats to their wealth and privileges. This meant that young ideologues seeking to enthuse workers with *revolutionary* ideas were mostly ignored. So Britain was able to proceed from an agricultural society to an industrial one – a huge change – with minimal dislocation. The tenets of capitalism – using capital to set up businesses, to hire and fire as the business requires and to enjoy the full fruits of success – have been more or less accepted by British people and still are. They may complain bitterly about the unfairness of fabulous wealth being manufactured from the labours of the poor but rising up to dispossess the wealthy has never been an idea embraced by Britain's poorer classes, even when urged on by middle-class idealists.

Most would like to earn more money and enjoy an ever-improving standard of living; Britons are substantially accepting of materialistic values. Marx would have condemned such *false consciousness*, whereby, as he would argue, the ruling class has used the media and state institutions to inculcate the subordinate masses into ignoring the fact of their exploitation.

THE CONSTITUTION

Their famous constitution is venerated by Americans and its provisions are widely known. Britain's lack of anything similar means its system of government is generally not very well understood. This may help explain why support for and participation in the political system has declined over the past few decades. But the truth is that parts of the system are well supported, others less so and still others are quite unpopular. Take the example of *free speech*. We tend to take many such basic *human rights* for granted, but imagine the uproar if any criticism of the government were suddenly to be banned by the home secretary. This would certainly ignite passionate demonstrations and protests, which could easily become violent. Having our liberal democratic rights snatched away might remind us how valuable they are, like setting up voluntary bodies (political parties) to represent common interests and to have the right, through voting, to dismiss any government of the day. Some aspects of the constitution are more controversial; ancient ones are sometimes seen as past their usefulness. Five examples follow.

Firstly, the European Union is increasingly seen as an institution to which British affiliation is inappropriate.

Secondly, the House of Lords is widely seen as beyond any utility, despite the fact it plays a vital role in amending bills. It has been stripped of much of its powers and *hereditary* entitlements. The debate about its future occurs mostly below the radar of the average voter and is intensely fought over only in the *Westminster village.*

Thirdly, the role of the monarchy is disputed by some who believe an elected head of state would be preferable. Since the lives of the royals have become something of a soap opera, respect for them has declined, though Prince William, his marriage and Prince George have caught the public's imagination and the Queen is still revered as wholly dedicated to her role.

Fourthly, the Church of England, while being the 'official' church of the United Kingdom, headed by the Queen, commands very little support in the present day. Over half the general public claim not to be 'religious' and only 5% regularly attend church.

Fifthly, the Police and Crime Commissioners (PCCs), elected November 2012, were elected officials the purpose of whom was unclear both regarding the detail of their role and, more importantly, the need for their creation in the first place. Average turnout in these elections was only 10–20% of the *electorate* and to date the PCCs have been the recipients of more criticism than praise.

Other elements are not yet fully accepted but nonetheless appear to be on the way to being so. *Devolution* offers an example here. The devolved assemblies were created in 1997–98 and have had four elections to date. The Scottish Parliament won a high degree of acceptance but faced a powerful challenge from the Scottish National Party (SNP), the governing party since 2012, which called a *referendum* for September 2014 when the 'yes' to independence case lost 55–45. The Welsh Assembly was initially regarded coolly by its electors but it would now be hard to imagine politics in Wales without it, after over a decade. The Northern Ireland Assembly is founded on the unstable foundation of a province still simmering with *sectarian* differences below the surface but, again, it would now be hard to imagine this part of the UK without its devolved assembly.

EXTREMISM

British history does not manifest any clear leaning towards the ideological extremes. The political fringe in Britain has included all the usual exoticisms of *anarchists, Trotskyists, communists, fascists, Maoists* and the like, but on no occasion have such beliefs ever taken root. The Labour Party emerged from a marriage of trade unions and *socialist* societies of varying degrees of fervour. *Marxists* set out their stall as well as Christian socialists and the gradualist *Fabians*. During World War I, leaders of the influential Independent Labour Party (ILP) tended to be *pacifist* and some Labour activists were enthused by the 1917 Bolshevik Revolution.

But once the Labour Party found its identity, it proved to be one eschewing the Moscow-led Communist Party of Great Britain and closer to the safe reformism of the Fabians. During the 1930s Oswald Mosley created his British Union of Fascists, a version of what was happening in Germany, but it failed to ignite and became further proof that the British people do not respond to ideological extremes. It was also the case that British political methodology remained essentially parliamentary during even the most turbulent inter-war years; even the 1926 General Strike, while briefly threatening insurrection, soon deflated into resigned failure. This does not mean that violent displays do not occasionally occur; examples include the city riots of the early 1980s, the *poll tax* riots in 1990 and the city riots during the summer of 2011. But such episodic events were not any prelude to a wholesale rejection of the political system. However, a lurch into the extremes can never be ruled out. The erosion of democratic processes and the growth of cynical mistrust in politicians, within a context of economic austerity, create exactly the conditions in which a fringe ideology might suddenly take off; UKIP might be seen as an example of this tendency.

DEFERENCE

Political deference equates with respect for the law, government institutions and an absence of dissent. Social deference means the acceptance that some people are innately superior by virtue of the social rank. A 'gentleman' was seen as an educated person, speaking in a *received pronunciation* fashion, who dressed well, was polite and clearly had 'leadership' qualities. For this reason the military recruited only the privately educated into its ranks until World War I so depleted them that 'lower-status' replacements from the lower middle classes were deemed necessary. In similar fashion the traditional professions – the law, civil service, banking, not to mention the new profession of broadcasting – looked first to recruit from the same privately educated middle classes. The Conservative Party drew most of its MPs from the same sources. Labour, too, drew some of its leading lights – Attlee, Gaitskell, Crosland – from *public schools*. However, deference from party members and the working classes in general was often granted only through gritted teeth. The 1950s was probably the last decade in which British society could be described as deferential in this sense.

During the 1960s a cultural transformation occurred which swept away much of this type of thinking. Factors involved included: trail-blazing, taboo-breaking writers – Kingsley Amis, John Braine, Harold Pinter – who attacked the traditional order of things and poked fun at its representatives like the Edwardian Harold Macmillan and the aristocratic Alec Douglas-Home; jazz and rock and roll, which galvanised youth through the expression of individualism and rebellion; the emergence of an alternative grammar school-educated elite, who resented the hegemony of a class which in other ways had scarcely distinguished itself; and the decline of religion as a social glue which legitimised social difference and respect for 'superiors'. The consequences of this *cultural revolution* were made manifest in: the 'hippy' phenomenon, which rejected traditional materialism among many other things; reform of the law on homosexuality; and a tendency to regard politicians as objects of derision.

SATIRE

The magazine *Private Eye* emerged as a weekly *satirical* bible for this new way of thinking and the BBC's *That Was the Week That Was*, provided a hugely successful weekly send-up of all things traditional and serious. Politicians tried hard to understand the new *zeit-geist*; Tories elected two grammar school products, Ted Heath and Margaret Thatcher, to avoid appearing too old fashioned but neither displayed much of the sense of humour which underlay this new cultural consciousness. Later prime ministers, Blair especially, cleverly disarmed such attacks with self-deprecation and a realisation that the angry denunciations of Heath were counter-productive. Satire remains a strong element of British political culture, reflected in such television successes in recent decades as *Yes Minister*, *Spitting Image*, *Bremner, Bird and Fortune* and *The Thick of It*, plus a style of media reporting which often looks for the satirical angle.

CIVIL SOCIETY

Civil society is the densely complex web of relationships between citizens – social, economic and via voluntary groups. Such connections are vitally important in providing the 'soil' in which healthy democracies can grow. For example, membership of the cubs, scouts and sporting clubs fosters the ability to lead and be led, be part of a team, to lose as well as win with good grace. Studies in the USA, especially *Bowling Alone* by Robert Putnam (2000), suggests Americans are withdrawing from such voluntary activity into the cocoons of their own flat–screen–equipped lounges. Studies in Britain suggest the situation is not currently comparable but declining voter turnout and party membership removes the idea that the UK has nothing to worry about. One study of volunteering in the UK reveals that it correlates closely with income, with higher-income groups much more likely to volunteer than low-income groups.

CRIME

The decline of deference has also had an impact on crime. When people more or less accepted their position in society, they were not too unhappy that the upper social strata received more financial rewards and more power. However, as more and more people began to feel an equal entitlement to success, some of those lower down in the hierarchy were not willing to accept inferiority and turned to illegality as a means of advancing their socio-economic status. This is one of the reasons, perhaps, why there was a huge crime wave between the advent of Thatcher in 1979 and the demise of John Major's government in 1997. Tackling crime effectively has become a major political demand over recent decades. Ironically, the fact that crime figures have halved since 1995 has not convinced a large section of society, who continue to believe crime is on the rise.

WELFARE STATE

After the introduction of pensions in the early twentieth century, welfare measures were added incrementally until the major extension of them after 1945, when Labour won its historic landslide. The experience of combating the common Nazi foe for five long years had a transforming effect on British political culture: the sense of 'togetherness' was so intensely felt that once it was clear the war was going to be won, a consensus grew that measures should be taken to ensure that everyone, rich as well as poor, should benefit from national wealth. Free health care and education quickly became major expectations and very soon became part of the nation's life. Additional measures, like sick and unemployment pay, added to a raft of support measures from the state, which almost amounted to 'cradle to grave' provision. It is fair to now say that the British have become used to such assistance and are closely attached to the National Health Service, so much so that any party seeking to dismantle it would lose support – even the suggestion that the Conservatives might do so became a negative in 1997 and in 2001. It would be fair to say that the British have become habituated to *welfare services*, expect to receive them and until recently would punish at the ballot box parties proposing to cut them.

Support for those receiving benefits shows a different pattern. During the 1980s Thatcherite policies were very unpopular and sympathy was extended towards the unemployed and those on other benefits, as Figure 3.1 illustrates. However, the recession that began in 2007 led to a distinct hardening of views towards those in need, as shown by research quoted by David Binder on the 'Politics and Policy' website of London School of Economics (22 August 2013):

> 15% of the public in 1994 thought people live in need because of laziness or a lack of willpower, compared with 23% in 2010. During the same period, adherence to the view that people live in need because of injustice in our society declined from 29% to 21%.

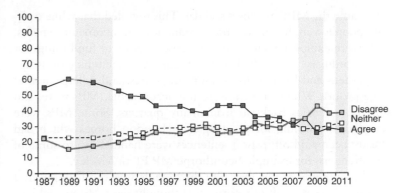

Figure 3.1 Views on whether the government should spend more on welfare
benefits for the poor, by UK recessions, 1987–2011

Source: Office for National Statistics.

IS BRITISH SOCIETY TOO OPEN?

Some suggest British political culture has become too liberal, plac-
ing too much emphasis on free speech and freedom generally. A
2008 report from the Royal United Services Institute suggested that
British society's relaxed attitude.

> is in stark contrast to the implacability of the Islamist terrorist enemy.
> 'Fractured institutional integrity' means that when the unexpected
> occurs, the response is likely to be incoherent, ad hoc, short-term and
> uncertain. . . . We look a soft touch. We are indeed a soft touch. (Prins
> and Salisbury, 2008)

MPS' EXPENSES AND THE EROSION OF TRUST

The banking crisis in 2008–09 produced a deep economic recession with widespread redundancies and bankruptcies. Anger was
felt against the bankers, with loathing focused especially on Sir Fred
Goodwin, former head of the Royal Bank of Scotland, who, after
presiding over a cataclysmic £28 billion loss, was rewarded with a
£700,000 pension (he later agreed to a £200,000 reduction). And

then came the MPs' expenses scandal. This revealed that while ordinary people were having to absorb reductions in income or benefits, MPs were exploiting a generous expenses regime to fund things for which ordinary people had to pay themselves, including landscaping gardens and buying up London properties (and selling them at huge profit). While bankers were not accountable, MPs were, and suffered a furious backlash from many quarters. Some MPs were revealed as claiming for mortgages on London homes which had already been paid off; prison sentences were handed out to some of the offenders, for example Scunthorpe MP Elliot Morley.

The outcome of this fusion of discontents was a shift in political culture whereby a raft of reforms was thought desirable and achievable. While some did take place, for example (as expected) reform of the expenses system, fixed-term parliaments, election of select committee chairs by committee members rather than appointment by the whips, many others were quietly dropped or, as with voting reform, defeated in the referendum of May 2011.

CONCLUSION

'A civic culture'? Writing in the 1960s, Almond and Verba produced *The Civic Culture*, a major study in political culture. They saw Britain as having the 'ideal civic culture', that is, one that 'combined or balanced the values of citizen participation and self-confidence with a trust in the elites and a responsiveness to their laws' (quoted in Jones and Kavanagh, 1994: p. 25). In the UK, judged the authors:

> Citizens are sufficiently active in politics to express their preferences to rulers, but not so involved as to refuse to accept decisions with which they disagree. Thus the civic culture resolves the tension between popular control and effective governance. (Quoted in Watts, 2003: p. 18)

Clearly, such an analysis requires an update. Participation rates have plummeted, along with trust in our elites, and perhaps stability is no longer so assured. The erosion of deference has made the country easier to live in for many people but at some cost to authority and trust. A more enthusiastic embrace of market forces has added dynamism to the economy but also instability as wealth and income gaps have grown apace. Our civil society is still robust but has suffered a decline since the days of Almond and Verba's book. It is by no means certain that, if written today, such a study would produce such an optimistic set of conclusions.

QUESTIONS FOR DISCUSSION

1. How different are the political cultures of the USA and the UK?
2. What changes to UK political culture have been introduced by *digital technology*?
3. Would you say UK political culture over the past two decades has moved to the right or to the left?

FURTHER READING

Books on UK political culture are not abundant but good starts are Almond and Verba (1965) and the two books by Beer (1982).

Almond, G. and Verba, S. (1965) *The Civic Culture*, Little, Brown.

Beer, S. (1982) *Modern British Politics*, Faber.

Beer, S. (1982) *Britain Against Itself: Political Contradictions of Collectivism*, Faber.

Jones, B. and Kavanagh, D. (1994) *British Politics Today*, Manchester University Press.

Kavanagh, D. (1972) *Political Culture*, Oxford University Press.

Mackenzie, R. and Silver, A. (1968) *Angels in Marble*, Heinemann.

Moran, M. (2011) *Politics and Governance in the UK* (2nd edition), Palgrave.

Rose, R. (ed.) (1974) *Studies in British Politics*, Macmillan.

Turner, A. W. (2014) *A Classless Society: Britain in the 1990s*, Aurum Press.

Watts, D. (2003) *Understanding US/UK Government and Politics*, Manchester University Press.

4

THE SOCIAL AND ECONOMIC CONTEXT

Understanding political institutions and behaviour without awareness of social and economic factors in the society of the country concerned is to understand only part of the complete picture. In democratic systems like Britain – where government, in theory at least, serves the people – it is political demands generated by society to which the system is supposed to respond. Elections, the legislature, executive and so forth are merely the shell, the structure within which political activity occurs. A country's economy will be of key importance, as it will help explain how wealth is generated and distributed.

ECONOMIC BEGINNINGS

Agriculture was the dominant economic activity from Roman times, through the Anglo-Saxons, Normans and beyond. The Black Death (1346–53) wiped out half the workforce, helping to push up agricultural wages. Wool became the dominant commodity in medieval times; it was produced in the heartlands of England and exported to the textile cities of Europe. So important was it that the Speaker's seat in the House of Lords was symbolically stuffed with wool: the woolsack. Textile production had evolved by the seventeenth century, ready for the huge expansions connected with Empire and the Industrial Revolution.

IMPERIAL BEGINNINGS

During the reign of Elizabeth I (1558–1603), intrepid British adventurers began to explore the extremities of the known world and push back its frontiers. The nation's maritime traditions and navigational expertise were substantial advantages in this competitive process. Britain did not access the kind of bounty exploited by Spain in the gold and silver mines of Latin America, but it did establish lucrative trading relations with India – for example, in spices and tea – as well as colonising the eastern seaboard of North America. Maritime interests grew rich on the slave trade, whereby, along with other nationalities, 12 million slaves were uprooted from Africa and taken across the Atlantic in often horrific journeys.

INDUSTRIAL REVOLUTION AND THE MARXIST ANALYSIS

During the eighteenth and nineteenth centuries a number of factors – inventions within the indigenous cotton manufacturing industry, abundant coal reserves and plentiful Irish immigration – combined to transform Britain's economy. For good or ill, this 'revolution' was destined to spread and engulf not just Britain but eventually the whole world. The consequences were manifold: an influx of workers from rural areas into cities to work in factories; the emergence of great metropolises in the north; the formation of municipal governments in response to related problems of health and sanitation; a surge of exports to the expanding Empire, creating huge individual and corporate wealth; the creation of a small number of super-rich 'capitalist' industrialists, often new entrepreneurs but frequently linked to the old aristocracy; and the corresponding creation of a huge 'proletarian' mass, who were more prosperous than earlier workers but hugely disadvantaged compared with the rich.

This new inequality had a transforming effect on the nation's society and politics. Emergent middle-class business people were determined to wrest away the power the landed gentry had enjoyed for centuries. The downside of capitalism – economic downturns, unemployment, industrial injuries, employment of women and children in dangerous industries like mining – prompted the growth of defensive organisations: trade unions. Once equipped with the vote, the working classes were wooed by both the major parties but it was the unions which set up a party to represent the interests of this newly defined capitalist-created class: Labour.

Karl Marx, a highly intellectual observer, of German origin, living in London during the nineteenth century, believed he had discerned the motive forces of history: conflict between differing 'classes' in society (Box 4.1). Marx argued that at every stage in human history there had been a dominant and a subservient class, with the former being the one which controlled the means of wealth production, be it agriculture, wool, cotton or whatever. The subservient class, argued Marx, would be convinced by the blandishments of the dominant class that these social arrangements were quite right and proper – no more, as they said, than 'common sense'. But this state of affairs was due to end: as capitalists maximised profits, workers would come to realise the extent of their exploitation and would begin to develop a 'revolutionary consciousness'.

This polarisation of society into what Marx called a small *bourgeoisie* and a *proletarian* mass would eventually express itself, he predicted, in a sweeping away of the former dominant class, followed by an interregnum period and then the formation of a 'classless society'. However, even though Marx's analysis of the forces creating and changing society was remarkably accurate, in the view of many historians, history's eventual narrative did not work out according to his 'scientific' rules.

Box 4.1   Classifying 'class'

Many sociologists have produced ways of classifying social strata but the most widely used is the ABC scale, which is as follows (with current approximate percentages of the overall population in parentheses):

A   Upper middle: professional, higher managerial (3% of all households)
B   Middle: middle managers (16%)

C1   Lower middle: junior managers, routine white collar (26%)
C2   Skilled: plumbers, carpenters, mechanics (26%)
D   Semi-skilled and unskilled: manual workers (17%)
E   Residual: dependent on long-term benefit (12%)

In April 2013 the British Sociological Association published a survey of British class divisions which saw: an elite middle class representing 6%; an 'established middle class' comprising 25%; a 'technical middle class' at 6%; traditional manual working-class members 14% (after substantial decline); 'new affluent workers' comprising 15%; 'emergent service workers' 19%; and, at the lowest level, the 'precariat', comprising 15% of the whole.

CHANGING CLASS STRATA

If class, as is usually the case, is defined primarily in terms of occupation, things have evolved differently to Marx's confident predictions – though see Eagleton (2011). We have seen neither an extreme polarisation of society nor the dawn of a classless one. In 1911 the working class comprised 74.6% of the labour force, while professionals, including managers and administrators, comprised only 7.5%. After Edwardian times, the economy grew rapidly to include mining, ship building and steel, but after World War II competition from other parts of the world reduced such industries to basket cases by the 1980s, along with the newer industries of vehicle production and electronics. By 1991 the equivalent figures were 37.7% working class and 34% professional. As Moran notes, 'The workers as traditionally understood, are now in a minority' (Moran, 2005: p. 43).

WHY NO REVOLUTION?

Marx was confident that revolutions would sweep through the industrialised countries but, despite a few wobbly moments (for example the 1926 National Strike), Britain survived quite comfortably. And this was despite astonishing levels of inequality in the nineteenth century, which have not narrowed significantly during the 20th or into the 21st. Why should this be? Why did the British masses not rise up in protest against the small rewards they were receiving, while the owners of capitalist enterprises lived in unprecedented luxury? Some commentators argue that the British are not ideological and reject extremist measures. Marxists tend to explain it in terms of 'false consciousness', the fact that the 'capitalist hegemony' of the institutions of the state – government, business, education, the media – enable it to 'brainwash' society into thinking capitalism is the only possible way of organising the economy and that inequality is a natural, unavoidable and necessary concomitant of such a system.

Others argue – perhaps more convincingly – that workers are extremely wary of risking what little they have for the speculative gains which might be won via the turbulence of revolution. It is perhaps not surprising that it is often young middle-class people who advocate revolution – the working classes cannot afford that luxury.

SOCIAL MOBILITY AND EDUCATION

The most usual way of moving 'up' in social class is through education, especially higher education. However, education itself mirrors class, with children from 'lower' social categories doing less well than those from higher strata; 80% of higher professional children attain five or more GCSEs at grades A★ to C, while only 30% of those from the lower supervisory group manage the same.

PRIVATE EDUCATION

Britain is unusual in having highly developed private primary and secondary educational sectors. Comprising only 7% of the whole, children who pass through them tend to do immensely better in exams and later careers than those who attend ordinary state schools. Schools like Rugby, Shrewsbury, Marlborough and, the most prestigious of the lot, Eton and Harrow, attract the children of the wealthiest upper middle class. Places in the elite universities of Oxford and Cambridge go disproportionately – about a half, even though they represent such a tiny part (7%) of the overall numbers of children – to privately educated people (or 'public school' educated as we oddly refer to it). These favoured recipients then go on to dominate most of the top jobs and professions: the law, directors of big companies, judges, top posts in the armed forces and the civil service (see Box 4.2).

Box 4.2   Private education

Writing in *The Guardian*, 23 February 2008, historian David Kynaston ruefully noted the conclusions of the autumn 2007 Sutton Trust report: 'Altogether, there were 27 private schools in the top 30, 43 in the top 50 and 78 in the top 100. Put another way, the 70th brightest sixth-former at Westminster or Eton is as likely to get a place at Oxbridge as the very brightest sixth-formers at a large comprehensive. I found it hard not to be angered as a citizen – and ashamed as an Oxford graduate – to see these figures.'

Importantly, this grotesque skewing is not confined to Oxbridge admissions. The Independent Schools Council (ISC), which represents the private schools, claimed in November that pupils at its schools were now five times more likely than the national average to be offered a place at one of the Russell Group universities, the top 20 out of more than 100 universities. 'These results show once again', justifiably boasted the ISC's chief executive, 'the superb job done by ISC schools in preparing pupils for entry to leading universities'.

A report in the next day's *Guardian* revealed that of the 30,000 candidates achieving three A grades in their A-level exams, only 176, or 0.5%, were drawn from those – the poorest – receiving free school meals.

MASS HIGHER EDUCATION AND SOCIAL MOBILITY

During the early 1960s, around 5% of children went on to university; by the end of the century the figure was closer to 40%. But studies show that the main beneficiaries were middle-class children – working-class children saw only a small percentage increase in their share of university places. This increase in no way broke the privately educated hegemony over powerful positions in business, the law, the civil service, parliament and the media. The massive post-war increase in white-collar jobs in both the public and private sectors enabled children born during the twentieth century to enjoy 'upward social mobility', that is, their eventual occupations were 'higher' than those of their parents. However, more recent studies suggest social mobility has 'stalled': white-collar occupations have ceased to expand so rapidly and those middle-class incumbents, already in place, are 'blocking' further mobility.

ECONOMIC INEQUALITY

Capitalism tends to create 'winners' – who establish successful enterprises or occupy high-income positions or have been born into the families of those who have done so – and 'losers' – who may have failed to obtain a good education or have lost their jobs. It has long been possible in both the USA and the UK for luxurious homes in big cities to exist side by side with slums or homelessness.

INCOMES

During the twentieth century, income inequalities began to decrease throughout most developed countries but towards the end of it the salaries gap between the high and low paid began to grow (see Figure 4.1) as British firms began to adopt US-style remuneration. At the same time, Margaret Thatcher brought down the top rate of tax to 40% and pursued economic policies – necessary or not – which caused widespread unemployment and loss of workforce expertise in key areas like engineering.

WEALTH

This relates to the assets owned by British people in the form of property, shares and savings accounts. Here the inequality is strikingly greater than in income, as Figures 4.2, 4.3 and 4.4 show.

The French economist Thomas Piketty published an influential book in 2014 called *Capital in the Twenty-First Century*. In it he claims to show that, apart from a period in the middle of the twentieth century, wealth has appreciated faster than wages have grown. This means that the inequality gap is much more related to inherited wealth than to annual income. He predicted that it will continue to grow unconstrained, perhaps until some calamity strikes. He called for an international redistribution of wealth to pre-empt such a disaster.

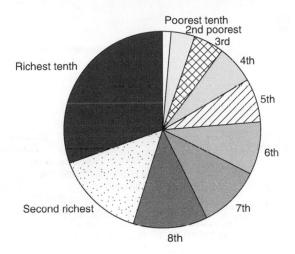

Figure 4.1 Income distribution: the income of the richest tenth is more than the income of all those on below-average incomes (i.e. the bottom five-tenths) combined

Source: Households Below Average Income, Department of Work and Pensions; the data are the average for 2006/07 to 2008/09, updated to August 2010.

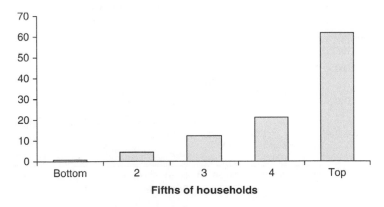

Figure 4.2 How total wealth is distributed, 2008–10 (% for each fifth)

Source: Wealth and Assets Survey, Office for National Statistics.

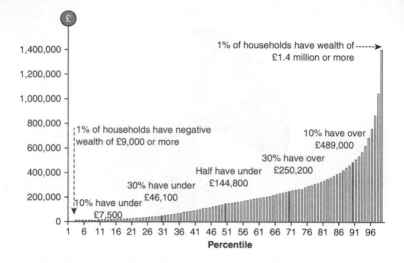

Figure 4.3 Household wealth excluding pensions, 2008–10

Source: John Hills (2015) *Good Times, Bad Times*, Polity Press, figure 6.1.

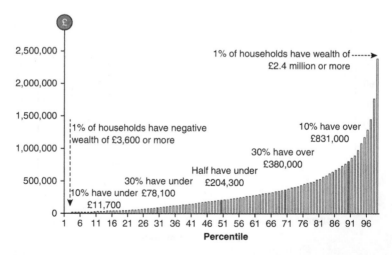

Figure 4.4 Household wealth including pensions, 2008–10

Source: John Hills (2015) *Good Times, Bad Times*, Polity Press, figure 6.2.

GINI COEFFICIENT

This is an index produced by relating the wealth and income of the richest 10% to that of the poorest 10%; a high rating means high inequality, while a low one means low inequality. According to this index Sweden, Denmark and Holland are at the low end while the UK is higher up the table, along with the USA and Canada. In his book, *Who Runs Britain?* Robert Peston (2008) reflects how the index soared during the Thatcher years of the 1980s, eased down a little under Major before climbing again under Blair and Brown, until Brown's redistributive policies after 2001 produced some slight reductions. This was only temporary, however, as the inequality gap took off yet again after 2005, as shown in Figure 4.5.

THE SUPER-RICH

This tiny minority cause substantial controversy as the media love to highlight their extravagant lifestyles. The *Sunday Time* 'Rich List' in 2014 revealed that from 88 billionaires in 2013, the 2014 figure was 104, representing a combined wealth of more than £301 billion;

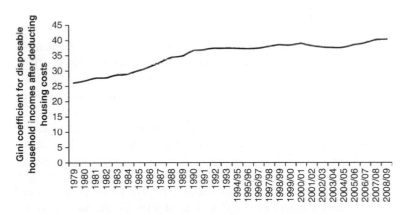

Figure 4.5 The Gini coefficient measure of overall income inequality in the UK (now higher than at any previous time in the last 30 years)

Source: Wealth and Assets Survey, Office for National Statistics.

the UK has more billionaires per head of population than any other country and London has more than any other city in the world, with 72 – its nearest rival being Moscow, with 48.

Should we worry? Well, the super-rich seem to have been chosen by party leaders as their funding 'cash cows': Labour seems to have chosen them to complement the trade unions, its traditional source of wealth; the Conservatives still depend on them for most of their income. Labour, surprisingly perhaps, when in office 1997–2010, did everything possible to persuade the super-rich to take advantage of lenient UK tax laws and live here, while their wealth in offshore tax accounts was left unmolested by the Inland Revenue. Most opinion polls show a large majority resent these huge rewards as immoral, yet even when very moderate tax proposals were aimed at them in the autumn of 2007, a barrage of objections were levelled at the chancellor, who eventually backed down. Maybe allowing people to become so very, very rich is morally bad for any society with even the slightest aspiration towards equality. On the other hand, it can be argued that having them live in one's country, distasteful inequality notwithstanding, creates advantages for the whole of society, as the super-rich spend their money and create new businesses within it.

UNDERCLASS

The US sociologist Charles Murray discerned a near permanent group of people at the 'bottom' of US society who were, in effect, not subscribing to the values of society: they did not live in stable families but often in single-parent ones, where children were allowed to run free and lacked good male role-models of steady workers and caring fathers. Murray suggested such a group also thought little of living off welfare and indulging in crime or drugs. It followed that their children tended to grow up with an inadequate moral compass and very vulnerable to anti-social influences. He called this group – maybe 5% of society – an 'underclass'. In the 1990s he journeyed over to Britain where he diagnosed, in articles for the *Sunday Times*, a similar phenomenon.

In 1998 he wrote an article entitled 'New Victorians, new rabble', in which he predicted rich middle-class people were likely to retreat to 'gated' communities, where they would live protected and isolated lives while the rest of society lived at the mercy of a 'rabble' expressing many of the underclass values. Most commentators dismissed this as highly unlikely but, it has to be said, that in July 2007, Professor Danny Dorling of Sheffield University published a report which suggested that, indeed, an increasing segregation in urban centres could be discerned where middle-class people lived lives wholly separate from working-class people, and vice versa (see Dorling, 2014; and Lee and Dorling, 2011). In January 2015, the Joseph Rowntree Foundation reported that, as a result of poverty, poor education and employment, as many as 40% of British families were 'too poor to play a part in society' (see Wintour, 2015).

REGIONAL DIFFERENCES

Britain has a major north–south divide, with a more prosperous south and a more depressed north, where so many of the traditional industries died out a couple of decades ago. London is relatively untypical, too, having not only a vibrant financial and business service economy but a multicultural society as well. Attempts to devolve businesses to other regions have been only partially successful. In the summer of 2014 chancellor George Osborne called for further investment in northern cities and infrastructure, his so-called 'northern powerhouse'. Labour's economic policy, too, adopted a similar stance on northern cities. In the wake of the Scottish independence referendum of 2014, devolution of power within England reignited as a political issue, when local government leaders in the north, like Manchester's Richard Leese, demanded more power over their budgets and more options for economic development. On 3 November 2014, Osborne announced just such a deal for Manchester and its region. A report appearing on 19 January 2015, from the Centre for Cities, suggested that government attempts to close the north–south gap seem to have failed. From 2004 onwards cities in the south have grown at twice the rate of cities elsewhere: 11.3% compared with 5.5%. In 2013 there were 26.8% more businesses in the southern cities than 10 years earlier, compared with 13.7% in the rest of the UK.

GENDER

As in so many countries, women in Britain have been treated unfairly compared with men for most of its existence; in the nineteenth century it was possible for a man to beat his wife and own her property while she had no legal redress and could not divorce an abusive or unfaithful spouse. In the late twentieth century many of these legal inequities were removed but social attitudes take longer to change and many women still receive lower wages than men for similar work and tend to be employed in lower-status jobs: clerical assistants, cleaners, shop assistants and the like. They are often, moreover, employed only part-time and can suffer discrimination should they have children and wish to return to their jobs. It remains the case that women suffer from various kinds of inequality which frequently feature on the political agenda:

1. Up to 3 million women and girls across the UK experience rape, domestic violence, stalking, or other forms of violence each year.
2. The full-time gender pay gap is 10%, and the average part-time pay gap is 34.5%.
3. Women make up only 22% of MPs and 17% of board directors in FTSE 100 companies.

ETHNICITY

It would be fair to say that, over the past half century, ethnicity has become almost as important a dividing line in British society as class. Successive influxes of refugees, such as the Huguenots (French Calvinists) in the fifteenth and sixteenth centuries and Jews fleeing pogroms in Russia during the nineteenth century, were absorbed without too much dislocation, but the thousands of impoverished Irish immigrants during that same century was less problem-free and they, often responsible for massive infrastructure achievements, had to face forms of discrimination.

Immigration after 1945 was initially from the Commonwealth and during the 1950s black Caribbeans, working often in the public services, were the victims of crude racism. It was the same with those from the 'New Commonwealth' – India, Pakistan and then Uganda –

when new immigrants became 'ghetto-ised' in certain areas, for instance Asians in Southall and West Indians in Willesden. In 1968 Enoch Powell, a prominent Tory MP, delivered his infamous 'rivers of blood speech' prophesying violent civil strife if immigration was not checked.

Those seeking asylum from world trouble-spots like Bosnia, Iraq and Afghanistan provided another stratum of difference to be integrated not without difficulty. But the most severe problem with immigration occurred during the first decade of the twenty-first century, when thousands of east Europeans from Poland, Romania and Bulgaria entered the UK by virtue of being members of the European Union (EU), which had 'freedom of movement of labour' as a founding principle. Various pressure groups emerged seeking to change an 'over-liberal' open-door policy, for example Migration Watch UK and then the United Kingdom Independence Party (UKIP), which argued withdrawal from the EU was the only way to solve the problem. It was true that such an influx, while contributing economic benefits, put excessive strain on public services in some parts of the country and might have forced wages down in certain unskilled occupations. On top of that, an unknown number of illegal immigrants regularly manage to enter the country and this adds fuel to the flames created by newspapers like the *Daily Express* and *Daily Mail*, UKIP and the right wing of the Conservative Party. In 1986 the foreign-born population was 6.2%; by the 2011 census the figure was 11.9%. David Cameron pledged in 2010 to keep net immigration to 'tens of thousands' but the figure resolutely refused to fall and registered around a quarter of a million in 2013. The refugee crisis in the summer of 2015, largely caused by the war in Syria, created great political pressure across Europe.

QUESTIONS FOR DISCUSSION

1. Why is it that the gross inequalities of capitalist societies manage to survive without any genuine political threat that they might be removed?
2. Are socio-economic inequalities harmful to society?
3. Have women achieved anything like genuine equality with men in the UK?

FURTHER READING

Provocative ideas can be read in the book by Eagleton (see below), who argues that Marx, far from being discredited (which is the current consensus), has been proved more and more right in his analysis as events unfold, suggesting the formation of monopoly capitalism and its possible collapse. The book by John Hills is a cornucopia of facts and arguments destroying popular myths about the welfare state.

Cadwalladr, C. (2008) It's the clever way to power, *Observer*, 16 March.

Clark, T. (2014) *Hard Times: The Divisive Toll of the Economic Slump*, Yale University Press.

Crump, T. (2010) *How the Industrial Revolution Changed the World*, Robinson.

Dorling, D. (2014) *Inequality and the 1%*, Verso.

Eagleton, T. (2011) *Why Marx Was Right*, Yale University Press.

Elliot, L. (2015) The regions cannot thrive with Whitehall in charge, *Guardian*, 19 January.

Halsey, A. and Webb, J. (eds) (2000) *Twentieth Century Social Trends*, Macmillan.

Hennessy, P. (1992) *Never Again*, Jonathan Cape.

Hills, J. (2014) *Good Times, Bad Times: The Welfare Myth of Them and Us*, Policy Press.

James, L. (2006) *The Middle Class: A History*, Abacus.

Kynaston, D. (2007) *Austerity Britain, 1945–51*, Bloomsbury.

Kynaston, D. (2008) The road to meritocracy is blocked by private schools, *Guardian*, 22 February.

Lansley, S. (2012) *The Cost of Inequality*, Gibson Square.

Lee, C. and Dorling, D. (2011) The geography of poverty, *Socialist Review*, October.

Miles, D. (2005) *The Tribes of Britain. Who Are We? And Where Do We Come From?*, Phoenix.

Wilkinson, R. and Pickett, K. (2009) *The Spirit Level*, Penguin.

Wintour, P. (2015) Joseph Rowntree Foundation report on poverty, *Guardian*, 19 January.

WEBSITE

Office for National Statistics: http://www.ons.gov.uk/ons/index.html.

5

THE UNWRITTEN CONSTITUTION

Constitutions provide the 'rules of the game' for states, in that they determine how their political systems are allowed to operate. If they know nothing else about its constitution, most British people know that their country has no written document upon which it is inscribed. But, like many other well known 'truths', this is not quite correct. Much of the constitution is actually written down, in the form of acts of parliament relating to, for example, who can vote. What Britain lacks is a complete *codified document* like the American constitution. Part of the explanation for this is that the monarchy from which the British system evolved existed at a time when the idea of basing royal behaviour on an explicit set of rules would never have been even considered.

Perhaps the closest Britain came to it was the 1215 document Magna Carta, which King John was forced by his barons to sign at Runnymede. In consequence of John's arbitrary style of rule, this laid down that excessive taxation should not be levied by the King and that nobody should be imprisoned without a proper trial. This was not a constitution as we now understand such a document but, as a historic limitation, in writing, of the monarch's hitherto unlimited power, it was a vital *part* of one. Magna Carta was a crucial component in what has become Britain's constitution, assembled piecemeal over the centuries. The US constitution, probably the world's most famous, came about because the separation of the 13 colonies from Britain essentially 'invented' a new country, the nature of which could be planned by its remarkably able founding fathers.

'DIGNIFIED' AND 'EFFICIENT'

Walter Bagehot, the most famous authority on the British constitution, made a distinction between those aspects which were 'dignified' – that is, had a mostly ceremonial function, like the monarchy, Privy Council and, to a degree the House of Lords – and the 'efficient' or 'working' aspects – like the Commons, departments of state and the law courts.

PARLIAMENTARY SOVEREIGNTY

Basic to the whole system of British government is the notion that it is only the Queen in parliament who can make the law, or indeed unmake it. Unlike in the USA, the courts cannot strike down a law as being contrary to the constitution: no other body can set aside parliament's statutes. After the so-called Glorious Revolution of 1688, the King agreed to be bound by the laws of parliament, and his courts of law too. The centuries-long conflict between monarch and parliament had ended in the latter's favour. Parliament is at the peak of the constitution and, as the Commons is the dominant element of it, elections to that body determine which party forms the government.

SOURCES OF THE CONSTITUTION

This is a complex subject but, arguably, the most important sources could be identified as follows.

STATUTES OR ACTS AFFECTING THE RIGHTS OF THE STATE

For instance, the Habeas Corpus Act was passed in 1679; it built on the Magna Carta in limiting the right of the state to detain anyone without trial. The Prevention of Terrorism Act 1974 increased state powers against terrorist offences on a 'temporary' basis but was renewed annually thereafter, with the Crime and Security Act 2001 strengthening it further.

'SUPER STATUTES'

Moran (2011) identifies these as laws so important that parliament cannot easily over-rule them, despite the ability of parliament to do so via simple majorities in both chambers. These include membership of the 1957 Treaty of Rome and other treaties of the European Union (EU), like the 1992 Maastricht Treaty, and acts relating to the devolved assemblies or the abolition of hereditary peerages. These are laws of heavier timber than the normal ones applying to electoral law and who has the right to vote.

CASE AND COMMON LAW

Case law comprises the interpretations of various laws in court cases when frequently problems encountered in application establish a new nuance. Common law dates back to Norman times and is distilled from 'custom and precedent' relating to traditional rights and freedoms upheld by courts over centuries; freedom and free speech are prominent among them.

ROYAL PREROGATIVE

These are the powers once exercised by the monarch like dissolving and summoning parliament, signing treaties, declaring war and so forth. Because they were the prerogative of the King or Queen, parliament's consent was not necessary. Over time, however, prime minister and cabinet have come to exercise these powers, still immune from parliamentary control. In 2007 Gordon Brown declared he would pass over these powers to parliament; the Constitutional Reform and Governance Act 2010 (CRA) did transfer some powers but only very partially.

CONVENTIONS

These are very British in that they lack the force of law but have been followed for so long that they have come to be seen as automatically applicable. Examples include the practice whereby the prime minister has sat in the Commons since the early twentieth century. The 'Ponsonby rule' was a convention whereby treaties were laid before the House before being signed; the CRA finally gave the rule legal force.

INSTITUTIONAL RULES

Erskine May's nineteenth-century work *Parliamentary Practice* (often known just as *Erskine May*) has become virtually an element of the constitution. Similarly, there are a number of hugely respected works on the constitution, such as Coke's *Institutes of the Law of England* and A. V. Dicey's *An Introduction to the Study of the Law of the Constitution*, which have considerable persuasive power where clarity is lacking.

AMENDING THE CONSTITUTION

In the USA there are several hurdles to be cleared before any aspect of the constitution can be amended; Britain is unusual in having no special 'entrenchment' of its constitution. However:

- Bills with constitutional content usually have their committee stage on the floor of the Commons rather than in a standing committee.
- It has now become (virtually) accepted that major constitutional proposals should first be subject to a referendum – as in the case of devolution or the voting system.
- Devolution itself has arguably removed some constitutional items away from the orbit of Westminster but power is still only delegated: it can be limited or abolished altogether should the parliament in Westminster so decide.

SEPARATION OF POWERS

French political thinker Baron de Montesquieu believed England had achieved a balance whereby the legislature, executive and judiciary checked each other. The framers of the US constitution were influenced by his analysis and embodied such a balance within their creation. However, he was mistaken, in that the executive is actually formed from the largest group in the legislature and its 'independence' is thus mostly a fiction. In the US, the executive and legislature are elected separately and the senior judiciary are appointed by the president. Separate elections endow separate legitimacy and powers not found in British government; indeed, the British prime minister has more power in some respects than the US president, who has to negotiate deals with a more independent Congress. The prime minister, though, can be deposed if party support is lost, while the president is guaranteed office until it expires after four years.

'CORE' AND 'CONTESTED' ELEMENTS OF THE CONSTITUTION

In the USA the constitution occupies a revered place in national life: its authority is accepted as a matter of course. In Britain, there is no such respect: indifference would probably be a better description. Michael Moran (2011), recognising that such distinctions comprise an element of 'political culture' (see Chapter 3), makes a useful distinction between those aspects of the constitution which are accepted without cavil (the core elements) and those which are contested.

CORE ELEMENTS

These include:

- *The rule of law.* Government is not allowed to transgress its own rules lest it offend by being *ultra vires*, in which case it can be challenged in the courts.
- *Procedural democracy.* These are the rules whereby the government is elected, seeks to fulfil its promises and is then subject to re-election by voters.
- *Accountability.* Governments have to explain themselves to voters, are subject to challenge and their dismissal is never questioned.
- *Liberal freedoms.* In the same way, basic liberal values like freedom of speech or assembly are essentially guaranteed. However, security fears born of terrorist activity have caused some qualifications to such fundamental tenets during the last half century.

CONTESTED ELEMENTS

- *Territorial unity.* Rather contrary to plans, devolution has unleashed powerful nationalist sentiments, especially in Scotland (see Chapter 17 for more on Scottish independence).
- *Parliamentary supremacy.* Membership of the EU has made its laws superior to those passed through parliament. This has nourished intense opposition from *Euro-sceptic* opponents of UK membership.
- *European Union.* See below.
- *Crown legitimacy.* The Queen still commands wide national support but the behaviour of some of the royal family has increased doubts as to their usefulness. At the time of writing, for example, there is one section of public opinion which would prefer Prince William to succeed as king rather than his father, Prince Charles.

CURRENT CONSTITUTIONAL ISSUES

REFORMING THE VOTING SYSTEM

When the coalition government was formed in May 2010, a key policy objective for the Liberal Democrats was a reformed voting system. Under the 'first past the post' system, small parties with widely dispersed voting support lose out; unless small parties have their support concentrated in certain constituencies, they will lose virtually every contest. The Lib Dems realise they are unlikely to win power in the long term unless the voting system becomes more proportional.

The Conservatives were willing to allow them a referendum on the voting system based on the *alternative vote (AV)*. This system was not very proportional at all but the Lib Dems saw it as first step along the way to possible proportional representation. David Cameron had hinted he would take a back seat in the campaign but was pressed by his backbenchers into reversing this half promise. His full-throated opposition to AV helped defeat the idea two to one in May 2011. The Lib Dems were dismayed by their defeat but still hope that their chance will come again.

REFORMING THE HOUSE OF LORDS

Again, the Lib Dems took the lead on this, submitting a bill to reform the upper chamber, but Conservatives in both Houses ensured it foundered. To show his anger at being let down by his coalition partners, Clegg refused to support a reform of constituency boundaries which would have delivered an extra 20 seats to the Conservatives in 2015.

EUROPEAN UNION

British opinion on the EU has become increasingly negative, with some polls showing a majority for withdrawal. In the May 2014 European elections, the anti-EU United Kingdom Independence Party (UKIP) came top of the poll.

SCOTTISH INDEPENDENCE

On 18 September 2014 Scotland held a referendum on independence. The vote was won by the 'No' campaign 55–45% but the vibrant 'Yes' campaign energised the Scottish nation and some of its energy leaked south of the border to reinvigorate the question of whether only English MPs should vote on English issues and the question of regional devolution.

DISCUSSION QUESTIONS

1. Should the UK acquire a written constitution?
2. Would it be fair to describe televised partly leaders' debates as accepted conventions of UK campaign practice?
3. Is Scottish independence eventually inevitable?

FURTHER READING

A useful short study of the changing constitution is provided by Philip Norton in Chapter 13 of Jones and Norton (2013). Another useful study is Chapter 4 of Moran (2011).

Bogdanor, V. (2009) *The New British Constitution*, Hart.
Brazier, R. (1994) *Constitutional Practice*, Oxford University Press.
Foley, M. (1999) *The Politics of the British Constitution*, Manchester University Press.
Institute for Public Policy Research (1992) *A New Constitution for the United Kingdom*, Mansell.

Jones, B. and Norton, P. (2013) *Politics UK* (8th edition), Routledge.
Moran, M. (2011) *Politics and Governance in the UK* (2nd edition), Palgrave.
Norton, P. (2011) *A Century of Constitutional Reform in the UK*, Oxford University Press.

WEBSITES

Ministry of Justice: http://www.justice.gov.uk.
The Electoral Commission: http://www.electoralcommission.org.uk.

6

POLITICAL IDEAS

This chapter examines British political ideas that emerged through the narrative arc of events as theory met practice in terms of changed political realities over three turbulent centuries of British political history. People are motivated to act on the basis of what is important to them, often, for example, the material comfort of themselves and their families, but also on what they believe is important: their country and, maybe, the future of the human race itself.

THE EMERGENCE OF POLITICAL IDEAS

It is easy to forget how political ideas as we understand them are of such recent provenance. During the medieval era there were debates around the religious and political status quo but they were limited in scope and dissemination. The Civil War (1642–49) saw the emergence, with the development of printing, of a fierce pamphlet debate about kingship. In 1647, however, this debate surfaced within Cromwell's New Model Army, when it was headquartered in Putney, creating the *Putney debates*, chaired by Cromwell himself. Here a vigorous discussion began between those who wanted to compromise and keep the monarchy and those, like the so-called

Levellers, who wanted a radical new system of politics based upon one man one vote, biennial elections plus new constituencies with authority based in the elected House of Commons. The leader of this radical group, Colonel Thomas Rainsborough, declared famously 'I think that the poorest he that is in England hath a life to lead as the greatest he'. Debate was terminated once Charles I escaped and new battles loomed – Cromwell was in any case worried by the radicalism displayed – but the first and influential outline of a possible new political order for Britain had been articulated.

The Enlightenment – that ferment of liberal ideas which swept through Europe during the seventeenth and eighteenth centuries – emphasised the application of reason and the prime importance of the individual as opposed to reverence for an omniscient church plus the monarchy as the natural form of political rule. Such views seem unexceptional in the present day but at the time they were perceived as subversive, if not revolutionary. These ideas, in fact, were the midwife of democratic ideas in the nineteenth century, which successively saw the extension of the voting franchise and the emergence of the Conservative and Liberal political parties. It was the advent of democratic government which saw political ideas take off to become the source of inspiration and route to power for political movements.

From concentrating on favoured forms of government, the focus of political ideas now moved on to such questions as: the desirable degree of state involvement in everyday life; the health of the economy; levels of poverty and government's obligation, if any, to alleviate it; not forgetting the role of the state in foreign affairs. During the nineteenth century the founding political ideas of our age were established; they were destined to be heavily amended by political events and practice

CORE PHILOSOPHIES IN THE NINETEENTH AND TWENTIETH CENTURIES

LIBERALISM

Liberalism (with a small 'l') originated with seventeenth–century British and European Enlightenment philosophers such as John Locke (1632–1704) and Jean-Jacques Rousseau (1712–78). Their writings marked a break with traditional unquestioning deference towards church and state. Locke believed in applying reason to all aspects of life, as well as in toleration of different ideas and beliefs, and the idea that people had 'rights' or natural entitlements. These ideas helped break the straightjacket of traditional acceptance of the then dominant monarchical rule, but during the nineteenth century they were further developed by the likes of Adam Smith (1723–90), Jeremy Bentham (1748–1832) and John Stuart Mill (1806–73).

Their works helped create a 'liberal' body of ideas: people should be free to do as they wished as long as their actions did not impinge on the freedom of others; government should only intervene in our lives if absolutely necessary ('minimal government'); and government should evolve towards genuine representative democracy. In the middle of the century the Liberal Party emerged out of a combination of former supporters of the Tory Robert Peel, the Whigs and the Manchester Radicals led by Richard Cobden (1804–65) and John Bright (1811–89). This last group contributed towards so-called *classical liberalism*.

Adam Smith (1723–90) argued that business should be allowed to produce the goods people wanted at the price they were prepared to pay. Provided competition remains fair, he maintained, the 'invisible hand' of the market will ensure goods are produced at the lowest possible prices at the quality levels consumers desire. This fundamental statement in favour of market-led, free enterprise capitalism did not initially gain the acceptance of Conservatives but, ironically perhaps, was warmly embraced by them later, in the twentieth century, not least by Margaret Thatcher.

Liberals also argued that government interference with 'markets' would seriously harm or disable their potency: capitalism should be left to work its own magic. However, towards the end of the nineteenth century thinkers like T. H. Green (1836–82) and Alfred Marshall (1842–1924) – the *New Liberals* – came to the conclusion that the inequalities produced by the free enterprise economy disadvantage the prospects of the poor compared with the rich. Liberal thinker L. T. Hobhouse (1864–1929) urged a levelling of the playing field through taxation to fund a minimum standard of living and old age pensions for the poor. Yet while the Liberal Party was one of the dominant parties of the nineteenth century, with

William Gladstone (1809–1898) becoming prime minister four times, their fortunes withered during the twentieth century, partly through the personal conflict between the brilliant David Lloyd George (1863–1945) and Herbert Asquith (1852–1928), not to mention the rapid rise of the Labour Party, with its socialist ideas.

SOCIALISM

Socialism put the economy at the heart of its argument. This was because industrialisation had transformed traditional society into new forms, which some applauded and others hated. It followed that applause tended to come from those who had benefited – in some cases hugely – from the changes; and the criticism from those who had not done so well or felt they had fared badly. *Capitalism* or free enterprise was the process whereby energetic entrepreneurial people set up the means to make the things people wanted – food clothes, furniture, jewellery – and employed (paid) other people to produce them.

Employers saw this as a virtuous circle in which everyone became better off, but some critics argued that the rewards of this new system were distributed unfairly. While the owners of businesses grew fabulously rich, able to buy huge mansions, employ scores of servants and live away from the dirt and noise of the town and city, workers were often paid a tiny fraction of the wealth they created and were forced to bring up their families in insanitary and squalid conditions. Moreover, capitalism had a cyclical tendency: business could 'boom' vigorously and everyone might indeed benefit for a period; but it also had 'busts', when economic activity would slump into recession. When the latter occurred, most successful owners of business could live off their savings for a while and wait for the business upturn; workers, however, usually had few savings and faced unemployment, poverty and even starvation. In hard times it is always those in low-paid employment who seem to pay the highest price.

Those who made this critique of capitalism elaborated the set of beliefs and arguments known as 'socialism'. This asserted that the inequalities produced by capitalism made it dysfunctional as the means by which people lived their lives. Instead, they advocated, depending on their radicalism, a series of alternatives. Revolutionary socialists like Karl Marx (1818–83) and later Lenin (1870–1924) and Trotsky (1879–1940) urged workers to rise up, throw off their 'chains' of poverty and employment, and establish a new 'classless' society in which distinctions between 'rich' and 'poor' would disappear and everyone would live in equal relationship to each other.

The dangers which attended revolutionary action, however, were not to everyone's political taste and many adopted a reformist – or social democratic – attitude, whereby inequalities would be reduced through gradual reform. The Labour Party contained some revolutionaries but in practice its leadership tended to favour incremental reform. They tended to agree with and adopt the ideas of the New Liberals and, as the twentieth century wore on, those of the liberal John Maynard Keynes (1883–1946), who favoured government intervention to manage the economy effectively, and William Beveridge (1879–1963), whose report in 1943 urged the birth of the *welfare state* to eliminate the 'five giants' of want, ignorance, squalor, idleness and disease.

CONSERVATISM

Conservatism as a philosophy is harder to define, as it lacks recognisable core elements. Rather, it comprises a series of tenets plus something which Lord Hailsham (1907–2001) called an 'attitude of mind' and a non-ideological, pragmatic approach to problems. Conservatives argue that business is the source of hugely beneficial outcomes for everyone. According to them, it is people with energy and organisational skills who set up businesses, often putting all their wealth and resources at risk. They have to toil and graft for days on end to make their business work; few people are prepared to make that sacrifice and few have the skills to succeed; they therefore 'deserve' to succeed and to receive the accompanying wealth as their reward.

Conservatives' attitude to socialism's critique is that paying people more is fine if the business climate allows but if wages go up too much products will not succeed at selling in the marketplace, business will fail and maybe thousands of workers will end up unemployed. Their response to 'equal pay', for which some socialists used to call, is that human nature is such that those who are not inclined to work hard will merely do less to receive the same pay as those who work very hard, resulting in a situation where the rich and energetic support or subsidise those lazy and talentless 'parasites' on other people's efforts.

Far better, they argue, that people should be paid according to their talents and contribution: you work hard, you earn money and prosper. Result? Everyone is content. If you lazily refuse to work, you fail to prosper and your family suffers. It's your fault. Any attempt to assist the feckless will merely encourage others to adopt the same lifestyle. Conservatives love Herbert Spencer's (1820–1902) comment: 'The ultimate result of shielding men from the effects of folly, is to fill the world with fools'. Who decides how much workers should earn? It will depend on the market concerned. If certain skills are in short supply – skilled surgeons for example – then high salaries are required to attract able people to enter the long training required for the medical profession. A surgeon will be paid more than, say, a plumber whose skills are easier to develop and require only a short period of training. But plumbers will be paid more than, say, shop assistants, as the skills required for working in a shop are abundantly available and so can command only modest rewards. In this way the hierarchy of rewards in a free economy is constructed. As technology has advanced, advanced education and training have increasingly become a requirement of employment.

HUMAN NATURE

Conservatism is based on a more pessimistic view of human nature than the other two ideologies mentioned above. Tories believe that people need to be *forced* to be law-abiding, requiring heavy penalties if they steal property or otherwise break the law. They also believe society requires elites, specially trained in elite schools and universities, to fill the most influential and powerful positions in business, the professions, public administration and politics. Socialists and liberals tend to be more optimistic, believing people are basically good but are more likely to become less so as a result of the environment in which they are brought up. They are opposed to 'elitism' and prefer an open society where anyone with the ability can ascend to the highest positions in the land.

Conservatives, almost by definition, are keen to respect the past and 'conserve' the present, to support the status quo. As they are usually the people doing well out of the present, they are less keen to rock the boat, hating the idea of revolution and distrusting any rapid change. Liberals, on the other hand, are not afraid of change, especially regarding political structures, where they have always argued for democratic improvements. Socialists, too, favour change – in some cases radical change – so that wealth is distributed more fairly in society and opportunities for advancement are equally available to everyone. Redistributing wealth, however, is not easy, as those who possess wealth fight hard to hang onto it.

POST-WAR DEVELOPMENTS IN POLITICAL IDEAS

THE POST-WAR CONSENSUS

So we see that the emphasis of political ideas shifted from forms of government before the middle of the nineteenth century to the social and economic health of the nation in the later nineteenth and early twentieth centuries. In the 1945 election, Labour astonished everyone, not least themselves, by defeating the massively popular war leader Winston Churchill (1874–1965) in a landslide election victory. Now in power with a huge majority, of 146, Labour under Clement Attlee (1883–1967) for the first time had to face the responsibility of government. From the early days, Labour members had viewed private ownership as the evil heart of capitalism and had called for public ownership of the economy. However, their zeal seemed to stop once Labour had *nationalised* one-fifth of the economy, the result being dubbed the *mixed economy*.

Their version of 'common ownership' was to dispossess owners of the major utilities, such as the providers of gas, electricity and water, take them over and then run them through boards accountable to government ministers. They also hugely extended government-funded welfare services, including free education and, most importantly, the National Health Service (NHS), established in 1948.

In 1950 Labour won a small majority, of five, despite, owing to the vagaries of the first-past-the-post system, winning a million and a half more votes than the Tories. The Liberals continued their half-century-long decline, returning only 12 MPs. After 20 months in power, Attlee sought to increase his fragile majority at another election. However, this time, despite another record number of votes for Labour, it was the Conservatives who won, with a majority of 16; the Liberals slipped even further, garnering only nine seats.

In office, the 76-year-old Churchill, displaying perhaps traditional Tory pragmatism, decided to accept Labour's substantial changes. A period ensued when, despite rancorous political argument, basic agreement persisted on the *post-war consensus* of the mixed economy plus the welfare state. How long this settlement held is a matter of dispute but by the end of the 1960s it was looking decidedly thin. British people had enjoyed a steady improvement in living standards following the austerities of the war and the immediate post-war years; however, the British economy was not performing well relative to its chief rivals abroad.

This hurt and had political salience, especially as the two major nations defeated in 1945, Japan and Germany, were both enjoying an economic renaissance. In power through 1964–70, Labour governed cautiously; 'revisionist' socialists believed equality now could be achieved via social reform, without the need for more nationalisation; left-wing Labour members continued to urge for 'more socialism' – meaning more state control – producing a divided party. Now Conservatives to the right and Labour MPs to the left were calling for radical change: Tories a return to a genuine market economy and left-wingers a more full-blooded programme of state control. The 1970s was a troubled decade, ravaged by inflation and industrial action. The Labour Party was dominated by the big unions. The 1980s, however, was about to usher in a remarkable change in British political life and the ideas which informed it.

THE 'THATCHER REVOLUTION'

Margaret Thatcher (1925–2013) came to power when the British economy was failing to compete abroad, much of it surviving only through government subsidy. She instantly announced an unremittingly tough new approach, soon to attract the 'ism' placed after her name: end inflation through raising interest rates; end over-manning; allow non-profitable industries to go bankrupt; reduce taxation drastically; and, most important for many Tories at that time, take on and overcome trade union power.

This extreme version of market force capitalism she drove through with a resolution reinforced by her famous victory in the 1982 Falklands War over the Argentine aggressors. A massive domestic battle ensued in 1984–85, when the miners' union under Arthur Scargill (1938–) led what some described as a heroic, others a reckless, strike against the government's plan to close scores of pits all over the country. After a period of intense civil and political conflict, the miners were defeated and along with them the power of unions for the indefinite future.

Thatcher believed in rewarding hardworking individuals, returning nationalised industries to the private sector as well as demanding that citizens act responsibly regarding payment of local taxes. She introduced a highly successful policy of enabling council house tenants to buy their own houses; over a million did so. Applying similar logic, she set about returning nationalised industries to the private sector. Among the enterprises she 'sold' back to the public were British Telecom, British Gas, British Airways, Rolls-Royce, British Steel, and the water and electricity companies. Her reforming enthusiasm did not stop there: she introduced a system of tendering in local government so that many of its functions were put out to tender and then taken over by private owners and employees.

She also introduced a new form of local government finance. Concerned that those paying the highest rates were often wealthy Conservatives, while many of the lower-paid (often voting Labour) enjoyed exemptions and subsidies, she introduced the community charge or *poll tax*, whereby everyone was obliged to pay the same basic charge whatever their income. For many, Thatcherism marked a high point of very necessary, brave political reform of a failing economy; for others, it epitomised the callous disregard the champions of capitalism reserved for the ordinary people who manned the British economy and its public services. But even her Labour opponents could not deny that 'Thatcherism' did much to revive the faltering British economy.

NEW LABOUR AND 'BLAIRISM'

SOCIALISM DISOWNED

After 18 years in opposition, having lost elections in 1979, 1983, 1987 and 1992, Labour realised it had drastically to change its approach if it ever wanted to re-enter 10 Downing Street. Labour's vowed intention to replace the capitalist economy with a 'socialism' which most voters associated, negatively, with inefficient, over-manned and corrupt nationalised industries had not proved a recipe for success. Party leader Neil Kinnock (1942–) began a process of reinventing his party as one comfortable with a free enterprise economy and perceived as capable of running both the economy and public services successfully. 'Socialism' became a dirty word and it somehow disappeared from Labour policy documents. Two young MPs, Tony Blair (1953–) and Gordon Brown (1951–), assisted by a gifted media manager, Peter Mandelson (1954–), set about rebuilding their party according to a different set of beliefs.

MEDIA MANAGEMENT

These three worked tirelessly to create 'New Labour'. It was certainly something of a public relations process – the nation had to be convinced Labour ideas had changed for the party to become electable – but it was hugely assisted by Brown's convincing display of economic competence in opposition and Blair's brilliant command of television and other media. With Labour's working-class constituency sharply reduced by Thatcher's winding-up of traditional industries, Labour needed someone to appeal to middle-class voters in the south. Blair, with his public school and Oxbridge background plus his youthful good looks and attractive family, was the ideal person to sell this message of a party transformed and now 'safe' to run the economy. Having accepted, or rather 'embraced', free enterprise capitalism, New Labour arguably became one of the most pro-business governments of modern times. However, critics argued that New Labour, having improved Labour's poor public relations, soon became obsessed with news management and *spin*.

ECONOMIC POLICY

Critics also claimed that Brown and Blair ran the economy pretty much along lines Thatcher would have approved of. Far from restoring privatised concerns to public ownership as they had earlier promised, Labour accepted them as *faits accomplis*, and, further, the Labour government even privatised some more public bodies, leading some to detect a 'post-Thatcher consensus'. Such a unity of view, however, did not extend to public expenditure.

Few could deny that the NHS and education had been starved of the funds they needed during the 1980s and 1990s. After a two-year period of restraint, Gordon Brown began to inject billions into these two central public services. This behaviour would seem to place New Labour squarely in the tradition, if not of the now discredited socialism, then certainly in that of 'social democracy', as practised in many European countries: using the fruits of capitalist economies to benefit the lower-paid. New Labour's liberal approach to social issues like equal rights for women and gay people tended to confirm such an analysis.

ROLE OF THE PRIVATE SECTOR

A major issue for New Labour, however, concerned the role which might be played in public services by the private sector. It has long been a tenet of Conservative thinking, reinforced by Thatcher, that private business is more dynamic and efficient than public services, because of the discipline applied by the profit motive. The private sector has to pay its way and be efficient in minimising costs, while the public sector frequently allows 'good money to be spent after bad', with nobody brought to account.

Once into their second and third periods in government, it became clear that Blair tended to agree with this Conservative axiom in relation to the NHS and other services, while Brown, who desperately resented Blair's continuing presence in Downing Street, apparently did not. Brown's position appealed to the unions, who feared the private sector would introduce the profit motive where it did not belong and result in public sector workers suffering lower pay and less secure employment.

FOREIGN POLICY

Few in the party objected to Blair being conspicuously pro-EU, even to the extent, early on, of wishing to join the euro. He was, however, well out of step with a wide swathe of his party over other aspects of foreign policy. Successful military interventions in Kosovo (1999) and Sierra Leone (2000) led him to believe that British military power could be used to resist the malign power of arbitrary autocratic rule in other parts of the world. But such 'humanitarian intervention' ceased to produce easy victory in the case of Iraq, in the joint action with the United States, led by the right-wing George Bush Jnr (1946–): with Saddam Hussein (1937–2006) deposed, the post-invasion process swung hopelessly out of control and into a bloodbath.

THE 'CORBYN REVOLUTION'

After Ed Miliband resigned the party leadership following the May 2015 general election, Jeremy Corbyn, a hard-left rebel on Labour's back benches for 32 years, managed to acquire the necessary 35 nominations to stand for the party's leadership only through the kindness of colleagues but then discovered he was addressing packed meetings and, assisted by 16,000 volunteers, achieved a crushing 60% victory on the first ballot on 12 September 2015. He benefited from the anger of so many at the Conservatives' anti-austerity policies and the enthusiasm of young people for someone who offered hope, albeit in the form of ideas once mooted and then defeated during the 1980s.

Corbyn and his shadow Chancellor, John McConnell, offered a Marxist analysis of Britain's ills, with solutions varying from widespread renationalisation, higher taxes on the rich, an assault on corporate tax dodging, plus a wealth tax as recommended by French economist Thomas Piketty. In addition, they urged the removal of university fees and a living wage of £10 an hour. At the time of writing, the new leader's views had not been warmly endorsed by his fellow MPs who doubt his ability to persuade voters as a whole that they should vote Labour.

CAMERON'S CONSERVATISM

Having enjoyed 18 years in power (1979–97), the Conservatives themselves had then to accept the bitter experience of opposition for

13 years: 1997–2010. Rather like Labour in the 1980s, Conservatism was out of touch with the times. By hanging onto the memory of Thatcher, future home secretary Theresa May suggested in 2002 that they were seen as the 'nasty party': overly focused on business, unconcerned with the poor, hostile to gays and immigrants.

Under the successive leadership of William Hague, Iain Duncan Smith and Michael Howard, the party lost two more elections and during this period barely rose above 30% support in the opinion polls. This episode illustrates that political ideas *do* matter, not just in terms of a party running the country successfully, but, even more important politically, for how positively voters perceive it. Finally the message that something drastic had to be done penetrated the party's high leadership and one ambitious backbench MP began a journey to re-brand the Conservatives – in the process preparing his own application for the nation's top job. David Cameron's impressive 'no notes' speech at the 2005 party conference meant his 'interview' with the party had been a striking success and in December he easily won the leadership contest.

He then embarked on a series of well publicised policy projects designed to show that the Conservatives: were no longer hostile to gays and wanted more Conservative women in the Commons; were determined to provide the 'greenest' possible government; and wanted social policy to cater centrally for the less well-off. It was a brilliant campaign, worthy of New Labour's spin machine. The polls showed it worked. Within two years the Tories had relegated Thatcherism, for the time being at least, to the back burner and shouldered their way into the political centre ground. They were now again electable. However, it was clear also that, economically, their shadow chancellor, George Osborne, was still cut from traditional Tory cloth. It was also clear that a large section of the Conservative Party was still deeply hostile to the idea of an EU in which members moved steadily towards a position of 'ever closer union'.

LIBERALISM

The flame of nineteenth-century Liberalism flickered ever more feebly when the party returned only six MPs in October 1955 but in the October 1974 election the Liberals managed a minor breakthrough, with 13 seats. The party's political message had not changed a great deal – Keynesian economics, pro-welfare state, internationalism and pro-Europe – but it acted as a 'protest' outlet for people fed up with the other two big parties. During the 1970s it helped Labour survive when its tiny majority eventually disappeared and during the early 1980s it found an ally in the temporary flourish of the breakaway Social Democratic Party (SDP), which had formed after four senior Labour former cabinet ministers – the so-called 'Gang of Four' – could no longer stomach the left wing of their party, led by Tony Benn.

The left-dominated party produced a left-wing manifesto for the 1983 election, dismissed by Labour's Gerald Kaufman as 'the longest suicide note in history'. Labour lost disastrously and was nearly outvoted by the Liberal–SDP Alliance, which had formed in 1981. The SDP lasted only until 1988 before it faded away but its ideas – a continuation of the moderate social democracy of post-war Labour governments – represented a repository of ideas from which New Labour could fashion its voter-friendly prospectus during the 1990s.

Substantial elements of the defunct SDP merged with the Liberals in 1988 to create a new party: the *Liberal Democrats*. This party, capably led first by Paddy Ashdown and then Charles Kennedy, continued to proselytise its centrist ideas and, combined with its role as 'protest vote' party, managed to increase its representation to 62 by 2005. Lib Dem leaders variously offered themselves as either leaning towards fellow progressive Labour or as 'equidistant' and independent. As the 'third' party in the field, the Lib Dems could afford to offer ambitious policies, as there was little chance of them ever being in a position to deliver them. This all changed in May 2010.

COALITION AFTER MAY 2010

In May 2010 Labour (258 seats) lost the election but the Conservatives (307 seats) did not win a majority. They were forced to form a coalition with the Lib Dems (57 seats) to create a workable majority in order to deal with post-recession austerity. This laid the basis for what became successful political cooperation, but principles were stretched to the limit and beyond, and both parties were forced to abandon dearly held objectives. Coalitions remove the option for parties in government to automatically enact their most favoured political ideas. Instead, 'give and take' or 'compromise' both become elements in the quiver of ideas of any party participating in such a political alliance; voters, however, do not always recognise the need for compromise and react with dismay to 'abandoned principles'.

The major ideas to be frustrated for the Lib Dems were:

- *Access to education.* Lib Dems would have liked to abolish university tuition fees and won support from students for championing this, even signing public pledges to this effect. However, they were forced to renege when fees were increased by the coalition to a massive £9000 per year.
- *Constitutional reform.* Under the terms of the coalition, Cameron had allowed a referendum on replacing 'first past the post' with the 'alternative vote', but he broke his promise to take a low profile in the campaign and the vote was lost heavily.
- *Reform of the Lords.* Nick Clegg hoped this high-profile reform would be seen as a major Lib Dem achievement by the time of the 2015 election. However, Tory MPs and peers decided to sabotage it and it failed. In retaliation, Clegg refused to support reform of constituency boundaries, which would have given the Tories an extra 20 MPs in 2015.

In his 2013 party conference, Clegg listed 16 things which he claimed his party had prevented the Tories from doing since 2010, including: tax cuts for millionaires, the return of selective education, enabling employers to fire workers without any reason being given, and scrapping a number of welfare measures, including housing benefit for young people. Cameron, not to mention the serried ranks of his right-wing MPs, were adamant they hated coalitions and would try their utmost to win on their own terms in order to govern alone.

Labour, disillusioned with the Lib Dems, made the same point just as passionately. However, Nick Clegg, aware that 'good partnership' might prove to be a key political notion in any age of coalition government, declared at his conference that the Lib Dems in coalition would restrain the 'nasty' excesses of the Tories, whilst neutralising spendthrift Labour tendencies, should they be in coalition with them. For its part, Labour was careful to keep policy lines open with the Lib Dems, in case 2015 brought another hung parliament. In fact, though, that general election saw the party reduced to a mere eight MPs, an apparently hopeless position. However, the surprise elevation of the hard-left Corbyn as Labour leader in September 2015 allowed Tim Farron, Clegg's successor as party leader, to suggest that the party now had a chance, possibly along with moderate Labour supporters, to occupy the vacated centre ground.

UKIP

As we have seen amply demonstrated in this chapter, new political ideas form often in response to political problems, for example Britain's post-war relative economic decline. A present problem, exacerbated by post-recession austerity, is low-paid employment being snapped up by economic migrants from eastern Europe. A major section of voters, mostly on the right and usually older, together with Conservative Euro-sceptics and an unquantifiable number who feel frustrated with the inability of the two big parties to deliver things they want, has been gathering for a decade or more. In the 1990s this public opinion phenomenon manifested itself in the form of the United Kingdom Independence Party; it has been growing rapidly in size and political significance ever since.

In January 2014, Nigel Farage, the party's charismatic leader, disavowed his party's own 2010 manifesto as 'drivel' and declared that a new programme was in preparation. Despite these embarrassing lacunae in the party's ideas, it probably needs only two or three of its stock policies to sustain already high public interest: withdrawal from the EU and hostility towards immigrants, joined possibly by opposition to gay marriage. In an attempt to prevent UKIP stealing Tory votes, thereby threatening a raft of marginal seats, Cameron – who had earlier condemned UKIP supporters as 'closet racists' – shifted his party much closer to hostility to European immigrants and complete withdrawal from the EU; this an example of political necessity hardening certain political ideas. Labour's immigration policies reflected a similar shift. As economic times have worsened, many people seem almost to enjoy having something on which to project their blame and their anger: the EU and the related mobile workers seem as good a scapegoat as any. When the Lib Dems were in coalition government, their role as a destination for 'protest votes' seems to have been surrendered to UKIP.

GREEN THINKING

The Green Party's election of its first MP in 2010 had made it more than just a 'fringe' party, as indeed its broad environmental ideology arguably deserves. 'Deep green' thinking rejects 'industrialism' as a thoughtless waste of finite natural resources and calls for a radical restructuring of the economy and political system to make it sustainable, and genuinely fair and democratic as well. This degree of radicalism is way ahead of what most people are prepared to accept – how many would give up travel by car, for instance? – and so most of the main parties have clothed themselves in 'light green' ideas, which aim to reduce pollution, protect the environment and introduce renewable energy sources to combat climate change. This last topic, however, is controversial; for instance, at least one 2010 coalition cabinet member was accused of being a 'climate change denier'.

True to its radical core, the Green Party's manifesto for 2015 included: the renationalisation of the railways; a maximum of 10 times the wages of the lowest-paid worker for company bosses; and a universal wealth tax to reduce the inexorable increase in inequality caused by the appreciation of capital assets.

CONSERVATIVE VICTORY, 7 MAY 2015

This unexpected result stunned the political classes and at the time of writing it is too soon to discern much. However, it is clear that the Tories' overall majority freed up Cameron's government to be far more true to basic Conservative ideas: on the economy, welfare state, public taxation and expenditure, not to mention the question of whether the UK should remain within the EU. Labour, meanwhile, was left to lick its wounds and, after Miliband's resignation, engage in a leadership contest which opened up historical left–right disputes which many in the party had not expected to re-emerge.

CONCLUDING COMMENT

It would be fair to say that the three great sets of political ideas which emerged during the early period of our democracy have been reinterpreted out of all recognition. British left-of-centre thinking has eschewed 'socialism', but retained the principles which underlay it

Table 6.1 British political ideas timeline

Period	Ideas
thirteenth–sixteenth century (medieval era)	Justifications for monarchical rule, religious and economic status quo
seventeenth century (Civil War)	Pamphlets for and against royal rule. Putney debates (1647) discuss detail of democratic government
seventeenth–eighteenth century	Enlightenment introduces new ways of thinking: apply reason to social questions; religious toleration; rights of individual to include right to vote; limited government; separation of powers; limit power of kings and all governments
nineteenth century	Socialism emerges mid-century: critique of capitalism's malign social effects; common ownership for private property; remove gross inequalities; introduce genuine democratic government
	Conservatism emerges as ideology. Conservative Party: approves capitalism and justifies its inequalities; defends power structure's status quo; resists socio-economic reform
	Liberalism based on liberal philosophers emerges as ideology. Liberal Party seeks: representative democracy; political and economic freedom; *laissez-faire* economy; welfare reforms
1939–45 (World War II)	Labour adopts Keynesian economic management and welfare state ideas from Beveridge
1945–51	Labour in power under Attlee nationalise 20% of the economy (the mixed economy) and establish the welfare state, including the National Health Service (NHS)
1951–64	The Conservatives in power basically accept the consensus on the mixed economy and welfare state
1964–70	Labour in power is less radical: no more radical economic reforms
	Liberalism is fighting for survival

1974–79	Labour is in power but 'revisionists' oppose more nationalisation while the left-wing members urge more of it; revisionists form breakaway Social Democratic Party, which allies with Liberals in 1988 to form the Liberal Democrats
1979–90	Conservatives in power under Margaret Thatcher see a low-tax, high-interest economy, end subsidies to ailing industries, fight union power, reform local government finance, privatise as much of the public sector as possible
1997–2010	New Labour, with Blair then Brown in power, rejects socialism and defeat of capitalism in favour of aspects of Thatcherism (e.g. privatisation) but maintains views on welfare state and public services (which are generously funded); liberal on gays and equal rights; Blair favours 'humanitarian intervention' abroad and joins US invasion of Iraq
2010–15	Coalition government, led by Cameron, between Conservatives and Lib-Dems
	Under David Cameron, Conservative leader from 2005, Conservatism becomes centrist; he rebrands the previously 'nasty' party's image on gays, women, environment and social policy but retains traditional Thatcherism on the economy. Party opposed to political integration with the EU
	The Liberal Democrats win support as a 'protest' party that is pro welfare and EU
7 May 2015 (general election)	Chief idea is to remedy government indebtedness
	Tories increasingly hostile to EU: in response to UKIP's success, Tories turn up heat on economic migrants
	Labour seeking to rebuild economic reputation and find new policies to regain power while keeping options open re coalition with Lib-Dems
	Conservatives win overall majority against all expectations and set fair to have possibly a decade in power

regarding the need for social policy to alleviate hardship suffered by the poor. Yet, economically, New Labour adopted more than a few of the prescriptions issued by the 'hated' Thatcher. Why? Because they worked and no alternatives seemed to be available.

But this transference of key ideas – 'political cross-dressing' as it is sometimes called – was not just one way. Cameron and Osborne greatly admired Tony Blair and noted how, under him, Labour had managed to gauge the tenor of contemporary society correctly regarding homosexuality, race relations, the environment and questions of equality. Modern Conservatives happily drew upon New Labour ideas when it suited and, again, crucially, when they worked. As political ideas are usually published and publicised, it is easy for parties to 'poach' the ideas of others; this has been very much the fate of the Liberal Party during the last century.

John Maynard Keynes was a Liberal and a very great economist. His ideas of government managing the economy to achieve specific ends, like full employment, were freely available and adopted by Labour during the war. The famous wartime report produced by a fellow Liberal, William Beveridge, was also adopted by Labour to provide a major part of Labour's 1945 programme for government. As for the future, it is worth recalling that all political ideas arrive as frail and delicate saplings and many perish before they find the fertile soil of political circumstance and people willing to be their champions. 'Socialism' had to wait many decades before it could boast a majority government dedicated to its principles. Which ideas will survive the future? UKIP's nostalgic isolationism maybe, or perhaps the environmentalism of the Green Party?

QUESTIONS FOR DISCUSSION

1. Do Conservatives merely reflect the self-interest of the wealthy?
2. Do Labour ideas entail too much control over everyday life?
3. Has there been a 'post-Thatcher consensus'?

FURTHER READING

A fairly full treatment of current political ideas can be found in chapters 4, 5 and 6 of Jones and Norton (2013). Hennessy (2006) is a wonderful political and social history of Britain after 1945; it is essential reading for a full understanding of the period and the ideas which underlay it. Heywood (1998) is a very good analysis of the main political ideologies of our time. Marshall and Laws (2004) reflect on how a section of the Liberal Democrats developed enthusiasm for market forces, in contrast to more traditional progressive views in the party.

Hennessy, P. (2006) *Having It So Good*, Allen Lane.

Heywood, A. (1998) *Political Ideologies*, Macmillan.

Jones, B. and Norton, P. (2013) *Politics UK* (8th edition), Routledge.

Marquand, D. and Seldon, A. (1996) *The Ideas That Shaped Post-War Britain*, Fontana.

Marshall, O. and Laws, D. (2004) *The Orange Book: Reclaiming Liberalism*, Profile Books.

WEBSITES

Conservative Party: http://www.conservatives.com.

Labour Party: http://www.labour.org.uk.

Liberal Democrats: http://www.libdems.org.uk.

Green Party: http://www.greenparty.org.uk.

THE MEDIATING AGENCIES

This section, in three chapters, moves on to address what I am calling the 'mediating agencies'. These are the means whereby in a democracy the people communicate, via parties and pressure groups, with the institutions of government – the legislature and the executive – and how communication is facilitated and 'mediated' throughout by political parties, pressure groups and possibly the key agency of them all: the mass media.

III

THE MEDIATING AGENCIES

7

POLITICAL PARTIES

Parties have already been introduced in the previous chapters but this chapter aims to shed more light on how they work in practice.

FUNCTIONS

HARMONISING

Parties perform the vital role in a democracy of organising and articulating the multifarious interests within society, many of which are in sharp conflict. Trying to make sense of what 60 million people think or want would be impossible without the intervention of parties. They offer broad 'churches' of ideas and policy objectives which attract support from the different sections of society. So if you are a farmer, you know that the Conservative Party, the traditional party of landowners, is likely to offer you support. If you are a trade unionist, you might feel the same about Labour. Parties help put together coalitions of interest and provide coherence for them before feeding their demands into the political system. Parties make democracy possible.

RECRUITMENT OF PERSONNEL

Parties draw in people to run the political system, providing a means whereby people can be turned into candidates and then 'politicians' operating at local, national or even at European Union level. Such recruits come from all sections of society, though proportionately, it has to be said, much more from the well-off middle classes. Ramsay MacDonald, the first Labour Prime Minister, was the illegitimate son of a Scottish crofter; David Blunkett the blind son of an impoverished Sheffield family who overcame his disability to become home secretary. At the other end of the social scale Conservative cabinet minister Douglas Hurd and Prime Minister David Cameron came from privileged backgrounds, went to Eton and Oxbridge before smoothly entering, and then rising in, the world of politics. But it has to be said that a proportion of public-school-educated MPs sit on the Labour benches, as do a proportion of working-class MPs on the Tory side.

PARTICIPATION AND EDUCATION

Parties not only involve people directly through their activists and candidates, but they also encourage and educate society to become aware of and engaged in a system ultimately dependent on public involvement.

CHOICE

Parties organise coalitions of interests to provide all voters with (admittedly) broad but clear choices at election time.

ACCOUNTABILITY

The party in opposition is a government in waiting and through its questioning and challenging of the government it holds it to account for the whole of the electorate. In democratic politics, parties tend to claim that their collection of policies will be best for the country as a whole; quite often, though, they go on to govern along the lines they advocated in opposition. Given that such policies have been crafted to serve particular sections of the electorate, voters might conclude at the end of the parliamentary term that the party in power has not succeeded in serving anything approximating to the national interest. It follows that voters might well proceed to vote that party out at the next election.

CONTROLLING THE EXECUTIVE

The leader of the winning party at election time becomes prime minister, who then chooses the 100 or more senior and junior ministers required to run the government. These elected ministers represent the line of democratic control bestowed upon the winning party by voters. It is assumed these party political ministers will govern in harmony with the majority opinion expressed in the election. Whether they succeed in doing so is often the subject of sharp controversy, itself the essence of democratic politics. Few would argue that democratic government is possible without parties: they provide the crucial link between voter and government and enable the link to make the system work to the extent that it does.

PARTY GOVERNMENT FROM THE MID-NINETEENTH CENTURY

Conservatives and Liberals shared government from 1867–1914, their efforts made more difficult by the 80 or so Irish Nationalist MPs present in the Commons.

The Labour Party was originally set up in 1900 as the political arm of the trade unions, socialist societies and working class voters; by 1924 it had already briefly held power, albeit as a minority government.

The Liberal Party was dominant during the late nineteenth century and before the war, but the party thereafter began to fracture, due to a rift between Asquith and Lloyd George and the increasing relevance of Labour's message as the champion of the recently enfranchised workers. Its number of MPs had shrivelled to a handful by the 1950s but slowly grew during the 1960s and 1970s. During the 1980s it allied with the breakaway Social Democratic Party, and morphed into the Liberal Democrats in 1988. The Lib Dems went on to rally the centre ground, winning 62 seats in 2005.

The Conservative Party is arguably Britain's traditional party of government: its prime ministers held power for 57 years of the twentieth century. Nonetheless, after 1945, a Labour and Tory duopoly dominated for two decades, until the Conservatives began an extended period in power, initially under Margaret Thatcher, from 1979. Then 'New Labour' in 1997 ('new' was merely a rhetorical suffix) established the first of four governments, three under Tony Blair, but the fourth, under Gordon Brown, failed to win the inconclusive May 2010 election, when the Conservative David Cameron allied his 307 MPs with Nick Clegg's 57 to form a coalition government. In May 2015 the Conservative Party won its first overall majority since 1992, with a majority of 12.

Concern about Britain's membership of the European Union (EU) and related incoming east European migrant workers gave rise to the United Kingdom Independence Party (UKIP), which, under Nigel Farage, commanded around 17% support in December 2014 opinion polls. It had done well in local elections and handsomely won the European Parliament Elections in May 2014. In the autumn of that year Tory MPs Douglas Carswell and Mark Reckless had defected to UKIP and successfully fought by-elections in their own constituencies under their new banner. The May 2015 election saw it muster 13% of the vote but – disappointingly for its supporters – only one MP.

On the political fringe in Britain, parties can command reasonable voting support but the 'first past the post' voting system means they are not able to focus support in any one constituency and they end up failing to win the seats their vote might be seen to justify. The Green Party was perhaps the exception to this rule, with one MP, whose seat was won in May 2010; Caroline Lucas was re-elected in 2015. The various left-wing Marxist parties are nowhere near winning a seat and the neo-fascist British National Party is also riven by internal disputes – its support almost disappeared in 2015; the Islamophobic English Defence League is not dissimilar.

THE CONSERVATIVE PARTY

The nineteenth-century Prime Minister Disraeli envisioned an alliance between the aristocracy and the working classes. Despite the party's defence of the landed and business interests, it has been able, crucially, to win sufficient working-class votes to achieve and maintain office on a regular basis. In 1945 it was crushed by the Attlee landslide but it was back in office only six years later, willing to accept Labour's mixed economy and the welfare state. After a period of Labour dominance in the 1960s and 1970s, Margaret Thatcher moved her party robustly to the right in the 1980s, winning three general elections, in 1979, 1983 and 1987.

John Major extended the party's run of success with victory in 1992; this was perhaps a victory too far, as his loss in 1997 was dramatic and foreshadowed 13 years in opposition. David Cameron, following the failed leaderships of William Hague, Iain Duncan Smith (IDS) and Michael Howard, was the person who realised drastic changes towards centrist policies were required to win power, something he almost managed in the May 2010 general election, after which his party, though the largest, had to ally with the Lib Dems to create a credible government. His reward came in May 2015, when he unexpectedly won an overall majority of 12.

LEADERSHIP

Tory leaders used to 'emerge' through a series of soundings but after Alec Douglas Home's short period as leader (1963–65) elections were introduced, leading to Edward Heath as the first leader so chosen. Thatcher controversially stood against Heath in 1975 and won the leadership of her male-dominated party. She then went on to win the 1979 election and, after she achieved military victory over Argentina in the Falklands War, she was able to win a landslide in 1983, another victory in 1987 and proceed to leave the imprint of her right-wing philosophy on the nation after 11 years in power.

CONSTRAINTS

In theory and according to its rules, the Conservative leader is given much authority to lead but in reality he or she has to: avoid policy divisions – crucial, as voters punish parties which cannot agree; sustain morale and leads in the polls, even when events intervene; maintain a balance among the leadership – Thatcher had to compromise with her 'wet' or liberal Conservative opponents on several occasions; and keep leading figures onside. Thatcher and Blair both suffered from resignations by key colleagues (Lawson and Howe for the former, Cook for the latter).

ORGANISATION

The 1922 Committee is the body representing Tory MPs; it jealously guards its independence. Usually it conforms to party culture and supports the leader but with John Major and his successors (up to and including Cameron) it has often voiced its displeasure behind the scenes over trends in leadership policy or style.

Central Office is the party's bureaucracy and contains the important Research Department; IDS had to resolve some problems over the staffing of Central Office.

There are several party groups that represent strands of opinion in the party. For instance, there are the Tory Reform Group on the left, the Bow Group at the centre and the No Turning Back Group on the right.

William Hague introduced a number of reforms: a board to run the party's affairs; a rule that all parliamentary candidates should be chosen by all members of a constituency party; a rule that a motion of no confidence would require 15% of Tory MPs to request it; and a new party forum to discuss policy.

LABOUR PARTY

ORIGINS

Labour began as a 'bottom up' party rather than 'top down' like the Tories and its procedures reflect rather more democracy than one finds among the Conservatives, though this difference has narrowed markedly in recent times. The party was set up by the trade unions with the enthusiastic support of the socialist societies to help elect supporters into the Commons. They hoped thereby to improve their attempts to influence legislation by direct intervention. In 1918 the party acquired a socialist constitution and an annual conference with policy-making powers. The party has always had to resolve the tensions between those who favour rapid and radical reform and those who prefer slower, safer progress towards change through peaceful consensual parliamentary methods.

LEADERSHIP

Labour has always had an instinctive suspicion of authority and prescribed collective leadership as a substitute for any possibly over-powerful leadership. Ironically, the party has twice had leaders – Ramsay MacDonald and Tony Blair – who were indeed charismatic and powerful but were subsequently accused of betraying party principles and of being shallow and self-seeking. In 1981 a new system of electing the leader was introduced, involving an 'electoral college' comprising MPs, unions and members, each vested with a third of the voting power. This system was criticised in 2010 when Ed Miliband failed to win the MPs' and members' section but triumphed because of support only in the unions. The electoral college was later abandoned by Ed Miliband for a 'one member, one vote' system.

POWER CENTRES IN THE LABOUR PARTY

ANNUAL CONFERENCE

The 1918 constitution set this up as the 'policy-making parliament' of the party. Unions were allowed to represent their whole membership in numerical terms when casting their votes – the block vote – and so dominated the big decisions. It became a platform for fiery speeches, where a name could be made, and it was always more influential than the Tory equivalent, which is more of a rally of supporters.

NATIONAL EXECUTIVE COMMITTEE (NEC)

This is voted in every year by the membership, so trade unions have again tended to control it. Once, the NEC used to lead policy-making and in the early 1980s, with the left in the ascendant, it became a focus of left-wing interest. Under Blair, however, it lost this function and hence much of its importance.

TRADE UNIONS

Given that the unions created the party and provided most of its funding, they have tended to exercise considerable power. However, during the 1970s union power was perceived by voters as malign and, despite their loss of power after the defeat of the miners during the 1980s, the link has still been problematic, especially as Ed Miliband's election in 2010 was the result crucially of union votes.

Cameron delightedly made considerable political capital out of Ed being 'in the pocket' of the unions. Unions certainly wield substantial power in the party by virtue of being its main source of funding.

PARLIAMENTARY LABOUR PARTY (PLP)

As elected MPs, the PLP has special authority, but constitutionally it is only one power centre, and not the most important.

POWER AND LEADERSHIP ISSUES

CONFERENCE

Left-wingers in the party have tried to use conference to advance their political agenda through moving their resolutions and getting them passed. However, once the party is in power, the conference is only an external influence: the real decisions are made by majorities in parliament, not conference. Parliament, after all, is answerable to all voters in the country, not just trade union or Labour Party members. Nonetheless, in the 1970s, by ignoring conference decisions Harold Wilson and James Callaghan eventually found they had alienated the unions and thereby caused themselves considerable political problems.

IDEOLOGICAL DIVISIONS

Differences between the radical left, who wanted to advance rapidly towards left-wing goals, and the 'revisionists', who favoured the slower parliamentary reformist route, plagued Labour politics, especially during the inter-war years and the 1950s, through to the end of the 1980s. During the 1970s the party seemed to offer two programmes of action: an official revisionist one and an alternative left-wing one. In the early 1980s this conflict reached its zenith, with the left winning temporary control. Consequently, the 1983 election manifesto was described by Gerald Kaufman as 'the longest suicide note in history', an accurate prediction as Thatcher won the election by a landslide. By the later 1980s the party had learnt how to absorb such conflicts, as they prove unattractive to voters: as Lloyd George famously noted, 'you can't make a policy out of an argument'.

MacDonald was accused of 'betraying' the party when he joined the Conservative-dominated National Government in 1931. His successor a few years later, Clement Attlee, was an exceedingly modest man with little or no charisma but he proved an able prime minister as well as a highly respected one. Harold Wilson was a clever and devious politician who did not always carry his party. James Callaghan was pro-union and proved an able party leader but was eventually overwhelmed by union militancy and was defeated by Thatcher in 1979.

Michael Foot was a favourite of the left but the 1983 election was a disastrous defeat which crippled the party for many years. Using policy review groups, Neil Kinnock bravely and cleverly nudged the party away from the voter-unfriendly left-wing end of the spectrum but it was Tony Blair who swept it into the centre ground and everything else before him in 1997. Blair, a gifted politician and superb communicator, could do no wrong for several years; while not achieving a great deal in his first term, he won the 2001 election by another landslide.

However, by then a widespread suspicion had grown that Blair relied too much on media management or 'spin': his formidable spin doctors Peter Mandelson and Alastair Campbell were seen as part of the problem. In 2003 his decision to join George Bush's invasion of Iraq soon proved a disaster, as the aftermath turned into a protracted bloodbath. To make things much worse, Blair's chancellor, Gordon Brown, constantly plotted and lobbied to replace him and their enmity became widely and damagingly known. Blair won a third election in 2005 but by 2007, political support draining away, was forced to stand aside and allow Brown to take over. His fraught period in power, however, hugely disappointed Labour supporters and no doubt himself.

Apparently paralysed by indecision and beset by gaffes and other disasters, his premiership sank into ridicule until in 2008 the world economic crisis arrived. Brown was then able to make a major, if widely unappreciated, contribution to the amelioration of the effects but by then voters had mostly lost faith in him and his party and in May 2010 Labour lost over 90 seats in a crushing defeat. Cameron, however, was still some 20 seats short of the required 326 seats for an overall majority and struck a coalition bargain with Nick Clegg's

Liberal Democrats, an agreement which, despite frequent disagreements between the two parties, held firm. In 2015 Labour suffered an even worse defeat, losing by nearly 100 seats (Labour 232, to the Conservatives' 330), and at the time of writing faces possibly a decade or even more out of power.

LIBERAL DEMOCRATS

The product of the 1988 merger of the Liberal Party and the Social Democratic Party (a breakaway from the Labour Party), the Liberal Democrats initially embodied centrist political thinking, with affinities both to 'revisionist' Labour and left-leaning Conservatism. Its first leader, the energetic Paddy Ashdown, tended to side with Labour but his successor, Charles Kennedy, was less keen, being strongly opposed to the Iraq War. He was replaced by Ming Campbell in 2005, who, after failing to make any impact, gave way to Nick Clegg in December 2007.

It was Clegg who threw in his 57 MPs to enable David Cameron to command a stable majority in a coalition negotiated in May 2010. However, many people had voted for Clegg to prevent, rather than enable, a Tory-led government and, combined with the fate of a cuts-based economic policy, support for Liberal Democrats slumped from 24% in May 2010 to barely double figures in spring 2014, when the party came fifth in the European elections. Until the next election, the party could no longer assume the mantle of 'protest party', attractive to those unwilling to endorse either of the big parties. At his 2013 conference Clegg offered his party as a force for moderation which, in the event of another (not unexpected) hung parliament, would, in coalition with Labour, restrain prodigal spending, or, with the Tories, prevent excessive cuts hitting the poor. This perhaps made the best out of a parlous position but subsequently falling or static opinion poll rating for the party suggested this offer did not impress voters. Nemesis arrived on 7 May 2015, when the Lib Dems lost 49 seats and were left with a paltry eight; Clegg survived but many of its leading lights – David Laws, Danny Alexander, Simon Hughes and Charles Kennedy – failed to return to the Commons.

UNITED KINGDOM INDEPENDENCE PARTY (UKIP)

The progress of this party was remarkable after its creation in the 1990s, arguably establishing a four-party system in the UK. In spring 2014 came UKIP's sweeping successes in the local and European elections. However, despite its vibrant advance, the party suffers from a number of shortcomings: it is overly dependent on its charismatic, maverick leader, Nigel Farage; its supporters tend to be at the senior end of the age range; and, apart from wishing to withdraw from the EU and halt immigration, its policies – notably on the economy and public services – are not well understood or, indeed, coherently worked out. Some pointed out that the party's strength lies in the south of the country, in places affected directly by immigration.

However, by-election results in 2013–14, at Eastleigh, South Shields, Rotherham, Wythenshawe and, most dramatically, Middleton and Heywood on 9 October 2014, suggested the party was also making deep inroads into traditionally strong Labour areas. In May 2015 this proved to be the case, as UKIP votes contributed to many Labour losses in the north of England. The party went on to poll a massive 13% of the vote but failed to win any target seats, Farage managing only third place in Thanet South. Only Douglas Carswell, a former Tory who resigned his seat and retook it for UKIP, ended up representing the party in the Commons. A series of unappealing rows broke out in the party over Farage's leadership style but he survived and with over 100 second places the party is well placed for the next election.

NATIONALIST PARTIES

In Scotland and Wales the UK-wide political parties are augmented by the Scottish Nationalist Party (SNP) and Plaid Cymru (PC), respectively. The major UK parties fail to gain any traction in Northern Ireland, which has a very different political culture. The Devolution Acts which created the Scottish Parliament and the Welsh Assembly were originally designed to take the weight off Westminster and the heat out of nationalism, but in the case of

Scotland it seemed merely to whet nationalist appetites for genuine independence. On 18 September 2014 a referendum was held for Scottish voters on whether they wished to remain part of the UK. The SNP leader, Alex Salmond, led a sensationally successful 'yes' campaign, which generated enormous energy and passion throughout Scotland, especially reaching young people and those who, in the past, had not shown much interest in politics.

The 'no' campaign was led by a former Labour chancellor, Alistair Darling, who represented the pro-union Labour, Conservative and Lib Dem parties south of the border. Salmond lost the first television debate but won the second handsomely and, as polling day approached, the momentum seemed to lie with the SNP-led campaign. However, this was when the former Labour Prime Minister, Gordon Brown, entered the campaign with a series of barnstorming speeches which may have tipped the balance in favour of the pro-unionists, who eventually won 55–45. However, the excitement generated by the 'yes' campaign continued to resonate well into the 2015 general election campaign, with the SNP's membership swelling over the 100,000 mark. Labour had expected to lose a fair number of its 41 Scottish seats but was left traumatised by the loss of all but one of them as the SNP won 56 of the 59 available seats.

FUNDING POLITICAL PARTIES

To survive and function, Labour and Tory parties currently need well over £20 million a year each. However, income flows have reduced catastrophically since their individual memberships have plummeted, just when state-of-the-art communication requires yet more expenditure. Labour now has only 200,000 members and Conservatives possibly just over half that number. Other countries in Europe employ state funding but the disdain in which politicians are held in Britain would make that difficult, if not impossible. The result has been a reliance on big donors: trade unions for Labour plus a number of rich supporters and mainly rich business people for the Tories and UKIP. The problem with this is that such people seldom give away money without expecting favours in return and that makes the practice profoundly undemocratic. Even the Lib Dems can get into trouble this way: in February 2014 one of their biggest donors, Sudhir Choudhrie, was said to be involved in major international arms dealing. Sir Hayden Phillips' inquiry into the subject suggested a cap on donations of £50,000 – good for the Tories, but not for Labour, which relies on large union donations to survive.

CONCLUSION: TWO-PARTY SYSTEM IN DECLINE

In 1950, 97% of votes went to Labour and the Tories but during the 1960s support for the Liberals and the nationalists grew. During the 1980s the Alliance emerged, wining over a quarter of all votes in 1983, though its support soon fell. The Liberal Democrats, formed in 1988, made good headway during the 1990s, along with the nationalists in Wales and Scotland. By 2005 the two-party system appeared to be fragmenting, with smaller parties taking 28% of the vote and 78 seats; in 2010 the smaller parties commanded over 30% of votes and won 91 seats. However, the 2015 election, when the Tories won an overall majority, suggested that, despite fragmentation, majorities for the big parties are still possible.

DISCUSSION QUESTIONS

1. Is Labour a more democratic party than the Conservatives?
2. Why did the Liberal Party lose influence in the early twentieth century?
3. Do you think the Green Party is destined to become a major party?

FURTHER READING

Recent books on British political parties are still awaited, as most teachers and students now seem to use the bigger textbooks, which have appeared since the early 1990s, for coverage of such aspects. Readers seeking chapters on UK parties can find them in: Jones and Norton (2013), chapters 4, 5, 6 and 11; Kingdom (2014), chapters 2, 12 and 13; Moran (2011), chapters 14 and 15. A useful snapshot of how the main parties shaped up as the 2015 general election approached was given in four 'Why Vote . . . ' books, published by Biteback, which appeared December 2014: Conservative (Nick Herbert), Labour (Dan Jarvis), Lib Dem (Jeremy Browne) and UKIP (Suzanne Evans).

Bale, T. (2011) *The Conservative Party from Thatcher to Cameron*, Polity.

Beech, M. and Lee, S. (eds) (2011) *The Cameron–Clegg Government*, Palgrave.

Carswell, D. (2012) *The End of Politics and the Birth of iDemocracy*, Biteback.

Clarke, A. (2012) *Political Parties in the UK*, Palgrave.

Driver, S. (2011) *Understanding Party Politics*, Polity.

Jones, B. and Norton, P. (2014) *Politics UK* (8th edition), Routledge.

Kingdom, J. (2014) *Government and Politics in Britain*, Polity.

Moran, M. (2011) *Politics and Governance in the UK* (2nd edition), Palgrave.

WEBSITES

Conservative Home: http://www.conservativehome.com.

Left Foot Forward: http://www.leftfootforward.org.

Liberal Democrat Voice: http://www.libdemvoice.org.

8

PRESSURE GROUPS

Pressure groups 'mediate', as do political parties, on behalf of the people but in their case it is between *groups* or *sections* of society and the government. They do not attempt to win control of government in the way parties do. Rather, they are organised groups in society that seek both to defend and to promote their own interests by influencing specific policies. Elections occur every five years in Britain, providing individual representation, but pressure groups, it can be argued, sustain their *functional* representation between elections.

TYPES OF PRESSURE GROUPS

ECONOMIC GROUPS

Trade unions seek to defend and advance members' interests in relation to pay and conditions of work. *Business groups* represent small to medium-sized concerns as well as the mega corporations, though the *multinationals* are often so large they deal directly with government rather than lobbying organisations.

CAUSE GROUPS

Sectional groups represent discrete groups in society, for example old people (Age Concern), the homeless (Shelter), children (National

Society for the Prevention of Cruelty to Children) or motorists (Automobile Association).

Attitude groups advance ideas they believe benefit society as a whole, such as human rights (Liberty), legal reform (Howard League for Penal Reform) and voting reform (Electoral Reform Society).

OTHERS

Other groups which can be discerned include: *peak* associations or umbrella groups representing collections of groups like the trade unions (the Trades Union Congress, TUC) or the Confederation of British Industry (CBI); so-called *fire brigade* groups which emerge to champion specific problems like the Road Traffic Reduction Campaign or the nineteenth-century Anti Corn Law League (ACLL); and finally *episodic* groups, for example groups which are not ostensibly political, like golf clubs or scout troops, but become so when needing to defend or advance their interests.

ORIGINS OF PRESSURE GROUPS

Even pre-democratic societies contained political groupings but democracies in effect give them licence to organise and apply influence wherever they can. William Wilberforce's Committee for the Abolition of Slavery was founded in 1787 and managed to persuade an unreformed parliament to ban the activity by 1806. Others in the nineteenth century included the Anti Corn Law League, the Salvation Army and the British Red Cross. In time, government began to appreciate the value of such groups, encouraging or even subsidising their activities.

As government began to extend its concerns in the twentieth century, especially after Labour's 1945 victory, groups formed both to inform and to influence government. Nationalised industries delivered something approaching monopoly power to their unions, which, in the case of the coal or electricity industries, could bring them and the country to a halt. Pressure groups became more professional, with skilled negotiators and press officers expert at using the media, frequently recruited at graduate level.

CIVIL SOCIETY AND PRESSURE GROUPS

'Civil society' was mentioned in Chapter 2. 'Political culture' refers to the 'non-political' relationships people have with families, business, church, school and voluntary associations such as scouts, guides, football and cricket clubs. These are the agencies whereby young people become engaged with and socialised into society; they learn how to lead, be led and perform as part of a team, to discuss and negotiate, to make both agreements and compromises. These relationships are the way young people the world over absorb the values and culture of their societies and provide the precondition of democratic activity, the soil in which it grows.

Britain has always had a plethora of voluntary bodies, suggesting its political culture is healthily receptive to democracy. However, there are signs such health might be waning. Membership of political parties has slumped since the early 1950s and membership of some voluntary bodies has declined severely. US political scientist Robert Putnam (2000) has charted the decline of his own country's voluntary groups and the growth of 'passive' members of many of them, doing nothing more than renew annual memberships. Other scholars, like Peter Hall (1999), suggest Britain's civil society is in a less parlous state; a 2001 'Citizen Audit' from Sheffield University (Pattie et al., 2004) reinforced this judgement. Survey evidence suggests, however, that it is people in higher-income categories who are much more likely than others to volunteer.

PRESSURE GROUPS AND GOVERNMENT

The relationship between these two is by no means as conflicted as might be expected given the potential clash of roles. Both sides of the table in meetings share certain objectives, in that they: seek policies which work to mutual advantage; share knowledge likely to make policies more effective; need to support new policies to ensure they are acceptable to the nation as a whole. Government therefore has much incentive to keep such groups onside. In the same way, pressure groups face every incentive to accept the code of discretion and passive support of the consultation process: to be an 'insider', to use Wyn Grant's term. Grant has argued that the vast majority of pressure groups aim for status close to the heart of the policy-making process: the place where influence can most efficiently be brought to bear. Such groups tend to apply their pressure quietly, steadily and effectively. 'Outsider' groups often pursue hard-to-achieve objectives – sometimes ideological in character – and engage in noisy public campaigns which, while possibly sowing seeds for the future, seldom achieve their objectives.

GOVERNMENT METHODS

While government and pressure groups share common aims and recognise their need to cooperate, there is also an element of conflict in the relationship: pressure groups try to apply influence which government often wishes to resist. The 'weapons' used can be identified as follows.

CONSULTATION STATUS

Groups bask in the warmth of government attention and are delighted to be given a permanent place on advisory committees.

PUBLIC RELATIONS

The government has vast resources to deploy in resisting the blandishments of pressure groups. Just how government can bring large organisations to heel was demonstrated by Alastair Campbell in his 'dodgy dossier' fight with the BBC in 2003; Campbell used every trick in the book to 'win' his side of the contest, bringing down the BBC's director-general and chairman in the process.

THE LAW

During the 1980s Thatcher's determination to subdue the miners' union was achieved in part through changing the law so that its funds could be sequestered if new laws were transgressed on balloting members before strike action. Labour also passed laws making certain kinds of demonstration against the Iraq War illegal.

FORCE

Ultimately, government can utilise force to overcome challenges from groups which contest its authority. In the past, the most common challenges originated in industrial action by trade unions; during that bitter miner's strike police were used to subdue striking miners, causing bitterness which remains to this day.

PRESSURE GROUP METHODS

In a scene from the 2014 film *Selma*, Dr Martin Luther King demands that president Lyndon B. Johnson change the law to make it easier for black people to register for voting. He replies, 'You have one issue, I have a hundred.' He may have been trying to refuse Dr King but his excuse was quite correct: the perennial problem of pressure group leaders is to find the approaches likely to make their single issue one which the government just has no option but to take seriously. These methods can be seen along a spectrum, from peaceful to violent.

PETITIONS AND LETTERS

If attracting sufficiently large numbers, these can feature in mainstream news and be quite influential. The arrival of online petitions, run by bodies like Avaas and 33 Degrees, can have a considerable impact, with signatures running into the hundreds of thousands. Letters to MPs and the press are usually less influential but if enough are received MPs can certainly be influenced to take further action.

MEETINGS

Groups seek to make contact with those who exercise executive power. One small local-government example is the Friends of Roundhay Park in Leeds, who ask senior members of Leeds Parks Department to attend and contribute to their meetings.

MEDIA CAMPAIGNS

Groups will focus much energy and resources on catching the media's attention, often with photo-opportunities to add appeal.

DEMONSTRATIONS

These are often marches with placards carried through the centre of towns and cities or could be colourful stunts like those tried by Fathers 4 Justice to attract attention to their cause.

VIOLENCE

This is a high-risk strategy, as public sympathies can as easily be lost as won by group action, as the early suffragettes discovered.

DIRECT ACTION

This approach can quite easily slide into violence but the technique of chaining oneself to blocks of concrete in tunnels close to a big development has been used to some effect by environmental campaigners. However, the Darley Oaks Farm case in 2006 illustrated the limits of direct action when activists stole the remains of Gladys Hammond, the mother-in-law of the owner of a farm which bred guinea pigs for experimentation. Public outrage resulted and middle-class leader of the group, Jon Ablewhite, was eventually sent down for 12 years. However, if handled carefully and if respectable middle-class opinion can be won over, direct action to prevent business development or airport runways can assist rather than detract from the causes involved.

APPLYING PRESSURE

Pressure groups are clever at spotting where 'power' or decision-making activity is concentrated and applying pressure accordingly.

GENERAL PUBLIC

Groups publicise their activities and hope to recruit activists as well as raise funds.

OTHER GROUPS

Alliances of like-minded groups emerge as groups realise this maximises their effect. It also helps neutralise those groups which work against their causes.

PARTIES

Groups will aim for the party likely to be most receptive. So business groups will head for the Tories, the Campaign for Nuclear Disarmament for Labour, though, significantly, while winning much support within Labour, official party policy has never been to give up nuclear weapons.

PARLIAMENT

Groups seek support in both Houses and look for officers for their executives for publicity purposes. They also work closely with MP allies, drafting amendments to legislation to which they are opposed.

MINISTERS AND CIVIL SERVANTS

Contacts with ministers are invaluable but civil servants often know more about the detail of what concerns groups and have the advantage of staying put, while ministers end up moving on.

EUROPEAN UNION

Some 3000 groups now apply pressure on decision-makers in Brussels, employing about 10,000 personnel.

PROFESSIONAL LOBBYING AND 'SLEAZE'

Professional lobby groups offer useful and lucrative employment to young politicians on the way up and to retired politicians looking for appropriate work to fund their retirement. These companies, of which there are over 50, essentially hire themselves out to establish contact with people or organisations – usually business ones – wishing to influence or change a particular policy or piece of legislation. In the mid-1990s there were 30 Tory MPs working for lobbying companies, being paid anything up to £10,000 a year or more to exploit their contacts with all the entry points described above.

This was not thought to be in any way shameful at the time, but when *Sunday Times* journalists, posing as businessmen, successfully asked two Tory MPs to ask questions on their behalf, there was outrage and such activities by MPs were quickly viewed as undemocratic and self-seeking. The case of Neil Hamilton, who was taking money from the owner of Harrods to do the same thing, was hugely publicised and condemned as 'sleaze'. Perhaps this case represented a change of our political culture regarding such activities from toleration to disapproval verging on condemnation.

The result was the judge-led committee of inquiry, the Nolan-chaired Committee on Standards in Public Life. This recommended that MPs should register any interests they might have with a new parliamentary commissioner. Sleaze did not disappear once the Nolan machinery began to work – far from it – but it did show that parliament can move to rectify faults in the way it works once they become evident.

POLITICAL THEORY AND PRESSURE GROUPS

PLURALISM

Robert Dahl, the US political scientist, argued that power should be, and largely is, distributed across a large number of groups in society and decisions should be reached through a process of negotiation, with the government acting as kind of 'referee'.

CORPORATISM

Phillipe Schmitter saw groups as intermediaries between government and citizen but saw government as suborning key groups onto its own side so that they become in effect part of the machinery of government influence. It was argued that Labour applied a 'corporate' approach during the 1970s when it recruited the unions as its agent and made them part of government, to the nation's detriment.

POLICY NETWORKS

This view, associated with Richardson and Jordan, sees groups forming 'communities of influence' around particular policy areas, being brought in to advise, offer information and often support in implementation. In this way groups provide essential cogs in the policy-making process.

QUESTIONS FOR DISCUSSION

1. Would you say that pressure groups are inevitably pitted against the government of the day?
2. Explain the difference between 'insider' and 'outsider' groups.
3. Have pressure or 'lobbying' groups virtually gained control of the policy-making process?

FURTHER READING

Professor Wyn Grant's writings on pressure groups (1989, 2000) are worth reading, if now a little dated; the book by Duncan Watts (2007) is also valuable and still reasonably up to date.

Ashford, N. and Timms, D. (1992) *What Europe Thinks: A Study of Western European Values*, Dartmouth.

Grant, W. (1989) *Pressure Groups, Politics and Democracy in Britain*, Phillip Allan.

Grant, W. (2000) *Pressure Groups and Politics*, Macmillan.

Hall, P. (1999) Social capital in Britain, *British Journal of Political Science*, 29(3): 417–461.

Pattie, C., Seyd, P. and Whiteley, P. (2004) *Citizenship in Britain: Values, Participation and Democracy*, Cambridge University Press.

Watts, D. (2007) *Pressure Groups* (Politics Study Guides), Edinburgh University Press.

WEBSITES

Friends of the Earth: http://www.foe.co.uk.
Greenpeace: http://www.greenpeace.org.uk.
Outrage: http://www.outrage.org.uk.
TUC: http://www.tuc.org.uk.

9

THE MASS MEDIA

The most important 'mediating' agency in any democracy has to be the mass media: the press, radio, television plus the 'new' media spawned by the internet and the digital revolution. This is the means whereby government learns about voters and citizens learn about their government. It is also how the different institutions of government learn about each other. In other words, the media enable any and all political systems to work. As they are the means whereby society receives information from government, control of the media is a sensitive subject: in autocracies, like modern-day Russia, they are rigidly controlled, so that only approved messages are transmitted downwards to the people and anyone offering dissenting messages to other members of society is seen as a risk and often action is taken against them. This is *not* to say, however, that, in democracies, governments do not seek to exert control over the media, as they most assuredly do, every day they are in power.

It is relatively easy for autocracies to control traditional print and broadcast media though less so the relatively unregulated 'new' media like Facebook and Twitter. It is in democracies that the media play the most central role because where expression of views is not controlled it follows that many will wish to express them, whether supportive of government or not. Freedom of expression is the key foundation of democracy; for a political system to be genuinely democratic its media have to be substantially free from interference. While the law can guarantee such freedom from government control, those with the means to own or influence the media can pose threats to the viability of democracy.

EVOLUTION OF POLITICAL COMMUNICATION

Britain, as one of the first democracies, has a wide range of media outlets, each with distinctive histories. Printing technology was imported from Germany in 1476 by William Caxton, who built up his business around Oxford, the first book he produced being Chaucer's *Canterbury Tales*. Printed versions of the Bible during the sixteenth century, especially in English translation, broke the church's control on its teachings but the Civil War (1642–49) witnessed the first propaganda war via printed pamphlets. Regular newspapers appeared in the eighteenth century and then in the late nineteenth century cheap daily papers arrived, together with the phenomenon of their owners, the so-called 'press barons'.

Table 9.1 Circulation of national daily newspapers, UK, 2015

Rank	Title	Number of readers
1	*The Sun*	7,772,000
2	*Daily Mail*	4,741,000
3	*Daily Mirror*	3,087,000★
4	*Metro*	3,287,000
5	*Daily Telegraph*	1,680,000
6	*The Times*	1,565,000
7	*Daily Star*	1,571,000
8	*Daily Express*	1,427,000
9	*The Guardian*	1,103,000
10	*The Independent*	532,000

★The *Daily Mirror* has a Scottish edition, the *Daily Record*, which has a further 884,000 readers.

Table 9.2 Circulation of Sunday newspapers, UK, 2015

Rank	Title	Number of readers
1	*News of the World*	7,537,000
2	*Mail on Sunday*	4,896,000
3	*Sunday Mirror*	3,690,000
4	*Sunday Times*	2,952,000
5	*Sunday Express*	1,466,000
6	*Sunday Telegraph*	1,442,000
7	*Sunday People*	1,273,000
8	*The Observer*	1,030,000
9	*Sunday Mail*	1,067,000
10	*Daily Star Sunday*	919,000

THE PRESS

Tabloid newspapers sell in the greatest bulk and their content, on balance, does little to create an informed democracy (see Tables 9.1 and 9.2). *The Sun* and *Daily Mirror* offer many pages on sport and celebrity gossip but give little space to political news and analysis. The tabloids tend to be directed at less well educated readers: for example *The Sun*, it is alleged, aims to cater for those with a reading age of 10. The 'mid-tabloids', the *Daily Express* and *Mail*, however, contain more news and comment. The so-called *broadsheets* or 'quality' press – *The Times*, *Telegraph*, *Guardian*, *Independent* and *Financial Times* – allocate plenty of space to political news and comment by well known, respected columnists. Despite usually supporting specific parties, 'quality' papers at least affect a degree of objectivity and consider opposing arguments. In theory, this latter section of the media ideally informs our democratic system but, aiming at more educated strata, their circulations are a fraction of that of the tabloids.

While top columnists might influence the political class in government or opposition, during election campaigns it is probably the tabloids which cause more votes to be switched through their robust, unashamed campaigning for the parties they have decided to support. During the 1990s most of the print press supported the Conservatives but then disillusion with the Major government caused the press to turn to Labour. During the next decade, much of this support fell away from Labour and when *The Sun*, after 12 years of supporting Labour, decided to back David Cameron in September 2009, the press was again dominantly and raucously pro-Conservative and helped Cameron win his 2015 victory.

DECLINE OF THE PRESS

The circulation figures reported in Tables 9.1 and 9.2 do not reveal the annual decline they are currently suffering: nearly 3% each year for dailies and Sunday publications combined. According to the online Media Briefing, print journalism is suffering from the encroaching effects of the new media: news is now available, often free of charge, online and young people are not acquiring the habit of daily readership as their parents did. *The Sun* and *Daily Mail* have been declining at a lesser rate, of 2% per year, but the downward direction is clear: within five years, overall circulation is predicted to decline by almost a quarter.

This decline explains why newspapers have tried a multitude of techniques – endless competitions, including bingo, expanding sports sections – to revive their fortunes, but to little avail. This economic imperative helps explain why 'common denominator' topics like celebrity gossip and scandalous exposures figure so highly on their pages, especially the tabloids. It also helps explain why the *News of the World* resorted to illegal 'hacking' of mobile phones to get celebrity stories at any cost (see Box 9.2, on p. 120).

It is true that the print media is not as important as it was three or four decades ago but it nevertheless still exercises significant influence, otherwise the 2011–12 Leveson inquiry into its behaviour would not have been so keenly followed and debated. Most newspapers support a particular party during election campaigns, but do they have any effect? It is fair to say that it is hard to measure the direct influence of reading a newspaper on how someone votes, but it is reasonable to assume lengthy exposure over time does have an impact. And some content can swing votes: studies have shown that *The Sun*'s vigorous anti-Labour campaign succeeded in the 1992 general election ('It's The Sun Wot Won It' boasted a *Sun* headline in the wake of the Conservative victory). Newspaper news coverage, furthermore, does tend to set the news agenda for the day in news bulletins and current affairs broadcast programmes, like BBC's morning *Today* programme on Radio 4.

Figure 9.1 reveals how press partisanship has varied over the years, indicating that the pro-right-wing bias of the press has been fairly consistent since 1945, apart from in the 1997 and 2001 elections. Table 9.3 shows how the party allegiance of newspaper readers broke down in 2005 and 2010.

THE BROADCAST MEDIA

Broadcasting, of course, is now the key medium when it comes to transmitting political messages. Radio was used by Hitler to great effect during his rise to power. Roosevelt also used it to augment his presidential power during the 1930s. British Prime Minister Stanley Baldwin's relaxed 'fireside chats' for the first time brought the voice of his office into every living room in the country. But even he could

Table 9.3 Party choice by newspaper readership, 2005 and 2010

	Labour		Conservatives		Liberal Democrats		Swing (Lab-Con)
	2005	2010	2005	2010	2005	2010	2005–10
Result	35	29	32	36	22	23	5
The Guardian	43	46	7	9	41	37	*3.5
The Independent	34	32	13	14	44	44	1.5
The Times	27	22	38	49	26	24	8
The Telegraph	13	7	65	70	17	18	5.5
The Star	54	35	22	21	15	20	10
The Daily Express	28	19	48	53	18	18	7
The Daily Mail	22	16	57	59	14	16	4
The Sun	45	28	33	43	12	18	13.5
The Mirror	67	59	11	16	17	17	

*Swing among *The Guardian* voters was from Liberal Democrat to Labour.

Source: Wring, D. and Ward, S. (2010) The media and the 2010 campaign: the television election?, *Parliamentary Affairs*, 63(4): 802–817, p. 808.

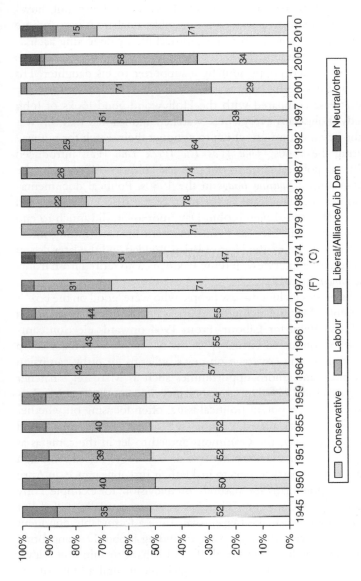

Figure 9.1 Newspaper partisanship at general elections, by percentage circulation, 1945–2010

Source: David Butler and Gareth Butler, *Twentieth-Century British Political Facts, 1900–2000,* published 2000.

not compete with Winston Churchill's stirring wartime broadcasts, which roused the nation to resist the Nazi threat. Churchill, however, proved ineffective on television, unlike Richard Nixon, whose 1952 'Checkers' speech saved his political life by deflecting accusations of sleaze with homely stories about his growing-up experiences and the so-named puppy sent by a supporter to his daughter. His presidential debate in 1960 was less successful: he appeared sweaty and ill at ease compared with the Hollywood good looks of John Kennedy. Politicians everywhere watched and learned that this was now the key medium on which to conduct their search for power.

During the 1960s, *That Was The Week That Was*, introduced hard-hitting political satire to our political culture – followed by the puppet-featuring *Spitting Image* in the 1980s. Political documentaries also became significant in the form of the BBC's *Panorama* and Granada's *World in Action*. Robin Day, moreover, did much to end the traditional deference to politicians with his hard-hitting interviews, followed up by the likes of Brian Walden and the later doyen of the aggressive interview, Jeremy Paxman (who retired from fronting *Newsnight* in 2014).

All the parties included a few people who were 'good on the box' – for example, Macmillan for the Tories and Anthony Wedgwood (later Tony) Benn for Labour. From 1964 onwards election campaigns were conducted virtually, via the television, with razor-sharp competition to win coverage on news bulletins for pithy campaign 'sound-bites' and photo-opportunities such as Margaret Thatcher cradling a calf in 1979. How television companies dealt with political issues became a potent political issue, often focusing on whether their coverage was biased or not (see below). After much soul searching and delay, the Commons agreed to let in the cameras as late as 1988; it took over another two decades for televised campaign debates between party leaders to make their first appearance, in April 2010. Some politicians are 'naturals' on television, for example Tony Blair and David Cameron; Thatcher was not naturally skilled but she worked hard to make herself over time a formidable opponent for even the cleverest interviewers, including Robin Day and Brian Walden. Others, like Ted Heath, found it hard to shine on television, while Ed Miliband seemed to lack the natural affinity of the likes of Blair or Cameron.

TELEVISED ELECTION DEBATES

The famous Nixon–Kennedy debates took place in 1960 but it was not until 2010 that Britain followed suit. The delay was because incumbent prime ministers did not want to provide a national platform for opponents. In 2010, Prime Minister Gordon Brown felt so unpopular that he decided the gamble of televised debates was worth the risk. In the event the Liberal Democrat, Nick Clegg, was the main beneficiary and because of this unwelcome success – Cameron's critics blamed his failure to win an overall majority on the debates – the Tory leader, fearful of allowing opponents the platform, tried his best to sabotage arrangements to repeat them in 2015. In the end he was successful in limiting televised debates to one occasion at the start of the campaign; but it was a seven-way leadership debate, 'diluted' by the small parties, and not the head to head with Miliband that Labour sought. Perhaps Cameron was wise to risk the accusation of being scared, as even in this forum Ed Miliband was able to show he was by no means the caricature of a weak and indecisive leader Cameron had tried so hard to create in his public utterances.

NEWS VALUES

Some question how certain trivial stories manage to claim front-page prominence in the tabloid press. It is important to remember that the print media are still essentially businesses, required to sell copies to survive. This means that their content has to attract the interest of buyers or the business fails; as sales have fallen off so 'news' has to some extent been redefined. Surveys show that detailed news and comment on political subjects are minority interests; only the more educated readers buy the quality press. The more 'popular' papers find that they have to be more hard-headed and offer stories on such subjects as personalities, especially if they have transgressed in some way, for example committed adultery or financial fraud. If celebrities are involved – pop singers, soap or film stars – then the story is seen as huge and likely to sell lots of papers. Other topics which dominate the news when they arise include major crimes or disasters: the public share a morbid interest in the misfortunes of others. On television, news items that can be accompanied by vivid pictures are often favoured, for example volcano eruptions and other natural disasters.

Clearly, news values dominated by celebrity trivia are not ideal nourishment for a mature democracy: only the quality press, up-market weeklies, BBC Radio 4 plus television channels BBC2 and BBC4 seriously address this requirement. Serious politics is a minority interest; without the assistance of television and radio it is hard to see how our imperfect democracy would function at all. Two minutes of exposure on prime-time television can enable a politician to make more contact with voters than several months of assiduous door-knocking. It follows that politicians need the assistance of people who understand how to manage the media to absorb and transmit their messages to voters.

'SPIN'

Political parties, in another sign of US-style professionalism, began to use advertising agencies towards the end of the twentieth century. Tories used Saatchi and Saatchi during the 1970s and Labour went on to use advertising men like Philip Gould and Stephen Carter. Close to leading politicians, 'spin doctors', like Labour's Peter Mandelson and Alastair Campbell and later the Tory's Andy Coulson, acquired a reputation as ruthless and possibly mendacious manipulators of the news. Campbell finally stepped down in 2003 after he tended to become the focus of too many stories rather than merely their source. Tony Blair also suffered from being associated with the deliberate massaging of news items – 'spin' – and in consequence lost credibility in office.

Writing in the *Sunday Times* (16 March 2003), Bernard Ingham, Thatcher's former press secretary, declared that 'spin is everywhere' and that 'Blair has forfeited the trust of the nation'. This is not to say, however, that Blair was not the most gifted political communicator of his generation, blessed with a near magical ability to transform hackneyed political phrases into what sounded like oratory. Maybe the public began eventually to notice the mismatch between what Blair claimed to be the case and what they perceived not to be. His passionate insistence before, during and after the Iraq War, that Saddam Hussein was hiding 'weapons of mass destruction' blasted a hole in his political reputation from which it has never recovered.

QUESTION OF BIAS

Many politicians complain that the media are 'biased' against them. Harold Wilson used to claim that while the print press was dominated by Tory-supporting papers, television was Labour's medium. However, in 1971, when *Panorama*'s 'Yesterday's men' asked how much money he had made out of his memoirs, he was able to detect a right-wing bias in the BBC. Margaret Thatcher was also convinced of the Corporation's bias, but to the opposite side. She tended to see the BBC through the same jaundiced lens as her colleague, Norman Tebbit: 'that insufferable, smug, sanctimonious, naive, guilt ridden, wet, pink, orthodoxy of that sunset home of that third rate decade: the 1960s' (Kureishi, 2011: p. 92).

The problem, however, probably lies with the politicians rather than with the media (although see Box 9.1). Committed to their beliefs, politicians tend to believe they are always right and that anyone who fails to agree with them must somehow be 'biased'. Thatcher, again, once said she would like to have four hours of airtime to get her message over, rather than the few minutes here and there which the media provided. This betrays another tendency of politicians: an urge to control the media so that it delivers more, to them, desirable messages. While this is easily understandable, democracy would collapse if control of the media fell to a single political force. It follows that it is autocrats and dictators whose rule is characterised by an iron control of the media.

Box 9.1   How accurate is John Lloyd's critique of the media?

An influential critique of the media was made in *What the Media Are Doing to Our Politics* (2004), by John Lloyd, himself a journalist, who has worked on a number of broadsheet newspapers. His argument is that the media have 'Decided that politics is a dirty game, played by devious people who tell an essentially false narrative about the world and thus deceive the British people'.

In support of his thesis Lloyd points to the aggressive interviewing techniques which assume politicians are dissembling liars. Tony Wright, MP, chair of the Administration Select Committee, argued, in *The Guardian*, 10 October 2005, that the media should accept some responsibility for the 'culture of contempt' which had contributed to a collapse of trust in politics and politicians. The late Anthony Sampson, in the same feature, reviewing a number of other contributors on Lloyd's argument, concluded that most felt he was right and that many distinguished people 'felt genuine anguish . . . at being misrepresented by the media'.

Finally, David Leigh, for the 'hacks', chipped in with his own experience that most politicians, when asked difficult questions, constantly evade or tell 'downright lies'. In addition, they utilise skilled PR firms or intimidating lawyers; 'They conceal what they can conceal and what they can't they distort'. If left unchallenged, he argues, power will invariably act in this way and in a democracy it is necessary for civil society to be 'truculent and unfettered'. His idea is that the media provide an essential counterbalance to power, even if it is democratically elected power.

Marxist critics – for example, Adorno and the so-called Frankfurt School – assert that, given that the privately owned capitalist economy includes the media in its orbit of control, then its outlets inevitably play a role in assisting societal control and the maintenance of the present unequal distribution of power in society. It is true that the press and large sections of the broadcast media are owned privately but against this it can be argued that media organisations strongly resist government attempts to control them, that investigative journalism regularly embarrasses and shames government, and that television journalism is much more bipartisan than press journalism, by law in the case of the BBC.

Box 9.2   The British press and 'phone hacking'

This explosive story first appeared on the news radar in January 2007, when Clive Goodman (royal editor) and his colleague Glenn Mulcaire of the *News of the World* were convicted of accessing messages – 'phone hacking' – left on the phones of newsworthy people. This procedure was relatively straightforward, being based on the default code settings of phone manufacturers; it is also illegal. *News of the World* editor

Andy Coulson resigned but his employer, Rupert Murdoch, who owned News International (NI), claimed Goodman was merely a one-off rogue reporter. Nick Davies of *The Guardian* refused to accept this and claimed phone hacking was more widespread; in September 2007 the *New York Times* implicated Coulson in backing up *The Guardian* story.

Despite these accusations and warnings from colleagues, David Cameron controversially appointed Coulson as his press secretary in July 2007 on the advice of his chancellor, George Osborne. Claims that Coulson was involved in authorising illegal activity continued to be made and in January 2011 he resigned as Cameron's trusted media guru. Then it was revealed that the phone of murdered teenager Milly Dowler had been hacked; police suggest there may have been 4000 people whose phones had been hacked. This prompted the Leveson inquiry, with much attendant focus on close Tory links to the Murdoch press. In October 2013 the trial began of Coulson, Rebekah Brooks (former editor of *The Sun* and chief executive of News International) plus several others. Coulson was found guilty of conspiring to hack phones on 24 June 2014; Brooks and her husband were cleared. Cameron faced criticism that he had shown bad judgement in employing someone under such a cloud and that he had done so only to curry favour with the Murdoch press.

REGULATION OF THE PRESS

Journalists are mostly dedicated to complete freedom in what they are allowed to write and publish. Freedom of speech is certainly a bedrock of democracy but in its pursuit of sales some newspapers, particularly the tabloids, have not been afraid to invade the privacy of people, especially celebrities. The Press Complaints Commission, mostly comprising leading members of the press, was supposed to provide some regulation but its strictures were frequently ignored. After a number of well publicised excesses by the press, particularly the illegal 'hacking' of mobile phones by the *News of the World*, it was decided that something had to be done (see Box 9.2). The result was the Leveson inquiry (July 2011–November 2012) into the culture, practices and ethics of the press. Its report proposed a new system of regulation, underpinned by a Royal Charter. However, most of the press rejected something which they felt smacked too much of 'government control' and instead set up their own body, the Independent Press Standards Organisation (IPSO). The deadlock continues into the present, with most newspapers having decided to support IPSO rather than the alternative backed by the Royal Charter.

NEW MEDIA

Less subject to the law and regulation are the so-called 'new' media which have burgeoned astonishingly over the past two decades. Just as printing in the fifteenth century caused a revolution in political communication followed by broadcasting in the twentieth century, so digital technology is causing further turbulent changes. At the most basic level there is currently an abundance of information about politics available online. People can now use email to communicate with a worldwide audience of people – so that we have MPs writing direct to constituents and online lobbyists like Avaaz pushing human-itarian campaigns. We also have the potential for 'online democracy', whereby people can be linked to decision-makers via their computers and can express 'instant' views or even vote online. While this could produce useful results it also runs the risk of misuse from power-seeking demagogues or, as we have seen, terrorists transmitting infor-mation about bomb-making or recruiting supporters.

'Blogs' or online commentary have become a regular part of the political universe, with sites like the right-wing gossip vendor Guido Fawkes attracting huge traffic and occasionally making the main-stream headlines. Some claim blogs are making newspapers obsolete but this is a gross exaggeration. Blogs spring up in their thousands but not many last more than a few years and, with most being staffed by sole bloggers, they lack the resources to provide a comprehensive news service.

Virtually everyone now owns a mobile phone and the 'smart' phones are in reality pocket-sized computers, capable of a wide range of functions which could have political significance: emailing, blogging, even voting or receiving news bulletins and broadcasts. 38 Degrees is a UK-based pressure group that seeks to inspire online petitions or write-ins to MPs and other decision-makers, mostly on left-of-centre issues.

Social networking also has huge potential politically. Campaigns which formerly might have included a word-of-mouth element can now exploit individuals' personal networks to advance messages from politicians to voters. Given the brevity of its messages Twitter has proved surprisingly effective at rapidly distributing messages over a huge area. George Galloway once told Radio 4's *Week at Westminster* that he could now communicate direct to the 150,000 people who follow him on Twitter. Writing in *The Times* on 17 October 2012, former spin doctor to Tony Blair, Alastair Campbell, marvelled at the dramatic emergence of social media – in particular Facebook, founded in 2004, and Twitter, launched in 2006 and now in Britain with over 10 million people on it (more than the number buying a daily newspaper). He went on to say that what politicians really fear is losing control:

> Nobody controls how the message lands. What this offers politicians is the opportunity to communicate directly without having to rely on the old media. There is an inescapable momentum behind the flow of political power to individuals and movements which recognise no national boundaries.

QUESTIONS FOR DISCUSSION

1. How much influence do you think newspapers exercise on voting attitudes?
2. To what extent has 'new technology' usurped the functions of the traditional print media?
3. Are interviewers justified in being aggressive with their politician interviewees?

FURTHER READING

The best book on the mass media up to undergraduate level is Street (2011) A still solidly useful review of theory is McQuail (1983). For a penetrating critique read Lloyd (2004). For an entertaining history of a tabloid paper, read Chippendale and Orrie (1992).

Chippendale, P. and Orrie, C. (1992) *Stick It Up Your Punter*, Mandarin.

Jones, N. (1995) *Sound-Bites and Spin Doctors*, Indigo.

Jones, N. (1999) *Sultans of Spin: The Media and the New Labour Government*, Orion.

Kureishi, H. (2011) *Collected Essays*, Faber.

Lloyd, J. (2004) *What the Media Are Doing to Our Politics*, Constable.

McQuail, D. (1983) *Mass Communication Theory: An Introduction*, Sage.

Moon, N. (1999) *Opinion Polls: History, Theory and Practice*, Manchester University Press.

Seymour-Ure, C. (1991) *The British Press and Broadcasting Since 1945*, Blackwell.

Street, J. (2011) *Mass Media: Politics and Democracy*. Palgrave.

WEBSITES

Excellent online newspaper: http://www.huffingtonpost.co.uk.

The Guardian: http://www.theguardian.com/uk.

Guido Fawkes Blog (most popular blog in UK): http://www.order-order.com.

The Independent: http://www.independent.co.uk.

The Telegraph: http://www.telegraph.co.uk.

The Times: http://www.thetimes.co.uk/tto/news.

UK Media Internet Directory, newspapers: http://www.mcc.ac.uk/jcridlan.htm.

IV

THE LEGISLATURE

Chapter 1 of this book explained how the legislature, starting from an advisory council to Anglo-Saxon and then Norman monarchs, emerged over centuries of British history as the body, by the late seventeenth century, ultimately responsible for making the laws of the land. In the fourteenth century the hereditary House of Lords, comprising mostly the aristocracy, separated from the (more or less) elected, though then less powerful, House of Commons. During the nineteenth century it was still possible for the prime minister to sit in the Lords but after the 1911 Parliament Act, the climax of a major struggle for power between the two chambers, the Commons emerged supreme. Since that year, no prime minister has ruled from a seat in the Lords. This is not to say that the Lords does not still perform important functions, as Chapter 11 explains. The chapter after that examines elections to the House of Commons, Chapter 13 examines the chamber itself.

THE MONARCHY

'Royalty is a Government', wrote Walter Bagehot in his classic study of the British constitution, 'in which the attention of the nation is concentrated on one person doing interesting actions. A Republic is a Government in which that attention is divided between many, who are all doing uninteresting things'. Thus did Bagehot declare his preference for a constitutional monarchy rather than a *republic* and define a role for the monarchy which, arguably, it still performs, at least partially. In medieval times the Plantagenets and Tudors were absolute monarchs, able to govern by whim alone, should they choose. To exercise this God-endorsed and indeed God-like authority was a seductive lure which caused the War of the Roses and many another bloody succession struggle. The Civil War (1642–49) was a conflict which put an end not only to Charles I but also to the idea of absolute, *divine right* monarchy itself. Within a few decades of this struggle, Kings and Queens were viewed essentially as figureheads, symbols of the nation; their effective political power, following the trauma of a beheaded King, had just melted away.

Now the monarch is seen by many as politically a mere shell, a useful fiction mobilised on national days, festivals and when foreign dignitaries visit. But others offer a more critical, more social analysis, for example the former editor of the *New Statesman*, Kingsley Martin

(1897–1969), who declared: 'The Monarchy . . . is the secret well from which the flourishing institution of British Snobbery draws its nourishment'. This view sees Britain as incorrigibly obsessed with class differences, with the monarchy at its fulcrum. Replacing it with an elected head of state, such critics insist, would remove a symbol, though antique, of the inequalities and class hatred which mar our present-day society.

Other critics claim the monarchy still exercises power, albeit only in the circumstance of a hung parliament. In such times historian Peter Hennessy sees the 'continuing political influence of the monarchy' as significant, in that he or she has the power to choose the prime minister. Ben Pimlott, biographer of the Queen, disagrees, arguing that should she ever seek to exercise such nominal powers they would soon be dismantled.

FUNCTIONS

Firstly, according to Bagehot, the Queen has 'the right to be consulted, the right to encourage, the right to warn', and over the years she has 'advised' 11 prime ministers, whom she sees at customary weekly one-hour meetings. She got on with some – Wilson and Callaghan – better than others – Heath and Thatcher. Prime ministers, it appears, are impressed by the Queen's knowledge of current issues: Wilson apparently thought her advice 'wise' but others, like Heath, saw the weekly meeting as something of a chore. Prime ministers do not lack for advice and, as such, the monarch's is unlikely to rank especially highly. Given that she has an hour's time every week of the most powerful person in the country, there is little or no evidence that her influence has extended much beyond preventing Tony Benn, when postmaster general, from removing the Queen's head from postage stamps in the 1960s.

Secondly, as the head of the armed forces, the monarch undertakes many ceremonial duties but because the Queen commands fervent loyalty from all three arms of the military, it is maintained that this command is more than just symbolic but rules out any possibility of a *military coup* ever being considered, let alone carried out.

Thirdly, the monarchy has traditionally been held to be a moral template for the nation: virtually *above* criticism. Thus, when King

Edward VIII, during the 1930s, fell in love with a woman who was divorced (a source of shame at that time), he was forced to abdicate. During the 1950s Princess Margaret was forbidden to marry a man she loved, Peter Townsend, because he too had been divorced. Since then, perceptions of the monarchy have changed. Bagehot reckoned that the key to the public's regard for the monarchy was its mystique or 'magic' upon which too much light should not be cast; maybe he was right.

Once the veil was lifted during the 1970s the inevitable downs as well the ups of royal family life were placed under the eager microscope of media scrutiny. It turned out that, with the exception of the Queen herself, the royals were no better and possibly a little worse than the rest of us, at least as regards marital fidelity and attitudes towards money. A poll in *The Observer*, 14 September 1997, revealed that only 12% were satisfied with the monarchy, with 74% wishing it to be 'modernised'; admittedly this was a low point and polls have varied before and since.

Fourthly, the monarch offers a symbol of national unity. Bagehot argued members of the public need a soothing and believable set of symbols to make them feel content with their government: the monarch provided precisely this. Ben Pimlott's 1996 study, *The Queen*, suggested the monarchy is a mirror in which the nation sees itself. In 1953 the huge ritual of the Queen's coronation was a triumphant ceremonial symbol of the nation, as successive royal weddings and events also proved and, indeed, continued to do so with the birth of Prince George in July 2013 to the Duke and Duchess of Cambridge.

CRITICISMS

One of the reasons for negative views of the monarchy is its allegedly excessive cost. In June 2014 Buckingham Palace said the cost of the monarchy – not including security – was the equivalent to just over one penny a week for every UK resident. Under the formula established in 2012, the sovereign grant rose to £40 million for the year 2014–15, which is perhaps not so huge a figure when it is considered that the Queen has given up luxuries like the Royal Yacht *Britannia* and now voluntarily pays income tax. When the economy is not doing well, however, and the government is making cuts, some ask why our monarchy cannot be as low-cost and low-key as those in Scandinavian countries.

PRESENT POWER OF MONARCHY

Bagehot placed the monarchy in the 'dignified' category of the constitution, as opposed to the 'efficient' parts, like the House of Commons. Political scientist and former Labour cabinet minister Andrew Adonis challenged that judgement:

> Add to its charismatic power the royal family's wealth, its influence over policy and government, its status as the head of the honours system and the hereditary aristocracy, and the monarchy looks every bit as 'efficient' as most departments of state. Indeed, it is a department of state, for the Court and royal household are an enterprise as elaborate and relentless about self promotion as any Whitehall ministry. (Adonis and Pollard, 1998: p. 134)

Should the monarchy be replaced by an elected head of state? To imagine the monarchy's future stretching ahead indefinitely does, indeed, seem unlikely, but, as Professor John Gray observed (*Observer*, 29 July 2007):

> Happily, we do not face in Britain any of the horrors that have accompanied the building of nation states in other parts of the world. Still, it would be unwise to take our good fortune too much for granted. The monarchical constitution we have today – a mix of antique survivals and post-modern soap operas – may be absurd but it enables a diverse society to rub along without too much friction.

THE MONARCHY AND POLITICS

By tradition our *constitutional monarch* steers well clear of political controversy, but occasionally the Queen has stated a political view. On her Silver Jubilee in 1977, in what was thought a Labour-inspired ploy to weaken the Scottish National Party, she said, 'I cannot forget that I was crowned Queen of the United Kingdom of Great Britain and Northern Ireland. Perhaps the Jubilee is a time to remind our-selves of the benefits which union has conferred, at home and, in our international dealings, on the inhabitants of all parts of this United Kingdom.' Again, in early September 2014 the government was so worried, following a poll showing the 'yes' campaign was in the lead in the run-up to the referendum on Scottish independence, that the Queen was prevailed upon to make her concern known. Given the Queen's need for political neutrality it was her private secretary and the cabinet secretary who stage managed the intervention – a much more nuanced one than in 1977 – by having her mention on 14 September 2014, to a woman outside the church she attends when at Balmoral, that, in respect of the referendum, 'people will think very carefully about the future' (see Carrell et al., 2014). This was so nuanced, one might think, as to be scarcely an intervention at all. If Prince Charles ever becomes King, his many written letters to ministers on a variety of topics and made public in May 2015 suggest limiting political interventions by the monarch might prove more of a problem.

QUESTIONS FOR DISCUSSION

1. Does the monarch wield any effective power in the modern political system?
2. Has publicity reduced the 'magic' of the monarchy?
3. Would an elected head of state be an improvement on our hereditary monarchy?

FURTHER READING

Walter Bagehot's *The English Constitution* is a good starting point for further reading, as it is on all constitutional topics; Lord Altrincham's 1958 *Is the Monarchy Perfect?* is also a useful introduction to the debate over the monarchy. However, the best short coverage of this ancient institution is by Philip Norton, chapter 14 in Jones and Norton (2013).

Adonis, A. and Pollard, S. (1997) *A Class Act: The Myth of Britain's Classless Society*, Penguin.
Altrincham, Lord, *et al.* (1958) *Is the Monarchy Perfect?*, John Calder.

Bagehot, W. (2001) *The English Constitution*, Oxford University Press.

Bogdanor, V. (1995) *The Monarchy and the Constitution*, Oxford University Press.

Bond, J. (2012) *The Diamond Queen*, Carlton Publishing.

Carrell, S., Watt, N. and Wintour, P. (2014) The real story of the Scottish referendum, *Guardian*, 16 and 17 December.

Hardie, F. (1970) *The Political Influence of the British Monarchy 1868–1952*, Batsford.

Haseler, S. (2012) *The Grand Delusion*, I. B. Tauris.

Jones, B. and Norton, P. (2013) *Politics UK* (8th edition), Routledge.

Pimlott, B. (1996) *The Queen*, Harper Collins.

WEBSITES

Constitutional Monarchy Association: http://www.monarchy.net.

Prince of Wales: http://www.princeofwales.gov.uk.

Royal family: http://www.royal.gov.uk.

11

THE HOUSE OF LORDS

The House of Lords emerged out of the Anglo-Saxon Witangemot and the Norman Curia Regis as gatherings which advised the King. By the fourteenth century it comprised earls and barons on a hereditary basis, plus leading churchmen: the church was probably the country's richest institution after the monarch and also wielded considerable political power. It met separately from the 'lower' House of Commons, which was elected and hence was more representative of the nation as a whole. During the nineteenth century the ramshackle elections to the Commons, vulnerable to corrupt pressures and with huge differences in voting qualifications, were reformed along democratic lines to create a uniform and coherent system.

This gave the Commons a legitimacy which the Lords, with its built-in Conservative majority, could not equal. In the first decade of the twentieth century conflict between the two chambers reached a climax when David Lloyd George's historic challenge was successful; from the 1911 Parliament Act onwards it could exercise only a two-year delay on legislation, and in 1949 this was reduced to one year. In 1958 the Life Peerages Act made it possible for individuals to be elevated to the peerage for the course of their lifetimes. Only three (non-royal) hereditary peerages were subsequently created (all by Margaret Thatcher).

The Peerage Act 1963 made it possible for hereditary peers, should they wish, to give up their titles, in the case of Lords Home (who became Alec Douglas-Home), Stansgate (Tony Benn) and Hailsham (Quintin Hogg) to pursue their political careers. Finally, the House of Lords Act 1999 abolished the hereditary principle, apart from 92 such peers, on a transitional basis, in lieu of a wholly reformed chamber.

PRESENT COMPOSITION

Membership of the Lords is controlled by the government of the day in that the prime minister suggests names for the Queen to approve. These are often retired senior politicians, or distinguished representatives of the business world, academe, civil service, army or the arts. In 1999 the nominal membership of the chamber was 1,300; since then it has been reduced (in 2015) to around 780. As mentioned above, hereditary peers have been largely abolished. Life peers now provide the dominant element; as Table 11.1 shows, there is no Conservative majority and cross-benchers hold the balance of voting power.

FUNCTIONS OF HOUSE OF LORDS

Some critics of the UK constitution argue that the House of Lords should be completely abolished as it serves no useful function. While

Table 11.1 Composition of the House of Lords by party group, 2015

Affiliation	Life peers	Hereditary peers	Lord spiritual	Total
Conservative	176	48		224
Labour	207	4		211
Liberal Democrat	97	4		101
Non-affiliated	21	0		21
Other	16	1		17
Cross-bench	145	30		175
Lords spiritual	0	0	25	25
Total	662	87	25	774

the overall utility of what it does is open to debate, there can be no doubt, however, that it does do a number of things and some of them not too badly.

CONSTITUTIONAL FUNCTION

The Upper House has the power of veto over any proposal to extend the life of a parliament beyond the present five-year limit. It can also delay a bill after its second Commons reading for a period of a year, and this is a useful weapon in the final year of a parliamentary term. The last time the delay was sanctioned was over the 2004 Hunting Act.

DELIBERATIVE FUNCTION

Regular debates take place in the Lords – some say that its unique mixture of experience and expertise make these debates superior to those in the Commons. This is especially so as peers are not as closely controlled as MPs by the whips and can more easily speak their minds. However, it remains the case that a debate in the Lords seldom attracts much attention unless the resultant vote defeats the government on an important bill.

LEGISLATIVE FUNCTION

The legislative process in the Lords is similar to that in the Commons in terms of the cycle of 'readings' and is accessible to amendments in similar fashion. Bills concerning finance do not concern the Lords, but all others do.

INITIATING BILLS

The Lords takes some pressure off the Lower House by introducing a number of non-controversial bills, especially those concerning local government. Peers can also move private members' bills, though they account for no more than 3% of the chamber's time.

REVISION AND AMENDMENT

This is probably the most important role performed by this chamber. A proportion of legislation, and some say it is a worryingly big proportion, is not very carefully drafted and contains loopholes and ambiguities. The experienced legislators sitting in the Lords are able to sift through the clauses of proposed new laws and iron out wrinkles which would otherwise make some laws difficult or even impossible to implement.

SELECT COMMITTEES

The Lords has its own array of select committees and can create more as its members think fit. The most important is the European Union Committee, which monitors draft EU laws through seven sub-committees, containing co-opted members.

JUDICIAL ROLE

The Lords used to perform the function of the highest appeal court in the land but since October 2009 this has been performed by the newly created Supreme Court.

REFORM

The reform of the Lords has been a perennial question in discussions about the British constitution since the dawn of democracy in the nineteenth century. But while its powers have been trimmed and its membership transformed, no comprehensive reform of the chamber has taken place. Why? It has not been for want of ideas; rather, there have been too many ideas and nowhere near a consensus on what would be best. Even on the subject of appointment there is no agreement. Enthusiasts for more democracy argue that any new chamber should be elected or contain a substantial elected component; more established members value their freedom from constituency pressures and, perhaps, recoil at the need to fight elections.

In January 2000 Lord Wakeham's Royal Commission offered a 550-strong chamber with the possibility of an elected component of 65, 87 or 195 members. The Commons rejected all the various options offered and the issue hung fire until May 2011, when Nick Clegg, Deputy Prime Minister, tasked with constitutional reform, came up with a new plan. He suggested a 300-strong chamber with 80% elected by proportional representation and the remaining 20% appointed as non-partisan cross-benchers. Each member of the new chamber would serve a 15-year term. On 6 August the proposal was abandoned in view of fierce opposition from Labour and 90 Tory MPs who voted against the measure. In retaliation Clegg withdrew support for the redrawing of constituency boundaries which Conservatives hoped would enable them to win an extra 20 seats in the 2015 election. When Cameron created 26 new peers in his August 2015 honours, he was heavily criticised for 'cronyism' and for elevating Conservative donors.

QUESTIONS FOR DISCUSSION

1. Is it possible to adduce a case for a hereditary element within political institutions?
2. What is the case for abolishing the Lords and having a unicameral democratic chamber?
3. How important is it that the upper chamber is elected rather than appointed?

FURTHER READING

Once again, Norton in chapter 17 of Jones and Norton (2013) provides an excellent short introduction to the chamber. Donald Shell (2007) provides a longer and more thorough treatment, as does another book by Norton (2013).

Baldwin, N. D. J. (2005) *Parliament in the twenty-first Century*, Politicos.
Barnett, A. (1997) *This Time: Our Constitutional Revolution*, Vintage.
Criddle, B. and Norton, P. (2005) The make-up of Parliament, in P. Giggings (ed.), *The Future of Parliament*, Palgrave.
Fitzpatrick, A. (2011) *The End of the Peer Show?*, Constitution Society/Centre Forum.
Jones, B. and Norton, P. (2013) *Politics UK* (8th edition), Routledge.
Norton, P. (2013) *Parliament in British Politics* (2nd edition), Palgrave Macmillan.

Russell, M. (2012) Elected second chambers and their powers – an international survey, *Political Quarterly*, 83(1): 117–129.

Shell, D. (2007) *The House of Lords*, Manchester University Press.

Tyrie, A. (1998) *Reforming the Lords: A Conservative Approach*, Conservative Policy Forum.

WEBSITE

Members of the House of Lords: http://www.parliament.uk/mps-lords-and-offices/lords/composition-of-the-lords.

12

VOTING BEHAVIOUR

EARLY HISTORY

Britain famously has had an elected legislative chamber since medieval times. But back then there were great variations as to who had the right to vote; most of those who did were qualified by virtue of owning a certain amount of property. Dunwich in Suffolk had only 32 inhabitants yet sent two MPs to the Commons while bustling industrial cities like Leeds, Manchester and Birmingham sent none. In 1780, a survey estimated the electorate numbered a mere 214,000: less than 3% of the 8 million total population. Calls for reform in the late eighteenth and early nineteenth centuries, in the wake of the French Revolution, elicited repressive reactions like the 'Peterloo massacre' in August 1819 – 11 people were killed by a cavalry charge at a meeting in support of parliamentary reform. But these forces and arguments eventually brought forth the 1832 Great Reform Act; according to Prime Minister Lord Grey (1830–34) it was to 'prevent the necessity of revolution'.

EXTENDING THE FRANCHISE

This famous Act did not greatly add to the size of the then 366,000 electorate but most of the smaller boroughs were abolished, and seats were distributed more fairly to the newer towns and cities. Further Reform Acts in 1867 and 1884 increased the electorate to approaching 8 million; the 1872 Ballot Act made voting secret, thus removing the ease with which votes could be bought or coerced. By 1918 voting lost its link with property and women over 30 also won the right to vote; in 1928 the voting age for women was made the same as men, 21.

In 1969 18-year-olds were given the vote. Voters have to be citizens of the UK, the Commonwealth or the Republic of Ireland; British citizens who have lived abroad for up to 20 years may also vote. Members of the House of Lords, those convicted of a crime and in prison, some categories of mental patients plus those found guilty of electoral malpractice are excluded from voting. Since the Electoral Administration Act 2006, *candidates* for public elections can be as young as 18 years, though civil servants, members of the armed forces and ordained members of the Church of England cannot stand as candidates.

THE ELECTORAL SYSTEM(S)

Traditionally, the British electoral system has been perceived as simple 'first past the post'. However, even though opponents of reform have been seen to have the upper hand for most of the recent past, several aspects of Britain's voting system have in reality been reformed, so that now it is more accurate to speak in the plural, of 'electoral systems':

SUPPLEMENTARY VOTE

This is used to select the London mayor and entails voters indicating a first and second choice. If no candidate wins 50% of the vote, second preferences are distributed, adding to the first preferences, until someone exceeds the halfway mark.

SINGLE TRANSFERABLE VOTE (STV)

This is most commonly associated with Ireland but, given its ability to be very representative, it has been introduced for all elections in Northern Ireland plus local elections in Scotland. Voters register their preferences right down the list of candidates in large multi-member constituencies. A quota is set based on the number of voters divided by the number of candidates plus one. Candidates who make it first time are elected outright and subsequent ones come through on the basis of second, third and if necessary, other preferences until the quotas are filled.

ADDITIONAL MEMBER SYSTEM

Based on the German system, this entails voters having two votes. The first is cast for candidates in a geographical constituency, the second for candidates in a 'top-up pool' and is for a party. The percentages won by each party – as long as they are over 5% – determine how many members of each 'party list' are judged elected. This system is used for the Scottish Parliament, the Welsh Assembly and for the Greater London Assembly; it has helped parties with thin support to improve their democratic representation.

REGIONAL PARTY LIST (PROPORTIONAL REPRESENTATION)

Voters choose from party lists in multi-member constituencies with the percentages gained by each party determining their share of the available seats. This is the system used for the elections to the European Parliament. Those at the top end of the lists are the candidates likely to be elected.

FIRST PAST THE POST (OR 'SIMPLE PLURALITY' SYSTEM)

This is still the one used at general elections for seats in the Westminster Parliament. While this system tends to deliver winning parties with large majorities, which are then likely to provide stable and decisive government, it has been found lacking from the democratic viewpoint:

1. Candidates can be elected on a minority of the vote; for example, with four candidates standing, all with similar levels of support, someone with 26% of the vote could win, with all remaining votes effectively 'wasted'. Reformers argue that the preferences

used in other systems help to make every vote count. In 2010, two-thirds of MPs were elected on minority votes.

2. The system favours the bigger parties, as any party with wide but shallow support will not win many individual contests. For example, in 2005 Labour won only 35% of the vote but 55% of the seats; in 1983 the SDP–Liberal Alliance won 26% of the vote yet under 4% of the seats. In 2015 UKIP polled 13% of the votes yet returned only one MP.

3. Given this bias towards the big parties, smaller ones have great difficulty in breaking into the level of voting at which they would begin to win large numbers of seats. This tends to perpetuate two-party dominance, when the reality on the ground might feature several varieties of political preferences.

The system as practised in the UK also tends to encourage parties which seek to maximise their appeal by offering a wide spectrum of ideas. Under proportional representation (PR), parties can afford to represent more specific groups in society; this tends to produce multi-party systems but most PR systems guard against excessive fragmentation by specifying that parties have to achieve a minimum percentage of the vote – e.g. 5% – before they are entitled to any seats in the legislature. Moreover, British MPs do not have 'substitutes' as in many PR systems and if someone dies or resigns their seat a by-election takes place. Because the deposit required to stand is only £500, a large number and wide variety of candidates tend to stand for the generally well publicised by-election contests, either for the fun or the fleeting publicity; virtually all of these 'joke' candidates lose their deposits, but succeed in adding some eccentric colour to our political life.

THE DIMINISHING INFLUENCE OF CLASS ON VOTING

Britain has often been perceived as having a 'class based' society, a reflection of the country's role as the initiator of the Industrial Revolution, which created a huge, largely impoverished working class, living in the older parts of cities and towns, and a small wealthy middle class, settled in the suburbs and the rural countryside. In 1911 three-quarters of the population were manual working class; by 1951 this percentage had trimmed down to around 65%. During the 1950s class awareness was still very powerful and votes tended to be cast along class lines. Working class voters tended to vote for 'their class' party, Labour, and middle-class voters for the Tories. In the 1960s Oxford political scientist Peter Pulzer produced a classic sentence often quoted in examination questions followed by the word, 'discuss': 'Class is the basis of British politics: all else is embellishment and detail.' The classification of class was discussed in Chapter 4 – see in particular Box 4.1.

In April 2013 the British Sociological Association published a survey of British class divisions which saw: an elite middle class representing 6%; an 'established middle class' comprising 25%; a 'technical middle class' at 6%; traditional manual working-class members having declined to only 14%; 'new affluent workers' comprising 15%; 'emergent service workers' 19%; and, at the lowest level, the 'precariat', comprising 15% of the whole.

SOCIALISATION

Voters cast their votes to a large extent on the basis of how they have been brought up and the way they have come to earn their living. Children from low-paid families might identify with Labour, traditionally, with its welfare policies, ostensibly the party of the disadvantaged, but as perceptions differ so much, they might easily prefer the Conservative approach of lower taxes and more economic freedom. The nurturing role of families is always important in forming attitudes, with children often reflecting parental views, though with a fair number of dissenting rebels.

PARTISAN DEALIGNMENT

The predictability of class allegiances was a feature of the 1950s; two-thirds of the working class voted Labour and four-fifths of the middle class voted Conservative. The fact that, in addition, 90% voted for one or other of the big parties made voting behaviour very stable. The country was also homogenous; swings from one party to another tended to be reflected throughout the country so that after only a few results in a general election it was often possible to predict the result with some accuracy. Voters used to identify strongly with one or other of the big parties. In 1964, 45% identified 'very strongly' with a party but by 2001 that figure had declined to less than half that figure: a major weakening in the moorings of voter loyalties, which had all kinds of implications. David Denver (2012) illuminatingly suggests a number of reasons why this 'partisan dealignment' occurred:

1. *Working-class occupations shrank* from around 50% of the workforce in 1960 to less than 20% three decades on, having been replaced by 'service' industries −70% of the workforce by 1991− mostly staffed by non-manual workers. These new industries were not extensively unionised, nor did their workers live in close proximity, as in the days of terraced housing close to factories. Social bonds which reinforced voting patterns were thereby weakened (see Tables 12.1 and 12.2).

2. *Rising prosperity enabled more people to buy their own homes* − instead of renting or living on council estates. By 2000 over half of non-manual workers lived in their own homes, a traditional middle-class characteristic. Margaret Thatcher's 'right to buy' policy enabled a million people to buy their own council home, thus weakening their connections with Labour.

3. *The deep recession of the early 1980s* greatly reduced union membership and thus the closeness of such voters to Labour.

4. *Public sector versus private distinctions became important* as workers in the former realised voting Labour would serve them best, while the latter discerned the same in Conservative policies.

5. Denver cites Crewe's analysis of how *the interests of the working classes had tended to fragment* so that home owners differed from renters or better-paid workers had more interest in tax cuts than the poorer-paid. Despite their possible class allegiances, working-class voters could be persuaded by these changes to consider supporting the Conservatives.

6. *Post-secondary educational opportunities* − 40% attended university by the end of the 1990s − encouraged a more sceptical and discriminating appreciation of political issues rather than the earlier knee-jerk class affiliations.

Table 12.1 How Great Britain voted (%), 1983–2005

	May 2005	May 2001	April 1997	June 1992	June 1987	May 1983
Conservative	32.4	31.7	30.7	41.9	42.2	42.3
Labour	35.2	40.7	43.2	34.4	30.8	27.6
Alliance/Lib Dem	22.0	18.3	16.8	17.8	22.6	25.4
Others	11.0	9.3	9.3	5.8	3.4	4.7

Source: Robert Leach, Bill Coxall and Lynton Robins (2006), *British Politics*, Palgrave, table 9.2.

Table 12.2 Decline of class voting, 1992–2005 (MORI)

	AB (middle class)	C1 (lower middle class)	C2 (skilled workers)	DE (unskilled workers)
Conservative				
1992	56	52	39	32
1997	41	37	27	21
2001	39	36	29	24
2005	37	37	33	25
Change 1992–2005	−19	−15	−6	−6
Labour				
1992	19	25	40	49
1997	31	37	50	59
2001	30	38	49	55
2005	28	32	40	48
Change 1992–2005	+11	+7	0	−1
Lib Dem				
1992	22	19	17	16
1997	22	18	16	13
2001	25	20	15	13
2005	29	23	19	18
Change 1992–2005	+7	+4	+2	+2

7. *Experience of parties in power* tended to engender a degree of cynicism about promises of parties and their capacity to deliver desired results. Labour in the late 1960s won few such prizes and neither did Ted Heath's 1970–74 government.

8. *Ideological polarisation* became so extensive in the early 1980s that activists became alienated from typical voters.

9. *Television coverage of politics* increased apace from the 1950s onwards and its statutory non-partisanship tended to encourage an appreciation of both sides of argument rather than a blind acceptance of either of the big parties.

VOTER VOLATILITY

All the above factors collectively served to weaken the emotional class link between parties and voters, with the result that voters were freer to use their own perceptions and powers of reason in deciding on which party to bestow their support. Apart from the smaller numbers who now gave more or less automatic support, voters' allegiance was 'up for grabs'. Denver points out that even the apparent stability of Conservative successes during the 1980s was not based on an unchanging, solid block of voters but on 'a temporary coalition of voters which then dissolved in the inter-election periods'.

So, it seems voters had emerged from the chrysalis of class loyalty into a butterfly which fluttered from party to party, depending on perceptions of their competence and the attractiveness of their policies. While party managers might complain at how their jobs of winning support have become so much harder, all these changes have, in fact, devolved more power to the individual voter, making the system, in theory at least, more democratic. However, voters did not necessarily view themselves as empowered by all these changes.

LOW ELECTION TURNOUT

Election turnout in 1951 was 81.91%; the previous year it had been 83.61%. It averaged well over 70% for the next four decades (Figure 12.1) but then it began to decline rapidly, to 71% in 1997 and then a worrying 59.38% in 2001. From there it climbed to 62.4% in 2005 and 65.11% in 2010, well below the average for the period

1950–92. Other elections fare worse than this, with those to the Scottish Parliament and Welsh Assembly averaging below 50%; in 2014 local election turnout was 36%; and in 1999 the UK figure for turnout to the European elections was a paltry 24%.

Does this matter? Yes it certainly does, if one values British democracy and wants it to work. Democracy is posited upon voter participation; if people fail to vote it suggests they have no faith in the system and it might in consequence fade away, to be replaced by something far less stable or acceptable to British society. Political scientist Paul Whiteley commented on the low turnout in 2001: 'If this is not a crisis of democratic politics, then is hard to see what is'. Others, like David Denver and Anthony King, disagree: all that was needed, wrote the latter, was 'a close fought election at which a great deal is at stake and, make no mistake, they will turn out in droves' (*Telegraph*, 17 May 2001).

Evidence of continuing apathy in 2005 and again in the close-fought 2010 election suggests Denver and King were far from ana-lysing this problem correctly. Especially worrying is that younger voters seem not to have absorbed the sense of voting as a civic duty: nearly a million of 18–24-year-olds are not registered to vote and in 2005 only 37% of this cohort bothered to visit the polling booth. However, if an issue genuinely galvanises, it can still bring voters out in their millions – the passionate Scottish referendum campaign in 2014 led to an 85% turnout and Jeremy Corbyn's campaign for

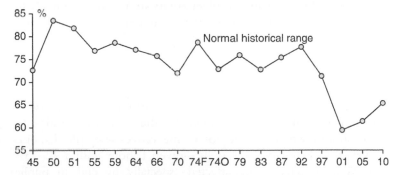

Figure 12.1 Election turnout in UK 1945–2010

Source: UK Political Info, http://www.ukpolitical.info/Turnout45.htm.

the Labour leadership in the summer of 2015 also reached thousands of new young voters. Turnout in the May 2015 general election was 66.1%, but this average hides some large variations, for instance in terms of age – 78% for those over 65 versus 42% for 18–24-year-olds.

OTHER FACTORS INFLUENCING VOTING BEHAVIOUR

RELIGION

Religion dominated politics during the sixteenth and seventeenth centuries. Even during the nineteenth century the Church of England was said to be 'the Conservative Party at prayer', while the Liberals and Labour attracted support from Methodists and Nonconformists. But, apart from Northern Ireland, which has its own distinctive history and culture, the UK has disengaged from religion so much that the country is virtually a secular one in practice. Nor do politicians seek to embrace religion; even Alastair Campbell, the spin doctor for the famously religious Tony Blair, once told a journalist, 'we don't do God'.

AGE

Voters tend to move towards the Conservatives as they age, which is an advantage for that party, as older voters are much more likely to use their votes than are younger ones (as noted above). UKIP supporters are predominately aged over 50.

GENDER

Women supported the Tories disproportionately during the 1980s but the pendulum swung to Labour for the next two decades. In 2010, 36% of women voted for Conservatives and 31% Labour. However, in February 2014 polls showed Labour with a 42–33% lead. Women tend to be affected especially by cuts in public expenditure and the Conservatives, with fewer women MPs, were perceived as not so 'women-friendly'.

NORTH–SOUTH DIVIDE

The declining economy of northern regions has inclined voters there towards benefits-friendly Labour, while the more prosperous south support the Conservatives. Of 158 MPs in the three northern regions, the Tories mustered only 43 at the 2015 general election and have only one MP in Scotland. For its part, south of a line from the Wash to Bristol, Labour held only 10 seats.

ETHNICITY

Ethnic minorities comprise some 8 million according to the 2011 census; their votes are crucial in determining a raft of marginal seats. Conservatives, with their harder line on immigration, tend not to be favoured by immigrant groups, as they detect an element of racism. Labour has traditionally won some three-quarters of the ethnic vote, though the Conservatives are striving hard to reduce the gap.

BIAS IN THE VOTING SYSTEM

Despite its apparent simplicity, the 'first past the post' system throws up some rather undemocratic anomalies. Firstly, it discriminates against smaller parties with thin national support: in 1983 the SDP–Liberal Alliance won 26% of the votes, yet only 3% of the seats. A more proportional system would reduce such distortions but in the referendum on the alternative vote in May 2011, the nation voted 2–1 against any change. Secondly, the fact that Labour seats tend to be won in inner-city areas where constituency size is small and turnout is low means that Labour votes win more seats than the same amount of Conservative votes, many of which are stacked up in their 'safe' seats in the south. This means that Labour can win an election with just 3% more votes than the Tories, while the latter need 11% more than Labour to seize victory.

According to the Electoral Reform Society, even if both main parties had polled the same number of votes in 1997, Labour would have won 336 seats and the Conservatives only 220, which is a huge difference. The Conservatives hoped to redraw the constituency boundaries in 2011 – which would have tipped an extra 20 seats their way – but Lib Dem support was withdrawn in retaliation when Tory MPs scuppered Lib Dem plans for reforming the Lords: yet another example of political considerations thwarting democratic reform.

THE MAY 2010 GENERAL ELECTION

The general election in May 2010 was a remarkable one in that it ended with no overall majority for either of the two big parties. The significance of the election was summed up by pollster Peter Kellner in the *Sunday Times*, 9 May 2010:

> Labour and Conservative no longer dominate politics as they once did. In 1951 only nine MPs did not take the Labour or Tory whip; in 1979 the number had climbed to 27, but the 70 seat Conservative lead over Labour delivered Margaret Thatcher a 43 seat overall majority. This time even a 70 seat lead would have been insufficient. As well as the 57 contingent of Liberal Democrats, 28 represented eight smaller parties. To secure an overall majority of just two, the Tories would have needed 86 more MPs than Labour.

The growth of third-party voting plus the systemic bias towards Labour meant that even a 7% lead by Conservatives over Labour was insufficient. Cameron led the biggest party but needed a solid coalition to govern for a full parliamentary term. Ironically, the Liberal Democrats, disappointed that their early campaign showing in the polls had not been reflected in the result, now found themselves as 'king makers'. Both parties wooed Lib Dem leader Nick Clegg and his colleagues but Cameron had the advantage with the arithmetic – an alliance with Labour would have entailed an awkward group of small parties – and a more skilfully handled negotiation. The result was the first formal coalition government since 1945. The factors identified above suggest it will not be the last, though the expected need for a coalition after the 2015 election did not materialise, as there was an overall majority for the Conservatives, as discussed in the next section.

THE MAY 2015 GENERAL ELECTION

COALITION YEARS AND THE CAMPAIGN

The general election on 7 May 2015 had been long and eagerly awaited. Since 2011 it was the first of the 'fixed term' elections consequent to the Act passed in September of that year. Ever since May 2010 opponents of the coalition government had waited for their revenge. Critics within the Conservative Party dreamt of the day they could govern alone, without the need to win the acceptance of those irritating Liberal Democrats. For their part, Labour could not wait to see its long-standing poll leads converted into at best an overall majority, at worst a Labour minority government. The coalition had initially been perceived as a weak arrangement and few had anticipated its longevity. But against the odds, it had proved surprisingly robust, its healthy majority enabling it to run the full five-year term with scarcely a wobble. For Labour, however, it was those poll leads which proved fragile.

Indeed, closer inspection of the polls – even when Labour's lead was in double figures – revealed Labour as less secure than its supporters hoped. There were two main problems for Labour: the party's 'economic competence' and the issue of leadership. The Conservative's poll lead over Labour was massive and sustained. As soon as the coalition was formed, its ministers and MPs had all relentlessly delivered the same message on the economy: Labour had ruined it and so was responsible for the recession, the resultant loss of gross domestic product (GDP) and growing unemployment. The Blair and Brown governments, ran their narrative, had overspent wildly, thus creating the chaos the new government was now forced to clear up. Liam Byrne's jokey note left to his Treasury successor that 'there is no money left' was carried around by Cameron on the campaign and displayed theatrically as an object of horror (*Observer*, 10 May 2015). For the period following its defeat, Labour had been locked into a leadership election, making refutation of this account difficult; those who made the attempt singularly failed to do so. This was also partly because of the second problem: the leadership of Ed Miliband.

After Gordon Brown resigned the Labour leadership following the 2010 general election, most informed opinion in 2011 expected former foreign secretary David Miliband to emerge as leader. The decision of his brother to stand against him was surprising, as was the support he quickly gained, partly through rejecting the Blairite 'New Labour' approach, from the trade unions. Indeed, it was union support which won him the prize, given that the majority of Labour's parliamentary and individual membership favoured the better-known sibling. This alleged 'union control' enabled Cameron to berate 'Red Ed' at prime minister's questions in the Commons, where the Labour leader was generally bested and bullied for five years. Indeed, Cameron did his best to establish a caricature of Ed Miliband as weak, far to the left and, if ever elected, likely to inflict economic disaster upon the country. The Conservatives' Australian election strategist, Lynton Crosby, confidently predicted 'crossover' in the polls would arrive by Christmas, allowing Cameron to coast to victory.

However, around February 2015 poll ratings for both main parties seemed to be tied, in the low 30s. Crosby's predicted crossover would occur at Easter but even when the campaign officially began there was no real movement. Most pollsters thought a late swing to the Tories was likely but the almost universal prediction was for the Tories to win around 280 seats, Labour around 265 and the Liberal Democrats 25–30. But what seemed certain and a huge blow to Labour was that the Scottish National Party (SNP) would sweep the board in Scotland. The September 2014 referendum campaign on Scottish independence had ultimately failed, but the excitement generated by the 'yes' campaign continued to fizz, with thousands flooding to join the SNP and the polls showing close to 50% support for the party.

The campaign opened with the single televised leaders' debate, on 2 April. These debates had aroused intense controversy, as it was clear Cameron, despite praising such debates as essential to democracy in 2010, had changed his mind. His Tory critics thought allowing Nick Clegg to participate on such an elevated platform was the reason why he had won so many Tory votes, thus denying Cameron an overall majority. Crosby, too, subscribed to this view and, having at first seemed to have denied the possibility of any debates at all, Cameron claimed to have 'broken the logjam' by agreeing to one between seven leaders, including those of the Greens, UKIP, SNP and Plaid Cymru. He had decided to take the 'hit' for appearing cowardly for the political advantage of denying his main opponent a nationwide head-to-head debate. The debates were watched by 7 million people and definitely made an impact. Cameron, confident, the well informed incumbent prime minister, scored highly, as did Nigel Farage for UKIP and Leanne Wood for Plaid Cymru, but there were two surprises: Ed Miliband, whose performance helped remove the image of him Cameron had assiduously sought to nourish; and the star of the debates, the SNP leader Nicola Sturgeon. The latter came over as very sharp, impassioned and much fresher than her predecessor, Alex Salmond; her star remained in the ascendant throughout the campaign.

The Tory campaign was criticised as narrow, over-cautious and over-personalised. Crosby's anti-Ed message was taken perhaps too far by Conservative MP Michael Fallon, who suggested that someone who had 'stabbed their brother in the back' to gain power would do the same to his country. Miliband's campaign – mercifully gaffe-free for once – was actually quite effective and his endorsement as 'best prime minister', though still well adrift of Cameron's, improved by over 10 points. His promise to end the tax-free status of 'non-doms' was well received, though the plethora of unfunded proposals by the two big parties – evidence of frustration at the stalled polls – towards the end of the campaign had little impact. Labour sought to exploit the Tory promise to reduce welfare spending by £12 billion but later in the campaign a much more effective scare story was deployed effectively by Cameron: that a minority Labour government would rely for its survival on left-wing SNP MPs intent on breaking up the Union.

THE RESULTS

On the eve of polling day most voters went to bed fully expecting a tied result of some 270–280 seats for each of the big parties and a high probability of minority government, given that the SNP and other nationalist parties refused to have any truck with the Tories. The anti-Tory voters sat in front of their televisions at 10.00 pm confidently expecting a change of government. The BBC exit poll, however, master-minded by Professor John Curtice of Strathclyde University, delivered a hammer blow to these expectations. This poll predicted: Conservatives 310, Labour 239, Lib Dems 10 and SNP 58. Paddy Ashdown, campaign leader for his party, declared this a re-run of the faulty 1992 exit poll and that if it proved right he would eat his hat on television. Alastair Campbell, for Labour and of Scottish parentage, offered, for good measure, to eat his kilt. Evidence that the Tory high command also believed the polls were mistaken is offered by the 'French kiss' which Osborne offered to give Lynton Crosby if his strategy proved successful (one political pledge which still remains unfulfilled: *Sunday Times*, 24 May 2015). Curtice was the most respected psephologist in the UK and his 2010 exit poll had proved uncannily correct. That his 2015 effort proved less accurate was no comfort for the aspiring hat-eaters as his prediction actually underestimated Tory seats, which, at 331, delivered an overall majority of 12 (Table 12.3). The other bombshell, of course, was the total meltdown of Scottish Labour: its tally of seats north of the border as Curtice predicted, slumped from 41 down to one, the same as for the Liberal Democrats and Conservatives.

As Table 12.3 shows, the headlong rush of the SNP stopped at a still incredible 56; the Lib Dems were massacred, only 8 surviving nationwide; Plaid Cymru retained its three seats; the Greens their one; UKIP, despite polling nearly 4 million votes, managed only to retain the by-election seat of Douglas Carswell. Farage, once thought a 'shoo-in' for Thanet South, eventually came third, as he did in his

Table 12.3 2015 general election results

Party	Seats (gains)	Vote share % (gains)
Conservatives	331 (+24)	36.9 (0.8)
Labour	232 (−26)	30.4 (1.5)
Lib Dem	8 (−49)	7.9 (−15.2)
SNP	56 (50)	4.7 (3.1)
Plaid Cymru	3	0.6
Green	1	3.8 (2.8)
UKIP	1	12.6 (9.5)
DUP	8	0.6
Others	10	2.5

2010 contest (see Figure 12.1). As for the poor Lib Dems, instead of their hoped-for 25–30 'balance of power' MPs, they lost 47 and were reduced to a tiny rump of 8 from their 7.9% of the vote, their lowest tally since Jo Grimond was leader of the Liberal Party, in the 1960s. In the wake of this total reversal of expectations, Ed Miliband and Nick Clegg resigned. Nigel Farage also proffered his resignation but when his party's executive refused to accept it, he remained in place, causing acrimonious rows to break out in the party. Criticism of the 'first past the post voting' system was reinforced by the combined vote of UKIP and the Greens, 16.4% of voters, returning only two MPs while the SNP's 4.7% delivered 56 MPs.

Clearly, the widespread 'expert' assumption that the growth of 'third-party voting' had bequeathed the UK a future of coalition government was premature. Cameron had followed his narrow campaign strategy, endlessly repeating his mantras of his government's economic turnaround, Ed Miliband's total unsuitability for Downing Street and the tartan danger lurking north of the border. Despite the doubts, he and his advisor Lynton Crosby had done the trick and routed their critics, not to mention the envious Tory opponents after his job. For a few weeks or months Cameron was master of all he surveyed, no longer shackled by the need to consult any coalition partner and free to contemplate the 'completion of the job' he and Osborne had promised in their campaign.

WHAT WENT WRONG WITH THE POLLS?

Certainly the nation's pollsters – with the exception of John Curtice – emerged from the election faces covered with egg. As in some previous elections they had underestimated the Conservative vote – by some 4.5% and overestimated Labour's – by 3%. Peter Kellner, president of YouGov, whose exit poll had predicted a hung parliament, acknowledged that a full inquiry into their failure would take place; the British Polling Council accordingly announced such an inquiry on 8 May. However, *Times* columnist Daniel Finkelstein possibly got close to the underlying truth in his article of 9 May. According to him, Cameron's pollster, Andrew Cooper, believed a significant group of voters, 3 million strong, existed who thought Cameron the best prime minister and the Conservatives best for the country, but could not bring themselves to vote for a party with whose values they disagreed. Finkelstein called them the 'Yes, yes, nos' and that Cooper was determined to win their crucial support:

> Mr Cooper repeatedly said this might not happen until polling day and no one would know whether it had worked until the votes were counted. He was correct.

Kellner said something similar in attributing polling errors to:

> people who don't like the Tories, consider them out of touch, for the rich and don't like their values. But in the end they think Cameron is better than Miliband, the Tories are better on the economy, and are fearful what Labour might do. So they honestly express an anti-Tory attitude to us, but in the polling station make a different choice. (*Sunday Times*, 15 May 2015)

Were these the famously elusive 'shy Tories', not willing to admit to pollsters that they might vote for, to use Theresa May's 2001 words, the 'nasty party'? Possibly. Something similar must have happened to the large numbers of voters who were undecided with just a day to go. Once in the polling booth and called upon to decide, a fair number decided to change that 'no' into a third 'yes'. The result confounded the whole political class in Britain, dashed the hopes of those to the left of centre (Labour and Liberal Democrats) plus Ukippers to the far right of centre. The Greens were pleased to have polled so well and retain the seat of Caroline Lucas.

But delight was unconfined for Cameron, with aides Ed Llewellyn, Kate Fall and Craig Oliver poised in front of his television in Chipping Norton. Anthony Seldon reported that when the exit poll is announced:

> there is a long pause. And then they start cheering. . . . 'Oh my God, I don't care about the Lib Dems' says Cameron. Later in Witney leisure centre he 'leapt into the arms of his closest aides and let out a primal roar: Yeeeaaaaaah'. (Anthony Seldon, *Sunday Times*, 10 May 2015)

Certainly, the inaccurate polls substantially helped the Tories, deflecting attention away from their future programme of austerity and towards the possible disadvantages of a minority Labour government propped up by the left-of-centre SNP. The spectre of such an outcome might well have unleashed the late inrush of support for Cameron. On the other hand, as Andrew Rawnsley, pointed out (*Observer*, 17 May 2015), knowing they were in reality six points behind might have made matters even worse for Labour.

ANALYSING THE VOTE

On 22 May, polling company Ipsos-Mori published a breakdown of the vote based on some 10,000 respondents which offers good estimates of how various social groups voted (see Table 12.4).

1. It was obvious that the Conservatives benefited greatly from those groups – the ABs social classes and the over-55s – who turned out at above-average levels. Average turnout was slightly up on 2010, at 66.1% but for the ABs it was 75% and the over-55s it was as high as 78%; among the over-65s Conservatives won 47% of the vote to Labour's 23%; within AB voters the respective figures were 45% and 26%.
2. Labour's support, by contrast, came from groups registering below-average turnout. For example, they had a lead of 9% among 18–24-year-old males, only 42% of whom voted, and a lead of 20% among women in the same age group, among whom turnout was 44%. They chalked up a massive 42% lead among black and minority ethnic groups, of whom, sadly for the party, only 56% voted. Predictably perhaps, Labour had a 14% lead among voters in social classes DE, only 56% of whom voted. Among 'social renters', Labour also had a massive lead of 32%, but turnout for this group was also a way below average, at 56%.
3. The Conservatives' lead among the key voters in social class C1, who so often determine UK elections, the largest single voting group, was a hefty 12%, the same as in 2010. Broadly speaking, the party's vote from five years earlier held up very well.
4. Labour managed to hold onto 72% of its 2010 support but lost 8% to the Tories, 6% to UKIP and 5% to the Lib Dems and the Greens. Liam Byrne in the *Sunday Times* (14 June 2015) wrote

Table 12.4 Breakdown of the vote

	Voting								Change Since 2010				
	Con %	Lab %	LD %	UKIP %	Green %	Oth %	Con lead over Lab %	Turn-out %	Con ± %	Lab ± %	LD ± %	Turn-out ± %	Con to Lab Swing %
All	**38**	**31**	**8**	**13**	**4**	**6**	**7**	**66%**	**+1**	**+1**	**−16**	**+1**	**0.35**
Gender													
Male	38	30	8	14	4	6	8	67%	0	+2	−14	+1	1
Female	37	33	8	12	4	6	4	66%	+1	+2	−18	+2	0.5
Age													
18–24	27	43	5	8	8	9	−16	43%	−3	+12	−25	−1	7.5
25–34	33	36	7	10	7	7	−3	54%	−2	+6	−22	−1	4
35–44	35	35	10	10	4	6	0	64%	+1	+4	−16	−2	1.5
45–54	36	33	8	14	4	5	3	72%	+2	+5	−18	+3	1.5
55–64	37	31	9	14	2	7	6	77%	−1	+3	−14	+4	2
65+	47	23	8	17	2	3	24	78%	+3	−8	−8	+2	−5.5
Men by Age													
18–24	32	41	4	7	8	8	−9	42%	+3	+7	−23	−8	2
25–34	35	32	9	11	6	7	3	55%	−7	+9	−21	−1	8
35–54	38	32	8	12	4	6	6	68%	+2	+4	−15	+1	1
55+	40	25	8	19	2	6	15	79%	−1	−4	−	+3	−1.5

Women by Age

18–24	24	44	5	10	9	8	−20	44%	−6	+16	−29	+5	11
25–34	31	40	5	9	8	7	−9	52%	−4	+2	−22	−2	−1
35–54	32	35	9	12	4	8	−3	68%	−1	+4	−20	+1	2.5
55+	45	27	9	13	2	4	18	76%	+3	−3	−12	+3	3

Social Class

AB	45	26	12	8	4	5	19	75%	+6	0	−17	−1	−3
C1	41	29	8	11	4	7	12	69%	+2	+1	−16	+3	−0.5
C2	32	32	6	19	4	7	0	62%	−5	+3	−16	+4	4
DE	27	41	5	17	3	7	−14	57%	−4	+1	−12	0	2.5

Men by Class

AB	46	25	11	10	3	5	21	77%	+2	+2	−16	+1	0
C1	42	27	8	12	4	7	15	68%	+2	−1	−14	+1	−1.5
C2	30	32	5	21	4	8	−2	62%	−3	−1	−14	+4	1
DE	26	40	4	18	3	9	−14	56%	−6	+5	−9	−3	5.5

Women by Class

AB	44	28	12	6	5	5	16	73%	+10	−1	−19	−2	−5.5
C1	41	31	8	10	5	5	10	69%	+2	+3	−17	+3	0.5
C2	34	33	7	17	4	5	1	63%	−7	+8	−18	+5	7.5
DE	28	42	5	16	3	6	−14	57%	−1	−3	−14	+1	−1

(continued)

Table 12.4 (continued)

	Voting								Change Since 2010				
	Con %	Lab %	LD %	UKIP %	Green %	Oth %	Con lead over Lab ± %	Turn-out	Con ± %	Lab ± %	LD ± %	Turn-out ± %	Con to Lab Swing %
Housing Tenure													
Owned	46	22	9	15	2	6	24	77%	+1	−2	−12	+3	−1.5
Mortgage	39	31	9	10	3	8	8	69%	+3	+2	−17	+3	0.5
Social renter	18	50	3	18	3	8	−32	56%	−6	+3	−16	+1	4.5
Private renter	28	39	6	11	9	7	−11	51%	−7	+10	−21	−4	8.5
Ethnic group													
White	39	28	8	14	4	7	11	68%	+1	0	−16	+1	−0.5
All BME	23	65	4	2	3	3	−42	56%	+7	+5	−16	+5	−1

Source: Ipsos Mori (https://www.ipsos-mori.com/researchpublications/researcharchive/3575/How-Britain-voted-in-2015.aspx?view=wide).

'Base: 9,149 GB adults aged 18+ (of which 6,202 were "absolutely certain to vote" or said they had already voted), interviewed 10 April - 6 May 2015. 3,196 interviews were conducted on telephone, 5,953 face-to-face (on surveys where voting intentions are asked as an analysis variable, but not comparable to our regular Political Monitor results without further weighting such as has been applied in these estimates). (Ipsos Mori)' that in the 24 seats Labour won, the constituencies were mixes of ethnic minorities and university-educated, middle-class, and quite possibly enjoyers of *The Guardian*. But of the 74 seats they lost south of the border, 'the Lib Dem vote collapsed by an average of 6,585 – but more than two-thirds sailed right past us and went to UKIP, their vote rising by an average of 4,853. . . . The Lib Dems quite simply were not and are not a reservoir of closet lefties'.

5. The Lib Dems lost two-thirds of their 2010 voters: 24% to Labour, 20% to Conservatives, 11% to the Greens and 7% to UKIP. Their only relative retention was among ABs and 35–44-year-olds. The biggest loss was among the under-34s.

6. One in eight voters voted for UKIP, but the party was third in every group apart from ABs (8%) and black and minority ethnic voters (2%). Again, predictably, UKIP scored most highly among C2 and DE groups and the over-65s. The party was slightly more popular with men (14%) than women (12%).

WHY DID LABOUR LOSE SO BADLY?

A post-mortem ensued for the traumatised Labour Party. David Miliband, in New York, offered the criticism that his brother and Gordon Brown had 'allowed themselves to be portrayed as moving backwards from the principles of aspiration and inclusion that are the absolute heart of any successful progressive political project' (BBC, 11 May 2015).

Many commentators judged Ed's message to have been too left wing. After the world economic crisis, Ed had assumed a leftward shift had taken place and fashioned an approach accordingly. In reality, voter choice, if anything, moved rightwards at this time, as evidenced by elections all over Europe. To compound the problem, Labour's selection of policies, while often popular in focus groups, did not cohere into any easily recognisable narrative: there was no overall vision. While Cameron claimed he would 'finish the job' with his 'long-term strategy', few could divine what Labour was saying it would do. Ironically, Scottish voters had indeed shifted to the left, in support of the left SNP, however, and not discredited Scottish Labour. Labour was hit by the double whammy: too left wing for England yet too right wing for Scotland.

A more in-depth analysis was given by Labour's respected former policy coordinator, John Cruddas MP. He thought that 2010 was the 'worst defeat for Labour since 1918; it was worse than the crisis of 1931 and worse than 1983. But a week ago (7th May) we suffered an even worse defeat than 2010 so this could be the greatest crisis the Labour party has faced since it was created. It is epic in its scale.' He identified several factors, starting with the double-digit lead Osborne's 2012 'omni-shambles' budget won for the party, instilling a sense of complacent confidence that Lib Dem losses would mostly accrue to Labour and that UKIP gains would eat into Tory leads in key marginal seats.

> so we bank what we have, we play it safe, in the common parlance, we 'shrink the offer', we play a 35% strategy, and we get over the line. . . . We gamed out the electorate but we got it wrong, and then we didn't realise the scale of it until one minute past 10 on election night. (*Observer*, 17 May 2015)

Cruddas was annoyed that much painstaking policy research – including a 'fantastic IPPR [Institute for Public Policy Research] rethink of social democracy when there is no money around. Despite all the work, in the end we had nothing to say on that. With Osborne pushing ahead with the "Northern Powerhouse", the Tories have taken more out of this work than Labour'. Meanwhile, David Skelton, director of the modernising Tory think-tank Renewal, suggested: 'The skilled working class deserted Labour in 2010 and didn't come back at all in 2015. Their heartlands, the ones they could once rely on, are dwindling and dwindling' (quoted by Boffey, *Observer*, 24 May 2015).

It is true that Miliband's minimalist campaign did not resonate even in stronghold areas, as Labour's brand had been so heavily depleted that even when voters agreed with its sensible policies they did not trust Labour to deliver on them. Ed's long-standing low satisfaction rating compared with Cameron proved fatal for Labour's attempt to engage with voters. Add to this the Tory's huge lead over 'economic competence' plus the potent scare story that a left-wing SNP would suborn a weak Labour leader, and the sledge-hammer defeat was set up to happen. Tory blogger Iain Dale pointed out that the 11.5%

swing Labour now need to win in 2020 was never achieved even by Tony Blair; party insiders fear it will take at least a decade.

THE SCALE OF THE CONSERVATIVE VICTORY

The win was historic in that it was the first time for over 100 years a governing party increased its share of the vote after serving a full term. That vote-share increase was only 1% but was deployed to maximum effect in the key marginal seats. Indeed, the increase in such seats, whether the main rival was Labour or Lib Dem, worked out at 4%. The party did not prosper in poorer areas of England and Wales, London or the north-west generally. The victory did, however, reflect long-standing weaknesses, as Rob Ford commented: 'Political divides by ethnicity, age and geography remain deep and the Conservatives will struggle to connect with groups whose numbers and political influence will grow' (*Observer*, 10 May 2015).

DISASTER FOR THE LIB DEMS

Their poll ratings had plummeted since 2010 and government had in no way enhanced their standing with voters. Not being the party of protest clearly destroyed a unique selling-point. Liberal Democrat activists had comforted themselves with the idea that their carefully established local loyalties and the strength of incumbency would limit their losses. Many, including the party leadership, hoped for at least 25–30 seats, enough anyway to play a key role in the minority-based administration likely to emerge from polling day. Negotiating machinery was already well in place for the Lib Dems. Harsh reality was possibly even harder to accept than it was for Labour: a 15-point exit of support compared with 2010; its top command destroyed (Simon Hughes and Vince Cable, and in Scotland Danny Alexander and Charles Kennedy). Their so-called 'banker' support of students and professionals moved in waves to other parties. The party which the Lib Dems had supported in government proved ruthless in swallowing up a huge and fatal chunk of their MPs. A Tory minister is quoted as saying: 'Angela Merkel said that coalition always destroys the little party and that was what we set out to do'. Tens of thousands of activists had visited Lib Dem powerbases like Twickenham and Yeovil where David Laws' 13,000 majority failed to save him. Nick Clegg was lucky to hold on in Sheffield Hallam, where Tory voters had been urged to vote tactically for him to keep Labour out.

MIXED FORTUNES FOR UKIP AND GREENS

When UKIP's poll rating was coasting along at around 20%, Farage allowed himself to dream of a possible UKIP Commons contingent of a dozen or more. His campaign, however, was marred by signs of conflict behind the scenes and all too frequently ill-advised remarks by his candidates. His own defeat in Thanet South must have been a big blow, as was the resultant election of merely a single UKIP MP, the incumbent member for Clacton, Douglas Carswell. However, UKIP did have achievements to savour. Its attractiveness to poor white voters with no educational qualifications garnered a not discreditable 13% of the electorate. UKIP polled strongest in eastern coastal areas and in declining cities in the north.

> UKIP's performance also confounded those who argued that the party would primarily hurt the Conservatives – UKIP's advance was slightly larger in Labour held seats and Labour did four points worse in the areas where UKIP advanced most, compared to a 2 point Tory drop. (Rob Ford, *Observer*, 10 May 2015)

Certainly UKIP's presence was instrumental in Labour losing some marginal seats, for instance the crucial 'bellwether' one of Nuneaton. UKIP managed to achieve second place in no less than 120 contests, meaning the party will be well placed to compete in 2020.

The Greens also emerged with a single seat, and in the local elections held on the same day lost control of Brighton council but, like UKIP, hugely increased its number of votes: 3.8% of all voters. Natalie Bennett, the party's leader, despite a few wobbles during the campaign, succeeded in enhancing her party's standing in the country, together with the salience of its message.

NATIONALISTS

While the smaller English parties suffered from the thin national spread of their support, the nationalist parties benefited from the advantage 'first past the post' delivers to small parties with concentrated geographical support. Plaid Cymru polled only 6 million votes yet returned three MPs. The SNP, however, took the prize, with its 4.7% delivering a stunning 56 out of the 59 Scottish seats. While Nicola Sturgeon was careful to separate a further independence referendum from her campaign, her landslide is bound to strengthen calls for another vote and in the wake of victory Alex Salmond, now an MP at Westminster, announced that 'The timing of a future referendum is a matter for the Scottish people first and foremost' (*Sunday Telegraph*, 10 May 2015).

CONCLUSION

Future election historians are bound to focus on the similarities between 2015 with that of 1992, especially the eventual margin of Tory victory. The breath-taking difference, however, was that, while the 1992 exit poll proved sensationally wrong, the 2015 version proved sensationally right. The much-anticipated dead heat in votes and seats together with the expected post-election government-building negotiations proved a chimera, with disastrous consequences for those who had invested hope in those possible outcomes.

QUESTIONS FOR DISCUSSION

1. How do you think political allegiances are formed?
2. Why is class less important in British voting behaviour now compared with the 1950s and 1960s?
3. Why have attempts at voting reform failed so frequently?

FURTHER READING

For a clear recent history of UK voting behaviour see Denver and Garnett (2014). The best short introduction for voting behaviour is Denver (2012).

Butler, D. E. and Stokes, D. (1974) *Political Change in Britain* (2nd edition), Macmillan.
Byrne, L. (2015) How Labour rebuilds the radical centre, *Sunday Times*, 14 June.
Clarke, H., Sanders, D., Stewart, D. and Whiteley, P. (2009) *Performance Politics and the British Voter*, Cambridge University Press.

Denver, D. (2012) *Elections and Voting in Britain*, Palgrave.

Denver, D. and Garnett, M. (2014) *British General Elections Since 1964*, Palgrave.

Farrell, D. (2011) *Electoral Systems: A Comparative Study*, Palgrave.

Pulzer, P. (1967) *Political Representation and Elections in Britain*, George Allen Unwin.

WEBSITES

Electoral Commission: http://www.electoralcommission.org.uk.

UK Polling Report, survey and polling news from YouGov's Anthony Wells: http://www.ukpollingreport.co.uk.

13

THE HOUSE OF COMMONS

Even autocratic political systems rely to some extent upon consent; so it was with the emergence of the English parliament. The counselling role of the King's advisers in medieval times slowly evolved into agreement to advance funding for the monarch's various projects: especially palaces and wars (the Hundred Years War was funded in this fashion). This became parliament's means of levering power away from the monarch into its bicameral structure. While the Lords remained the dominant chamber in the seventeenth century, Charles I's failure to extract money from the Commons was the trigger for the 1642–49 Civil War.

The execution in 1649 of Charles symbolised the institution's loss of power, though some historians argue Elizabeth's execution of her cousin Mary Queen of Scots, half a century earlier, had already unwittingly laid the trail for the regicide to follow. The Great Reform Act 1832 only marginally extended the number of people entitled to vote but it established the principle of representative democracy upon which later reforms were built. Some historians have seen the middle of the nineteenth century as the 'golden age' of parliament. A small electorate, loose party discipline and MPs with private means created a parliament in which debates determined the way MPs voted and, as one eminent scholar observed:

The House sacked Cabinets, it removed individual ministers, it forced government to disclose information, it set up select committees to carry out investigations and frame bills and it rewrote government bills on the floor of the House of Commons. (Mackintosh, 1962: p. 613)

DIMINUTION OF POWER

If, as some insist, the power of the Commons has diminished drastically since this time, what have been the causes?

EXPANSION OF THE ELECTORATE AND THE GROWTH OF A DISCIPLINED PARTY SYSTEM

As the number of voters grew, parliamentary party leaders realised they needed to organise them, try to make them supporters and to offer a programme of measures – a manifesto – on which to fight elections. The winning party then needed to implement its programme but, given the limits of time, had to introduce a disciplined voting regime for its MPs. This led to the 'tyranny' of the whips, insisting their MPs toed the line; they could debate as much as they liked but if they valued their party membership – and losing it would tend to make them unelectable – their vote had to be for the government's policy.

THE 'LOYAL OPPOSITION'

As the majority party automatically became the government after elections, so the second largest party became the official 'opposition': a kind of 'government in waiting' ready to fight an election and take over the government if necessary. To achieve this, opposition parties had to instil the same rigorous discipline as the governing party.

GROWTH IN THE POWER OF THE PRIME MINISTER

Ambitious MPs – and that means most of them – have always been keen to achieve ministerial office: junior, then senior, leading to a place in the cabinet. All such appointments depend on the prime minister and if MPs want to be considered for 'promotion', they cannot afford to be seen as a loose cannon or a 'trouble maker' by voting against the government. Former Liberal Democrat MP and cabinet minister Chris Huhne explained this clearly in *The Guardian* (16 June 2014):

> The ambitions of MPs to become ministers enfeeble its [parliament's] scrutiny. If they want preferment, they must be loyal to their party leader and future prime minister. In short, the prime minister has corrupting patronage over the people meant to hold him to account.

EXTENSION OF GOVERNMENT ACTIVITIES AND GROWTH OF BUREAUCRACY

During the twentieth century, the state began to intrude increasingly deeply into the everyday life of the nation. For example, the number of people employed by the government multiplied 10-fold with the arrival of the welfare state after World War II. With so many complex decisions to be made, MPs discovered they were not sufficiently well informed and that ministers preferred to take the advice of permanent civil servants or specialists brought in from pressure groups or elsewhere.

GROWTH OF PRESSURE GROUP INFLUENCE

The major pressure groups have become very important to government as sources of information and, if they support a measure, legitimacy. MPs, however, find themselves locked out of policy-making by the triumvirate of group leaders, civil servants, special advisers and ministers, who tend to be in charge of the process.

INCREASING INFLUENCE OF MEDIA

As the scope and influence of the media, including internet-related forms, has evolved to its present 24–7 intensity, those who control and edit the media processes have usurped some of the functions once performed by MPs in earlier times: publicising government activities and, more important, holding government to account. So important has televised coverage of election campaigns become that a row erupted in the lead-up to May 2015 when Cameron tried hard to avoid, and finally succeeded in avoiding, a head-to-head debate with Ed Miliband.

MEMBERSHIP OF THE EUROPEAN UNION

Since 1972 Britain has been a member of the European Community (European Union since Maastricht Treaty, 1992) and the authority of MPs and Parliament has been diminished as laws passed by this multinational body take precedence over those passed by the UK parliament. Euro-sceptics from Tony Benn to William Cash MP bitterly regretted what they saw as a loss of sovereignty and democratic accountability.

REFERENDUMS

These historically little-used instruments of democracy, based upon voters and not parliament through their MPs, have become more frequent: in 1975 to measure approval of the European Community; in 2004 to measure support for regional government in the north-east; and most recently in September 2014, to gauge aspects of nationalist opinion in Scotland and Wales. Cameron entered government in May 2015 committed to holding by 2017 an in–out referendum on UK membership of the European Union.

HOW MUCH HAS THE COMMONS DECLINED?

Having been drained of so much power by the above factors, does the chamber still exercise worthwhile functions? Is it still, to use Bagehot's term, an 'efficient' part of the constitution, as opposed to a merely 'dignified' one? During the 1960s critical voices were raised regarding the House's efficacy, with some suggesting it was no more than a rubber-stamp for ready-made government legislation. Professor John Griffith (2010) reported that during the first three sessions of the 1970s, virtually 100% of government amendments were passed while only 10% of government backbenchers' amendments did so; the figure for opposition amendments was 5%.

ESSENTIAL FUNCTIONS OF THE COMMONS

Despite the above observations, a number of essential functions can still be discerned.

SUSTAINING GOVERNMENT

It remains a fact that elections to the Commons determine the political complexion of governments, in the shape of the largest party – or coalition of parties – returned. Governments are occasionally defeated on key issues and, as in February 1979, this can cause a government to resign.

RESTRAINING GOVERNMENT ACTION

What the Commons will accept allows new laws to be made but what it will not accept is just as important. Its generally rational assessment of bills precludes the kind of absurd self-regarding laws passed by dictators and other autocrats. It can also amend and change a controversial proposal to accommodate critical opinion.

'SOUNDING BOARD' FOR THE NATION

Enoch Powell, a respected authority on the constitution, argued that a precise representation of the country, something which he accepted the current voting system does not allow, is not necessary for the House to provide an effective sounding board for the nation: MPs, insisted Powell, are always better informed after a debate and every section of society is able to contribute towards proceedings via their MP.

PASSING LEGISLATION

This passes through a well established procedure of first reading (purely explanatory of its aim), second reading (a major debate), committee stage (clauses examined by a standing committee), third reading (bill reassessed after committee stage), then up to the Lords, where a similar process awaits until it is returned to the Commons to consider Lords' amendments before going on to receive the royal assent. This extended process allows plenty of time for debate, amendment and redrafting, although it can be compressed into a few days or even hours if necessary.

RECRUITMENT AND TRAINING OF MINISTERS

Listening and participating in debates on complex national issues provides a period of training for MPs before they are called to accept the 'minister's seal' of office from the Queen. Some say this preparation is inadequate for the massive managerial task of running a department of state, but others, including (Lord) Andrew Adonis, argue that, as 'persuasion' is the key political skill, such training is wholly appropriate.

POLITICAL EDUCATION

Traditionally the Commons has been the platform on which the business of the nation has been discussed in public. Even though critics point out that MPs now often prefer to give television interviews on the grassy areas outside parliament, the floor of the House is still where the major dramas are acted out; significantly, during the summer recess the media find little purchase for political reporting and resort to so-called 'silly season' stories instead.

REDRESSING PRIVATE GRIEVANCES

MPs have to respond to the 200-plus letters they receive each week from their constituents. These may concern a whole host of topics, from immigration to benefit claims and special-interest lobbying from developers. Some argue that constituency business alone represents a full-time job for an MP: forwarding letters to ministers, raising questions in the House and sometimes moving such matters, for example, on adjournment motions, after 10 pm.

LEGITIMISING DECISIONS

This function is the one most societies adopt as a way of showing to themselves that a law has been passed, often entailing a degree of ceremony and ritual. The centuries-old procedures of the Commons, culminating in the monarch's signature, provide such a function admirably.

SCRUTINY OF THE EXECUTIVE

This function, possibly the House's most important one, takes place in a number of ways.

QUESTION TIME

Prime minister's questions (PMQs) take place for 30 minutes every week from 12.00 pm every Wednesday. This is the most watched piece of Commons business by far. The prime minister answers questions on anything MPs might throw at him or her. The spectacle is viewed with interest in the USA, where the president never has to face such rumbustious scrutiny. The leader of the opposition is allowed three or four supplementary questions and the leader of the next biggest party two. Often the question is a 'set-up' for the supplementary, for which the prime minister is unlikely to be prepared.

Sadly, however, PMQs have deteriorated into a slap-stick shouting match which edifies nobody but provides some entertainment and, not unimportant, boosts the morale of either the prime minister or opposition leader, depending on whose insults have been judged the best aimed and the most insulting. Some argue the two hours' preparation prime minister have to endure to survive this clamorous examination enables them to be much better informed on the whole range of government business. The prime minister is usually a skilled performer and with proper briefing usually wins the day, especially as he or she is backed by a whooping majority of MPs.

SELECT COMMITTEES

These investigatory committees used to be few in number but in the early 1980s were expanded to get one shadowing every major department. A third of all MPs are involved in them. The most powerful is the Public Accounts Committee, which scrutinises how public money has been spent and reports on malpractice or inefficiency by civil servants. A prominent opposition MP chairs this committee and, in this role, Labour's Margaret Hodge after 2010 established a formidable reputation as a fearless interrogator of witnesses, however famous or powerful they might be. Since the 2010 election the often televised select committees have been allowed to elect their own chairs, giving them more independence and adding to their ability to hold the executive to account. Distinguished service in the chair of such committees now almost represents an alternative career path for MPs and a 'qualification' for promotion to ministerial office, as with John Whittingdale in May 2015, who was promoted to culture secretary after serving as chair of the Culture Select Committee.

POWER OF THE COMMONS ASSESSED

While the Commons has lost a huge amount of its power to influence policy, it is still the defining forum of the nation's politics, providing the colour, atmosphere and drama of the decisions which shape the country's future. It lost power up to the 1970s but enjoyed something of a renaissance subsequently. Major's small majority after 1992 made many votes cliff-hanging ones and Blair's growing band of rebels asserted the power of MPs in the House, especially when one-third of his party opposed him over the Iraq War. The coalition government formed in May 2010 was itself a manifestation of the pivotal role of the chamber and how the need for an overall majority can dictate alternative forms of government. Studies by Philip Cowley and Mark Stuart reveal the fact that MPs have become more rebellious over time, the issue of the Britain's membership of the European Union proving the most contentious.

REFORM OF COMMONS

In 1978 the Select Committee on Procedure reported that the relationship between the Commons and the government 'is now weighted in favour of the government to a degree which arouses widespread anxiety and is inimical to the proper working of our parliamentary democracy'. Since then, a sea change has occurred in MPs' attitudes to the legislature, which has helped propel a number of reforms. Some reforms are structural and have a major impact while others are minor, procedural maybe. A number have occurred over the past two decades, outlined below.

HOUSE OF COMMONS COMMISSION

Set up in 1978 this in-house body gave the House more political and financial control over its own administration and personnel.

NATIONAL AUDIT OFFICE (NAO) AND THE PUBLIC ACCOUNTS COMMISSION

The NAO replaced the Exchequer and Audit department of the Comptroller and Auditor General (C&AG) – the official entrusted with the task of ensuring government funds have been disbursed as intended. Now the C&AG acts independently of Treasury control and on the basis of formal statutory authority, not convention as before.

'SPECIAL' STANDING COMMITTEES

These committees used only to scrutinise the clauses of bills but after 1980 some were allowed to hold hearings into the subject matter of the bills and to hear from witnesses.

OPPOSITION DAYS

Twenty-nine days used to be set aside for the opposition to choose topics for debate. In 1981 'supply days' were reduced to 19 but in 1985 they were increased to 20 and three given to the second-largest opposition party – usually the Lib Dems, but after the 2015 general election the Scottish National Party.

TELEVISING PARLIAMENT

In 1966 a proposal to televise the Commons was defeated – it was felt by traditionalists that the Commons in session had a unique, almost mystical quality which the cameras would ruin with their intrusive coarseness. Successive votes in the 1970s reinforced this rejection but slowly opinion was changing. In 1989 television was finally allowed its first shy peep and the world continued to turn, as before, despite dire predictions. People have become familiar with the Commons in a way not possible before, through the regular clips which appear on news bulletins – the famous chamber has never been more viewed. But television is a cruel master; MPs now prefer to queue up to speak to the cameras on Cromwell Green outside the Houses of Parliament, on the grounds that they will be seen by millions on the 'telly' but only by a few MPs if they declare their views in the chamber.

DEVOLUTION

Gordon Brown came to power brandishing proposed reforms, including reform of the voting system, abolition of the royal prerogative and consultation on the Queen's Speech, but, like so much during his premiership, nothing much came of any of them. Without doubt the major reform undertaken of the constitution bearing upon parliament was the devolution measures introduced in the late 1990s; these are considered in Chapter 17.

COMPOSITION OF THE HOUSE OF COMMONS

The 2015 election did not fundamentally change the social composition of the Commons. A third of all MPs were privately educated and a quarter went to Oxbridge: 52% Tory and 12% Labour. A quarter of MPs have hopped into the Commons from a 'political' job (for example a parliamentary aide or think-tank researcher). Only 3% were drawn from manual trades while 11% came from public relations and 10% from the media. A quarter of Tory MPs worked in finance before being elected, compared with only 4% on the Labour benches. The election benefited ethnic minorities, whose number rose from 27 in 2010 to 41. The gender balance also improved, with the 22% figure for woman MPs in 2010 increasing to 29%; Labour has 41%, the Scottish National Party 36% but the Tories only 20%.

QUESTIONS FOR DISCUSSION

1. Is the Commons too remote from ordinary people and too hard to understand?
2. Do the Commons procedures allow sufficient time for thorough discussion of proposed changes in the law?
3. How can the Commons be made more representative of women and their interests?

FURTHER READING

The best short book on parliament as a whole is still Rush (2005).

Bradbury, J. (2009) *Devolution, Regionalism and Regional Development*, Routledge.

Griffiths, J. A. G. (2010) *Politics of the Judiciary* (5th edition), Fontana.

Lodge, G. and Schmuecker, K. (2010) *Devolution in Practice: Policy Differences in the UK*, IPPR.

Mackintosh, J. P. (1962) *The British Cabinet*, Toronto University Press.

Mitchell, J. (2011) *Devolution in the United Kingdom*, Manchester University Press.

Rush, M. (2005) *Parliament Today*, Manchester University Press.

Smith, A. (2014) *Devolution and the Scottish Conservatives* (New Ethnographies), Manchester University Press.

WEBSITES

Parliament: http://www.parliament.uk.

Unlock Democracy campaign: http://www.unlockdemocracy.org.uk.

Philip Cowley and Mark Stuart's fascinating research on the behaviour of MPs: http://www.revolts.co.uk.

V

THE EXECUTIVE

The legislature creates the laws of the land and approves the broad policies by which the country is to be governed. But carrying out such policies, turning aspiration into reality, is the job of the executive. In the UK it comprises essentially: prime minister and cabinet; ministers and civil servants; departments of state; and non-governmental organisations or 'quangos'. Part V analyses how each element of the executive is constructed and how it operates.

Originally, in medieval times the tip of the executive pyramid was the monarch, ruling all he or she surveyed in a kingdom which morphed from England to incorporate Wales, Scotland and, until 1920, the whole of Ireland as well, not to mention, of course, an empire covering a quarter of the world's surface. These monarchs were often peripatetic; Henry II constantly patrolling the whole of England plus his possessions in France, ruling from the saddle of his horse. Usually the royal court, comprising principal officers and advisers, travelled along. Monarchs varied in quality and indeed longevity: some, like Henry, were talented administrators and lawmakers; others, like Henry V, were essentially warriors, while others were weak Kings, like Edward II, youthful tyrants, like Richard II, or just uninterested in the responsibilities of power, like Henry VI. Many of them had constantly to be aware that the absolute power they wielded was much sought after. Ruthless rivals might consider subversive propaganda, civil war or even straightforward murder well worth the risk as the means of donning the royal ermine and wearing it long enough to achieve legitimacy.

Most of the time early monarchs drew their officers and advisers from the ranks of the aristocracy or the church but this began to change. Henry VIII employed Thomas Wolsey, the son of a butcher and cattle dealer, as his closest adviser; when he fell from power, after being raised on high, he chose Thomas Cromwell, son of a blacksmith to take his place. Maybe his daughter with Ann Boleyn was a little influenced by this tendency; Francis Walsingham, the hugely influential principal secretary to Elizabeth I, was from the ranks of the gentry rather than the powerful aristocracy. Perhaps the major change was caused by the Civil War, 1642–49, in which the victorious revolt of parliament was led by the MP for Huntingdon, Oliver Cromwell, born into the lower ranks of the landed gentry. Thereafter the nature of executive power changed dramatically, with the monarch plus court gradually being superseded by the 'prime minister' and cabinet.

14

THE PRIME MINISTER AND CABINET

From the 1688 Glorious Revolution onwards, as explained in previous chapters, it was the dominant power in parliament which determined the membership and colour of the executive. When the Hanoverians were drafted in, in 1714, George I was not keen on the business of government and his English language skills were so poor he required an intermediary to communicate with his cabinet. This gave the opportunity to Sir Robert Walpole, an astute member of the landed gentry and a Whig, to dominate the first half of the eighteenth century in the new role of *prime minister*, as Britain's evolution towards representative democracy continued. After the Great reform Act 1832, prime ministers, rather than being the monarch's favourite, became the leaders of the majority party after a general election; this person now was more than the 'first among equals' Walpole was originally said to be: he chose members of the cabinet and was the prototype of the modern version we have today.

CABINET

By the late nineteenth century cabinet was the most senior 'committee' in government: it comprised all the major portfolios and took all the major decisions. To be a member carried authority and prestige; in effect it was, and still is, the talent pool, the 'short-list', from which prime ministers are usually drawn. So with the present government, candidates to succeed Cameron are found among his cabinet colleagues: Theresa May, George Osborne, possibly Michael Gove.

SIZE AND COMPOSITION

Cabinets have varied in size over the years but usually comprise up to two dozen ministers. During the exceptional periods of the two world wars, cabinets were a quarter of that size to facilitate effective decision-making. During peacetime, cabinet contains the main ministers – chancellor, home secretary, foreign secretary, health, work and pensions and so forth; also included are the more specialist jobs of leader of the House, chief whip and attorney-general, plus the occasional 'all purpose' archaic appointments like lord privy seal and lord president of the council, who often chair cabinet committees or perform specific tasks for the prime minister.

When making appointments, prime ministers will take into account such things as: ability and experience – it was obvious George Osborne would be Cameron's chancellor in 2010; gender and region – it is important cabinets should contain as many women as possible as well as a spread of regional backgrounds; groupings in the party – Cameron needed to reflect Euro-sceptic opinion, for example; and, of key importance, loyalty – Jeremy Hunt must have retained his place in cabinet as health secretary after the 2015 general election partly for this reason.

COLLECTIVE RESPONSIBILITY

This principle – that every member of the government should toe official party policy – is enshrined in 'Questions of Procedure for Ministers' (known as *the Ministerial Code*). The obvious aim of this rule is that the business of government is a collective effort; if even one of its members cavils in public it affects the viability of the whole enterprise. Resignation is the honourable route out of such a dilemma; being sacked is the less honourable one.

CABINET FUNCTIONS

As the foremost committee in the nation, cabinet: determines the main policy guidelines – often led by the prime minister's judgement; plans the handling of legislation – cabinet decides when to hold the major debates and who will speak for the government; and leads, along with the prime minister, the governing party in parliament and the country, with members of cabinet speaking accordingly in the House and on the media. In addition, the cabinet controls and coordinates the various government departments and provides a forum for the resolution of disputes between departments and between senior colleagues.

CABINET COMMITTEES

Government business is so weighty that cabinet would be over-whelmed without cabinet committees and subcommittees playing major delegated roles. When there is full agreement these committees carry the authority of full cabinet but when problems arise in a committee it might have to be referred to full cabinet for resolution. The work of these committees used, for no very good reason, to be secret but in recent decades their activities are much better known. During the 1970s their number rocketed to over 400 but during the 1980s Thatcher reduced them to just over 100.

CABINET BUSINESS

Typically, discussion in cabinet will flow from papers or verbal reports presented by ministers, with the leader of the House dealing with parliamentary business. In the 1970s cabinets dealt with voluminous papers and continued sitting for hours. Thatcher was less interested in discussion; as a 'conviction politician' she felt she knew what she wanted and merely wished her ministers to deliver it. Blair also shortened cabinet meetings, sometimes into mere series of brief verbal reports lasting less than an hour. Blair was also notorious for informal meetings – no minutes taken – with his unelected aides in which ways ahead were charted.

CABINET OFFICE

Until the early part of the twentieth century cabinet business took place without any record being taken. Sometimes members were unaware of decisions being taken at the nerve centre of the largest empire there had ever been. Cabinets in those days were 'informal affairs – delightfully simple' says Mackintosh, where members might well have attended school and Oxbridge together and been joined by ties of blood or marriage. As Mackintosh observed, 'it discussed with little pre-digestion and no secretarial assistance all the issues of any importance' (Mackintosh, 1962: p. 4). Sometimes members fell asleep and failed even to register that major decisions had been taken.

But during World War I, such a casual approach could no longer be tolerated: when so many lives were at risk, accurate statistics and good decisions were at a premium. David Lloyd George set up the Cabinet Office, headed by Sir Maurice Hankey. This grew rapidly, along with the hugely complex government responsibilities for the economy and public services, into a very high-powered unit which coordinates briefings for the cabinet on the top policy issues: security, foreign policy, the economy. It also provides management of the civil service, monitoring its efficiency; and it handles the disbursement of honours and appointments in the prime minister's gift.

It is staffed by about 1000 people, many of them high-fliers drawn in from all over Whitehall, who carry out these functions and, as important, follow up to ensure that policies are carried out in practice. It operates through six secretariats: Economic; Overseas and Defence; European; Science and Technology; Civil Contingencies; plus Security and Intelligence. In addition, it has seen the invention of several new units, including the Social Exclusion Unit, the Policy and Innovation Unit and the Future Strategy Unit, which used to employ Blair's friend, Lord John Birt, former director-general of the BBC. Britain lacks the kind of staff the US president has but the Cabinet Office provides, in effect, something not very dissimilar to a White House staff for the person at the pinnacle of UK government.

CABINET SECRETARY

The list of those who have filled the office since Sir Maurice Hankey (1916–35), including Sir Edward Bridges, Sir Burke Trend and Sir Norman Brook, is a roll-call of the most hugely important figures in the running of twentieth-century government and the forming of its policies. This is the key figure who connects the political side of the executive with the non-partisan side – the civil service – which implements government decisions. As such, the cabinet secretary sits at the prime minister's right hand, acting, in the words of Burke Trend, as 'the prime minister's permanent secretary'. Possibly this was why Sir Robin Butler resented the intimacy granted by Blair to aides like Alastair Campbell and Jonathan Powell, who, to a degree, shouldered him out of the role traditionally performed by his distinguished predecessors. Some analysts of public administration argue that the role of the cabinet secretary has diminished, losing the battle for the ear of the prime minister.

THE PRIME MINISTER

Some commentators argue that the UK prime minister (PM) has become so powerful the office is more like a 'presidency'. How did it become so powerful during the twentieth century? The reasons I suggest are fourfold.

Firstly, two world wars placed a huge focus and expectation upon the prime minister. Lloyd George became synonymous with victory in the first conflict and Churchill with the second. Resisting the same formidable enemy bestowed upon the occupant of number 10 a key importance as the leader of the nation.

Secondly, responsibility for wartime decision-making entailed a streamlining of the bureaucracy and the reduction in cabinet size, focusing more power in the hands of the PM.

Thirdly, the electronic media have transformed the prime minister from a distant figure in the nineteenth century to someone, by the late 20th, known, almost intimately, in everyone's home, not just voice, as with Baldwin but face, family and personality too. Even if prime ministers are not wholly in charge of their government machines, their media profiles make it appear as if they are.

Finally, given that the role of prime minister is not defined by any written UK constitution, two incumbents in particular extended the limits of prime ministerial power, in the persons of Margaret Thatcher and Tony Blair, and they have left a permanent legacy.

ROLES OF THE PRIME MINISTER

CHIEF EXECUTIVE – HIRING AND FIRING

PMs head up the government of the day: they have proved that they command trust and respect by winning an election. They appoint members of the cabinet and all the junior ministerial ranks too, though, unlike the head of government in many other countries, for example the USA, British PMs are limited in whom they can appoint, to members of either of the Houses of parliament, and even then there is a limit on recruits from the Lords. They also need to 'manage' these appointees, dismissing when necessary and implementing regular 'reshuffles' to refresh the energy, competence and appeal of the team. Critics argue that limiting ministerial appointments in this way severely diminishes the 'talent pool' available for top positions in the service of the nation.

CHIEF POLICY-MAKER

Departments generate the bulk of detailed new measures, based on their experience and expertise, but the general tone and direction of policy is set by the person at the top. Thatcher, for example, set the framework of lower taxes and market forces and departments sought to develop new measures within these guidelines.

In another sense, the aspirant PM, namely the leader of the opposition, has the job of leading policy in a way which will win voter support. When Blair became Labour leader in 1994 he worked hard, as Neil Kinnock had before him, to drag his party away from unpopular left-wing policy positions towards a new 'centre-ground' programme attractive to the electorate. After 13 years of opposition, Cameron, elected leader in 2005, performed a similar feat with his party as he approached the 2010 election.

PMs work very closely with departments of state in policy development but also like to have their own experts to armour them against the 'vested interests' of departments themselves. To this end, all PMs since Harold Wilson have maintained a Policy Unit within number 10; in 2015 the head was Camilla Cavendish, who had succeeded Jo Johnson, younger brother of London mayor Boris Johnson.

PARTY-POLITICAL LEADER

To maintain control of a regular majority in the Commons, the PM must be able to rely on party support. In the media age, the prime minister is the brand leader, synonymous with both party and government. It is the PM who opens the most important debates in the Commons or makes the announcements designed to persuade voters to keep faith with the government at the next election. If successful, MPs will give the PM their support. Prime minister's questions (PMQs) is a weekly period of 30 minutes which does little to illuminate the nation's understanding of issues but, depending on how the game of insult and be insulted goes, does help to maintain party morale. A party leader who is regularly trashed at PMQs – as Iain Duncan Smith tended to be – will not for long command the respect of back-benchers. During election campaigns, moreover, the PM must lead the contest for voters' favour, travelling the country, hosting press conferences, debating on television.

SENIOR UK REPRESENTATIVE

As the head of government, the PM travels the world meeting fellow heads and seeking to advance Britain's interests. Personal relationships can be crucial in winning support at key times, for example Thatcher's friendship with Ronald Reagan and the support he rendered during the Falklands War. Another example of strong personal relationships at head-of-government level was the hard-to-believe degree of support Tony Blair gave to George Bush over the invasion of Iraq in 2003.

HEAD OF PATRONAGE

During the eighteenth century, the PM came to access some of the patronage used by the monarch when awards of honours and allocation of government jobs were vital instruments of persuasion. Today, the use of patronage is more limited to rewarding with honours those people who have served the government, though it is an open secret that big donors, should they be seeking titles, can easily obtain them through donations to the main political parties.

This role has been assumed, probably unwillingly, by modern prime ministers by virtue of the media interest in their private lives. Margaret Thatcher found the eccentricities of her husband Dennis attracted media interest (mostly positive), the wayward accidents befalling her son Mark even more so (mostly negative). No prime minister can afford for any family member to be seen living less than squeaky-clean lives, as Blair discovered when an aide, (Carole Caplin) of his wife was revealed to have a conman boyfriend.

DIFFERING STYLES OF PRIME MINISTERS

Every prime minister has a distinctive style, which reflects both politics and personality. Clement Attlee, Labour PM after 1945, was astonishingly bland and colourless. 'He was a very modest man', quipped Churchill, 'who had much to be modest about'. This was scarcely fair; politics, so often crowded with egotistical colourful characters, can sometimes resent someone so totally lacking in charisma and therefore different. But while Churchill entertained his cabinets with stirring rhetoric, it was Attlee, as his deputy, who efficiently worked his way through cabinet agendas when, as so often during the war, the PM was away. Attlee did the same as PM, ticking manifesto objectives off the list until almost all were achieved, including nationalisation, the National Health Service and independence for India. Indeed, Clem was almost too business-like. One unfortunate minister whom Attlee sacked was summoned in to be told the sad news. Upon entering his office and being told he was sacked, Attlee continued writing something but noticed his former minister was still there, waiting. 'Might I ask why my services are no longer required?' he stammered. Attlee seemed surprised by the question: 'Oh . . . you're no good'.

HAROLD MACMILLAN

Macmillan offered a great contrast to Attlee. He was given to more reflective exposition, though much less so than Churchill; and he was infinitely subtle and diplomatic, eliciting opinion, leading the debate and then drawing conclusions which reflected the weight of agreement.

MARGARET THATCHER

The first woman prime minister, she was quintessentially a one-off. Coming to power after fighting male prejudice in her party, she took on Ted Heath in 1975 and won; persisting in her fight, she won the 1979 election and then took on those liberal Tories in her party's leadership. Her tough line of withdrawing government help for ailing industries and keeping interest rates high caused widespread bankruptcies and unemployment. Her position was parlous when she decided to fight against Argentina's invasion of the Falkland Islands in April 1982. Taking on the risk, she formed a small war cabinet; her steady nerve enabled her to emerge with a hugely enhanced reputation and a confidence which enabled her to take on all-comers within her party and the country as a whole, until her political force was finally spent in November 1990.

She tended not to be a good cabinet chair, preferring to state her position and dare others to challenge her. She was always amazingly well briefed, which intimidated colleagues, and she worked 18 hours a day (or on occasions more). She was also ruthless with those in whom she detected even the slightest disloyalty and crushingly dismissive of anyone of whom she disapproved in cabinet; the long-suffering Sir Geoffrey Howe was a prime target, though Howe's devastating resignation speech on 13 November 1990 hastened her departure from Downing Street. In politics as in life, enemies made will often in time gain their revenge.

JOHN MAJOR

Endorsed by Thatcher as her successor, Major was a totally different personality. His was a much more consensual style, seeking views and weighing them carefully. Initially he won plaudits for collegiality and being open to alternative views, especially when compared with his predecessor. But his small majority of 21 became a yoke when a hard minority of his MPs, shadowed by a similar one in cabinet, began to rebel over issues connected with the European Union. Critics tended to blame him for indecision and weak leadership when he was merely seeking to deal with his rebels, egged on, as they were by Thatcher in retirement.

Blair was more informal: 'call me Tony' he said at his first cabinet. But his informal unrecorded meetings on his Number 10 sofa were unpopular with civil servant traditionalists, like (now Lord) Robin Butler. Butler's asperity was palpable in the conclusion to his 2004 report on intelligence relating to the Iraq War: 'However, we are concerned that the informality and circumscribed character of the Government's procedures which we saw in the content of policy-making towards Iraq risks reducing the scope for informed collective political judgment.'

Also criticised was his liking for running things from the centre, making UK government even more centralised, despite his programme of devolution to the Scots and Welsh. Cabinet meetings were reduced in number and substantive content. Blair seemed to want to personalise his period in power, seeking out publicity as if too aware of his visibility, popularity and vaunted persuasive skills. Perhaps his most damaging character trait was to be obsequious to the very rich and the very powerful: abroad towards President Bush and at home to the likes of billionaires Bernie Ecclestone and Rupert Murdoch.

DEPUTY PRIME MINISTER (DPM)

There is no constitutional basis for this post but several PMs have found it useful to invent it, often for party political reasons. Geoffrey Howe was made deputy prime minister (DPM) in 1989, though Thatcher scarcely bothered to acknowledge that any power was being deputised. Michael Heseltine was also promoted DPM, though probably as a reward for supporting Major during his 1995 're-election' episode. John Prescott was Blair's DPM, in his case providing a vital link between the more right-wing 'New Labour' leadership and the left-leaning ranks of the trade unions. Finally, Nick Clegg assumed the title in May 2010 to reflect his party's role in creating the Tory–Liberal Democrat coalition. Interestingly, Clegg's title won him little in respect or influence outside his own party. In May 2015 Cameron decided to dispense with the post.

THE 'CORE EXECUTIVE'

What is meant by the term 'core executive'? It has become more popular in recent years as a more accurate description of how decisions
are made at the centre of government. A traditional way of thinking of
the government hierarchy is to envisage a pyramid, with the PM at the
top and junior ministerial ranks plus civil servants making up its body.
Traditional constitutional theory sees the tip of the pyramid controlling
the direction of policy and the lower administrative bands implementing it in practice. Michael Moran (2005) judges that, at the very top
stratum of government, distinctions between 'policy' and 'administration' are not really relevant: politicians and senior civil servants confer
on a more or less equal basis. Often, depending on the topic, external
experts, political advisers, maybe spin doctors too will be involved in ad
hoc groups discussing policy or trying to solve a government problem.
Moran discerns four characteristics of the core executive:

1. It removes the distinction between policy and administration, as
    explained above.
2. It emphasises interdependence and coordination: policies stream
    into number 10 from the departments and they have to be rec-
    onciled so that they do not conflict and can be made to appear
    to be part of an overall drive in a given direction – usually the
    main lines of the manifesto on which the government won its
    election to power.
3. It is based on roles rather than structures: members of the core
    executive will have multiple roles – slipping into its inner work-
    ings and then out, perhaps to attend to departmental business.
    Mere structures will not explain a great deal about the workings
    of government; roles explain more.
4. It focuses on decisions. Core executive members are trying to
    make the machine work, managing events together with several
    policies which may be in conflict. A sudden crisis might sum-
    mon a substantially varied group drawn from all over Whitehall.

WHAT DOES THE CORE EXECUTIVE COMPRISE?

It comprises a collection of policy-making units and 'actors' at the
centre of government:

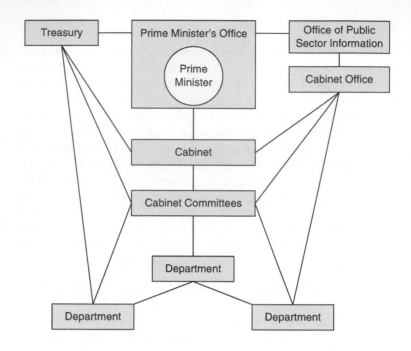

The core executive

Figure 14.1 The wiring of the core executive.

Source: Michael Moran, *Politics and Governance in the UK* (Palgrave Macmillan, 2005: p.118, figure 7.1).

1. Prime Minister's Office and related units. These include the PM's personal staff like his principal private secretary, parliamentary private secretary, chief of staff, foreign policy adviser, EU adviser, Forward Strategy Unit, director of communications and strategy, Office of Public Service Reform, Delivery Unit. PMs regularly tweak this machinery, creating and merging units as the need arises.
2. Cabinet, comprising ministerial heads of the big departments, plus others like the chief whip and the attorney-general. These meet weekly for at least an hour.
3. Cabinet Office, comprising a range of coordinating committees which seek to resolve disputes between departments. Cabinet Office personnel brief committee chairs and service them.

4. The cabinet secretary heads up the Cabinet Office and is in effect the most important civil servant, being officially its head. The cabinet secretary is always someone who has already pursued a successful career within a department.

5. Cabinet committees. These have become increasingly important as the business of government has increased exponentially in order to take the weight off the main forum. So there will be a number of key committees concerned with economic policy, future legislation and EU matters, plus any number of temporary ad hoc ones dealing with specific matters. Moran (2011) notes that while the aim of the committees is to be small to expedite business efficiently, so many departments and interests demand representation on them that they are often as big and unwieldy as the full cabinet itself.

6. Departmental heads. The permanent secretaries of government departments are also included in the network called the core executive; they will spend much of their time within their departments but will be drawn into the 'core' from time to time according to the topic and the unfolding of events.

QUESTIONS FOR DISCUSSION

1. Why do you think politicians strive so hard to become prime minister?

2. Rather than limit ministerial office to Members of Parliament, would you open up eligibility to anyone with the right abilities?

3. How useful is the concept of 'core executive' in the analysis of the British executive?

FURTHER READING

In the big textbooks good short but insightful analyses are found in: Moran (2011: chapter 6); Jones and Norton (2013: chapter 18); and Kingdom (2014: chapter 16). The book by Anthony King (1985) is a good place to start for a deeper understanding of the office of prime minister, followed by Hennessy's book on cabinet (1986). Kavanagh and Seldon's (1999) study provides good analysis and David Owen's book presents a theory of why prime ministers tend to overreach themselves after too long in the post.

Hennessey, P. (1986) *Cabinet*, Blackwell.

James, S. (1999) *British Cabinet Government*, Routledge.

Jones, B. and Norton, P. (2013) *Politics UK* (8th edition), Routledge.

Kavanagh, D. and Seldon, A. (1999) *The Powers Behind the Prime Minister*, Harper Collins.

King, A. (ed.) (1985) *The British Prime Minister*, Macmillan.

Mackintosh, J. M. (1962) *Cabinet Government*, Stevens.

Moran, M. (2011) *Politics and Governance in the UK* (2nd edition), Palgrave.

Owen, D. (2007) *The Hubris Syndrome: Bush, Blair and the Intoxication of Power*, Methuen.

Rose, R. (2001) *The Prime Minister in a Shrinking World*, Polity.

Seldon, A. (2005) *Blair*, Little, Brown.

Seldon, A. (2007) *Blair Unbound*, Simon Schuster.

Smith, M. (1999) *The Core Executive in Britain*, Palgrave.

WEBSITE

Cabinet Office: http://www.gov.uk/government/organisations/cabinet-office.

15

MINISTERS AND CIVIL SERVANTS

MINISTERS

It is in the minister's name that an Act of Parliament is granted, so legally ministers are of great importance in British government. Democratically they are even more important, as they represent the 'red line' of democratic accountability, running from voters, who return a majority of one party to parliament, through to the leader of that party, who, as prime minister, allocates colleagues to the 100 or so ministerial posts. Each department has several ministers, typically a cabinet secretary of state, maybe a minister of state (a 'senior' version of a junior minister) and perhaps two or three parliamentary under-secretaries (PUSs). In addition, ministers usually appoint an (unpaid) parliamentary private secretary (PPS), who represents the first rung on the ministerial ladder: these are often ambitious younger MPs who serve as aides to the minister and as conduits to back-bench opinion. They sit in on most policy meetings and, if they do well, and show promise and initiative, can reasonably expect promotion to PUS level.

Members of the Lords are often given junior portfolios and occasionally cabinet jobs but within a quota limit; since Lord Salisbury in 1902, no prime minister has sat in the Lords. Junior ministers are usually keen to become senior ones. Promotion is likely to depend on them showing their paces, usually in the Commons by: demonstrating expertise in the business of their department; speaking well in debates and committees; displaying loyalty to the government and the prime minister; and, when required, defending and promoting the government's cause via the media. Being close to a senior minister—sometimes they have something approaching an 'entourage'—can often be the means of advancing one's chances of preferment; Labour's Roy Jenkins, for example, was well known for his assiduity in advancing the careers of his younger protégés.

How long does it take to become a minister? Rarely are they appointed directly into the cabinet, unless a party has spent years in opposition, like Labour in 1945, 1964 and 1997, or the Tories in 2010. Usually MPs have to serve an apprenticeship on the backbenches, then as junior ministers. Sometimes careers are still-born early on, when periods in office are judged negatively and a stint as junior minister remains the zenith of an MP's career. But it is possible for sacked ministers to make come-backs: Harriet Harman was sacked in 1998 but was brought back into the fold in 2001, as solicitor general, but it took Gordon Brown to become prime minister before she could make it back into the cabinet, in 2007.

TYPES OF MINISTER

Philip Norton (in Jones and Norton, 2013) created a typology of five types of ministers: *team players*, who prefer collective decision-making; *commanders*, who have a clear idea of what they want and set about achieving it; *ideologues*, who have a clear vision of what they want, like the Thatcherite Sir Keith Joseph and Nicholas Ridley; *managers*, who lacks clear visions but are content to administer even-handedly, reaching balanced decisions (Douglas Hurd is perhaps typical of this type); the *agent*, put in place to do the prime minister's specific bidding; or, finally, the *weak minister*, who has been taken over by the civil service and is led by them.

MINISTERIAL RESPONSIBILITY

Ministers are individually responsible to parliament for the actions of their departments, whether they know of such actions or not. This is meant to accentuate political accountability and shield civil servants, as the neutral instruments of democracy, from any negative consequences. It follows that often clever civil servants who have inspired successful policies have to watch their ministers take all the credit. Their payoff is to escape censure when things go wrong. However, recent years have seen ministers prepared to blame their civil servants, for example the bidding fiasco over the west coast rail franchise in 2012.

RESIGNATION

Do ministers resign when things go wrong? The classic case was the Crichel Down affair, in 1954, when Sir Thomas Dugdale resigned over mistakes in his department even though he knew nothing about them. But apart from Lord Carrington's resignation as foreign secretary on behalf of his department's failings over the Falklands in 1982, examples of similar honourable resignations are hard to find. Carrington, incidentally, gains even more moral credit in that he was a junior minister to Dugdale in 1954 and actually offered to resign along with his boss but was persuaded not to.

CIVIL SERVICE

ORIGINS

The British civil service grew out of the medieval monarch's household, though the written communications and records of modern times were not so necessary when illiteracy was so widespread. Those serving the royal court were often connected to the church, as this was the main source of literacy in such times. Until the thirteenth century, Kings appointed 'justiciars' to provide support while they were away overseas; they developed into such powerful officers they eventually ceased to be appointed. Henry VIII continued the reforms initiated by his father, Henry VII, and appointed two successive secretaries famous for the extent of their power. Wolsey, the son of a butcher, accumulated such wealth his King eventually acquired it once the cardinal had, rather conveniently one has to conclude, been executed.

Then came his protégé the great Thomas Cromwell, maybe 'the first true civil servant' (Pilkington, 1999: p. 10), who organised the dissolution of the monasteries and sequestration into Henry's coffers of the church's wealth. 'An administrator of genius' (Elton, 1991: pp. 180–184), Cromwell used his 'constructive statesmanship' to extend Henry VIII's reforms from the household to the nation as a whole, setting up separate institutions which provided the embryo of modern public administration.

During the eighteenth century many public offices were filled by patronage, based on contacts and nepotism not merit. But one part of the emerging Empire had adopted a Chinese practice of basing public appointments on performance in common examinations. The East India Company had evolved from a successful commercial organisation into one which effectively administered large parts of India. It needed able young men, not effete sons of the aristocracy. In 1806 it set up a training college for its employees. This meritocratic model influenced the historic Northolt–Trevelyan report into the civil service.

NORTHCOTE–TREVELYAN REPORT, 1854

This report was the result of a realisation that an industrially advanced country, at the centre of a worldwide empire, desperately needed first-class public administration. The report advised a politically neutral civil service, appointed on merit, with clear distinctions made between three levels of staff. Staff of the administrative 'officer' class would advise ministers and run the departments; 'executive' non-graduate staff would perform the everyday tasks; and 'clerical' staff would do the essential but more routine tasks. This military-style hierarchy worked well enough for a long time, with 'class to class' promotion possible for the brightest from the lower strata. The Civil Service Commission was set up in 1855 to handle recruitment and end the practice of patronage. Senior civil servants are often called *mandarins* because of the Chinese connection with their selection method. For the next century this system served the nation well and its honest, efficient civil service was one of the nation's boasts. Strains began to appear, however, by the middle of the twentieth century.

FULTON REPORT, 1968

The civil service had been criticised for being too 'general'; British mandarins were good but maybe the École nationale d'administration, which from 1945 provided specialised training for the French senior civil service, offered a superior alternative model in the form of its multi-talented *énarques*? Critics pointed out that in 1963 the Treasury employed only 19 trained economists. Also mentioned was the bias towards a narrow middle-class, Oxbridge-educated recruitment pool; typically during the 1960s, only 3% of the administrative grade intake were drawn from the working class; inevitably this made them remote from the everyday life of the nation they were helping to govern.

Fulton reformed the caste system, and set up a Civil Service College, later known as the National School of Government (NSG) and the Central Policy Review Staff (which became known as Number Ten's 'think-tank') to advise the prime minister, but the other 150 or so recommendations were either ignored or quashed by senior mandarins worried that their traditional arm-lock on ministerial advice might be broken. Worse, in the eyes of some critics, is that the NSG was closed in 2011 with no replacement for such training.

THATCHER'S REFORMS

Margaret Thatcher suspected the civil service of embodying the post-war consensus which she so abhorred and of automatically expanding and defending their bureaucratic empires. She set about reducing their number from 732,000 in 1979 to 594,000 by 1986: an impressive reduction. She also believed the private sector to be much more efficient than the public and so sought to make the latter more like the former, by injecting market forces wherever possible and drawing business people into leading roles to apply business principles. Derek Rayner, from Marks and Spencer, was invited to set up an 'efficiency unit' and in the Ministry of Defence Michael Heseltine, himself a successful businessman, pioneered his so-called MINIS planning system.

THE *NEXT STEPS* REPORT

Perhaps the most important next reform was Sir Robin Ibbs – formerly of ICI – who produced the *Next Steps* report in 1988. This was something of a revolution in that it separated routine functions from the more complex business of advising and supporting ministers. Within a few years, scores of 'executive agencies' were set up, along the lines of the Benefits Agency, the Training Agency or the long-established Driver and Vehicle Licensing Authority in Swansea. By 1997 over three-quarters of civil servants were employed in 200 agencies. While the reform created increased efficiency, some criticised the agencies being at arm's length from ministerial accountability and parliamentary scrutiny.

PRIVATISATION

Part of Thatcher's zeal to reduce the public sector was manifested in her privatisation programme. Few had thought her aspiration to 'roll back the state' would be fulfilled – politicians frequently forget radical plans once in office – but she set about this task early on, without the benefit of anything similar having been attempted; it was the most radical reform since nationalisation itself in 1945–50. First up was British Telecom in 1984. Originally the General Post Office, it was converted to a public corporation before being floated on the Stock Exchange with great success and profit for the Treasury.

Former Tory Prime Minister Harold Macmillan (Lord Stockton) complained the government was 'selling off the family silver' but few in his party were listening as they celebrated what became a bonanza for the government: coal, gas, steel, forestry, electricity, water and the (arguably ill-fated) railways followed. By the mid-1990s almost all the enterprises nationalised after the war were back in private hands. Selling back to the public things they already owned was by no means an unqualified success. The result was increased efficiencies in some areas, for instance gas, but not in others, for example the railways. And voters had to live with job losses, higher charges in many cases and huge salaries for the senior management of the newly privatised enterprises. Workers in privatised industries, moreover, frequently had to put up with lower pay and less favourable terms of employment.

CIVIL SERVICE PERSONNEL

Top of the departmental hierarchy (Table 15.1) is the permanent secretary, usually a career official who will have spent his or her

Table 15.1 Senior grades in the home civil service

Old title	Grade	Often now known as . . .
Cabinet secretary (head of civil service)		
Permanent secretary (civil service head of each department)		
Deputy secretary	2	Director general
Under-secretary	3	Director
Assistant secretary	5	Director or assistant director
Senior principal and principal	6, 7	Deputy director, assistant director, team leader, policy manager, etc.

Source: www.civilservant.org.uk.

whole time in the same department (Box 15.1), with possible external secondments to business or the Cabinet Office. This official is directly answerable to parliament via the Public Accounts Committee, which checks that money granted to departments has been disbursed appropriately. Contrary to the Fulton philosophy, many of this most senior cohort are still Oxbridge-educated and generalists rather than specialists (see Box 15.2).

Box 15.1   Ministerial departments, 2015

- Attorney General's Office
- Cabinet Office
- Department for Business, Innovation and Skills
- Department for Communities and Local Government
- Department for Culture, Media and Sport
- Department for Education
- Department for Environment, Food and Rural Affairs
- Department for International Development
- Department for Transport
- Department for Work and Pensions

- Department of Energy and Climate Change
- Department of Health
- Foreign and Commonwealth Office
- Her Majesty's Treasury
- Home Office
- Ministry of Defence
- Ministry of Justice
- Northern Ireland Office
- Office of the Advocate General for Scotland
- Office of the Leader of the House of Commons
- Office of the Leader of the House of Lords
- Scotland Office
- UK Export Finance
- Wales Office

Box 15.2   The 'generalist' in the civil service

The 1968 Fulton report criticised the tradition of the generalist in the civil service. Unlike the French École nationale d'administration, many senior civil servants, or 'mandarins' as they are called, have been educated in subjects like classics, history or philosophy, politics and economics (PPE), not those most closely related to government: economics, statistics or, perhaps most importantly, law. Defenders of the 'generalist' argue that:

1. The people recruited are among the cleverest of their generation, coming, as they do, from the best universities.
2. Public administration is so complex and unique, it is hard to prepare anyone for its demands. Years doing the job are usually thought to be superior to education in any particular subject studied years before.
3. Ministers themselves are 'generalists', as few have specialised skills. The senior mandarin is therefore the public servant mirror

image of the elected minister in charge. Together they decide what is best for the national community.

Against this it can be adduced that:

1. Local government has no problems in vesting authority in specialised architects, planners, engineers and the like. Why should the highest advice to ministers be less expert?
2. French officials, with their specialised training, show that it can be worthwhile: the so-called, *énarques* who graduate from the École nationale d'administration are famed for their ability and populate the highest ranks of administration in just about every walk of French public administration.
3. There have been many government failures in terms of information technology disasters, inadequate equipment for soldiers serving abroad and a welter of other incompetence like the loss of details, including bank details of about 25 million people in autumn 2007. Surely, say, critics, better-trained civil servants would reduce the depressing catalogue of government failures?

POLITICAL ADVISERS

This group became controversial during the Blair years. Ministers have always drawn upon external advisers; often these connections were informal but political (or 'special') advisers ('temporary' civil servants appointed under article 3 of the Civil Service Order in Council 1995) began to be employed officially as long ago as the 1970s. Jack Straw, adviser to Barbara Castle, and Bernard Donoughue to Harold Wilson, were among the first, but their number grew rapidly thereafter. Blair employed 78 of them but in 2014 the figure was down to 68, with 18 employed in Number 10, including: a chief of staff (Ed Llewellyn), plus two deputies; a director of communications; a chief speech writer, plus advisers on Scotland, broadcasting, youth crime and women. Blair's advisers, especially Alastair Campbell and Jonathan Powell, created waves because they were so powerful, were allowed to give orders to civil servants and annoyed senior officials by usurping their traditional role as the prime minister's closest confidants.

WHO MAKES POLICY – MINISTER OR CIVIL SERVANT?

This is a traditional question in political science, often appearing in examination papers, and, as with all complex problems, the answer is not straightforward. Ministers have the authority to make decisions but it is easy to believe the plot of the sit-com, hugely successful worldwide, *Yes Minister*, that naïve, *temporary* ministers (few serve more than two years in a post) are easily outwitted by smooth, devious, highly educated *permanent* civil servants. However, in practice, most of the evidence suggests it does not work that way. In the first place, ministers are usually powerful personalities who understand power very well. They will mostly know what they want and will not allow even the most silky-voiced mandarins to lead them astray (Box 15.3).

Box 15.3   Civil servants and ministers: how they get their own way

David Blunkett, three times a cabinet minister in Blair governments, has recently published his diaries. In them he describes how civil servants brief ministers in such a way that the course they favour is adopted. A diary entry for March 2002 (Blunkett, 2006) reads:

> The civil service has a particular line that they've developed well over the years. First, if they don't want you to do something, they produce the lengthiest, most obscurantist document, with no clear recommendations, but in the text itself all of the so-called pluses and minuses, except with the minuses (which avoid them having to do what it is they do not wish to do) highlighted. The second element is to put up costings that make it impossible even to consider arguing with the Treasury, so everything is inflated beyond belief. . . .

Civil servants are socialised all their careers to play according to the rules and they are democratic ones: the minister represents the people's will and is the 'master' of the mandarins, however clever and senior they might be. So even if they complain about their minister – which they frequently do – civil servants will usually do everything they can to fulfil their remit within a representative democracy. The only area where civil servants might resort to delaying tactics and the rest is if civil service interests are involved; this might explain why many of the recommendations of the Fulton report were kicked into the 'long grass'. Also, if a minister is constantly undecided, civil servants are tempted to step in, if only to keep the wheels of the department turning.

Relationships between ministers and civil servants are usually characterised by mutual respect and cooperation. Ministers need to achieve the aims of the government – civil servants need to keep their departments running smoothly and effectively. Usually the minister will take a case to cabinet which seeks to achieve both ends. Finally, on this vexed question, any ministers who cannot impose their will on civil service staff will not remain ministers for long.

REFORMING THE CIVIL SERVICE

As we have seen, Britain's civil service has come a long way since the inefficient patronage dominated days of the eighteenth century. Following the 1854 report and, a century later, Fulton, the civil service has undergone constant change and development. The report *Context for Civil Service Reform*, published June 2012, revealed that numbers employed fell from 746,000 in 1977 to 435,000 in 2010. Further reductions continue. The Civil Service Reform Plan, published in the same month, foresaw an additional 23% reduction on the 2010 figure, to 380,000 in 2015. The Plan makes clear that some of this reduction is driven by the need to reduce the government's budget deficit.

For the future, the Plan suggests devolving the service away from Whitehall: 'the Civil Service will need to do less centrally and commission more from outside' (p. 7). 'Non-departmental public bodies' or 'quangos' (quasi-autonomous non-government organisations) are also targeted for reduction: from 500 down to 250 by 2015, with three-yearly reviews of their performance to ensure accountability and efficiency. To improve policy-making, the Behavioural Insights Team was created in the Cabinet Office to 'find new ways of applying insights from behavioural science to public policy' (p. 17).

An innovation designed to improve policy implementation as well as accountability, 'non-executive' members drawn from business have been appointed to departmental boards. Under the leadership of Lord Browne, 59 such people have been appointed. One of the most embarrassing failures of the civil service has been its inability to manage major projects, the £12 billion National Health Service information technology disaster being the most obvious example. The Major Projects Authority now oversees over 200 of the highest-value and highest-risk projects. A Major Projects Leadership Academy trains senior staff responsible for such undertakings.

QUESTIONS FOR DISCUSSION

1. Should ministers be appointed for a minimum period, to enable them to master their portfolios?
2. Education in which subjects do you think would be most appropriate for future civil servants?
3. How persuasive do you find the 'generalist' argument?

FURTHER READING

Still very useful for explaining the culture of the higher civil service is Barberis (1997). For good insights into working with civil servants see Barnett (1982). Hennessy (2001) is a fabulous volume on how the machine works. Kaufman (1997) is a classic 'must read' too. A thorough study of the civil service is Burnham and Pyper (2008). Finally, highly recommended is the perceptive and very amusing Lynne and Jay (1982).

Barberis, P. (ed.) (1997) *The Civil Service in an Era of Change*, Dartmouth.
Barnett, J. (1982) *Inside the Treasury*, Deutsch.
Blunkett, D. (2006) *The Blunkett Tapes*, Bloomsbury.

Brazier, R. (1997) *Ministers of the Crown*, Clarendon Press.

Burnham, J. and Pyper, R. (2008) *The Modernised British Civil Service*, Palgrave.

Cabinet Office (2010) *The Ministerial Code*, Cabinet Office.

Hennessy, P. (1992) *Never Again*, Jonathan Cape.

Jones, B. and Norton, P. (2013) *Politics UK* (8th edition), Routledge.

Kaufman, G. (1997) *How To Be a Minister*, Faber.

Lawson, N. (1992) *The View from Number 11*, Bantam

Lynne, J. and Jay, A. (1982) *Yes Minister: The Diaries of a Cabinet Minister by the Rt Hon James Hacker MP*, BBC.

Pilkington, C. (1999) *The Civil Service in Britain Today*, Manchester University Press.

WEBSITES

Cabinet Office: https://www.gov.uk/government/organisations/cabinet-office.

Civil service: http://www.gov.uk/government/organisations/civil-service.

16

POLICY-MAKING IN BRITISH GOVERNMENT

The latter part of the last chapter discussed the balance of power in policy-making between ministers and civil servants but the process involves many more players than just those two. 'Policy' is what affects us all in our day-to-day life. During the 1980s Margaret Thatcher pursued a very clear set of policies – privatisation, reduce union power, increase productivity, reduce taxation – which had a huge impact on Britain, for good or ill. By studying how a political system finally focuses on what it wishes to do, we find out something central and basic about its character. Throughout these chapters so far we have examined how the various 'players', be they in the legislature, executive, pressure groups, media or judiciary, impact upon the making of decisions. In this chapter we sharpen the focus a little and examine the process and the machinery at closer range.

POLICY-MAKING AS A 'SYSTEM'

One way of looking at the process is to see the machinery of government – legislature, executive and judiciary – as a 'system' of which political demands or 'inputs' are made and then which produces 'outputs' in the form of white papers, statutes, delegated legislation, benefit payments, ratified treaties and so forth, drawing upon available resources of finance, expertise and the like. Figure 16.1

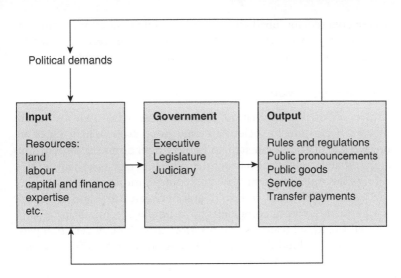

Figure 16.1 Input–output model of policy-making

Source: Burch, M. (1979) The policy making process, in Jones, B. and Kavanagh, D. (eds), *British Politics Today*, Manchester University Press.

illustrates the process. It also indicates a 'feedback loop' whereby outputs influence the situation which created the demand in the first place. Implementing outputs will call upon resources like land, labour, finance and expertise.

MODELS OF POLICY-MAKING

Scholars of policy studies have constructed 'models' of how policy is most often made in practice and consideration of such alternatives helps understanding. Just how policy is made is important: some of the models drawn from practice below are not exactly compatible with democracy.

WESTMINSTER MODEL

This is the 'official' model, according to the constitution, whereby, on the basis of the mandate provided by voters, the prime minister appoints ministers, who are placed in charge of departments and where civil servants obediently strive to implement their commands. Ministers try to convince us that this is how government works; political scientists argue the reality is often very different.

THE RULING-CLASS MODEL

This is essentially the Marxist analysis: those who own the means of wealth creation in society are the group from which elites are recruited, values disseminated and policy directions established. This argues that society's 'superstructure' of democracy is a sham, in that ruling-class interests manipulate and control, mostly in secret behind the scenes. With a contemporary gulf between rulers and ruled, this is a frequently voiced complaint, for example by comedian/agitator Russell Brand, who argues that decisions are taken by very rich people, standing behind the political system, in their own interests and not those of society as a whole.

PLURALISM

This approach, associated with US political scientist Robert Dahl, suggests that the various interest groups in society, connected to the economy, the professions and so forth, are all engaged in a competitive process to apply influence. He saw the government as the referee, holding the ring between participants and ensuring fair play.

CORPORATISM

Philippe C. Schmitter argued that a triumvirate of ministers, civil servants and interest-group leaders come together to 'fix' decisions at the top and then impose them on the nation. So, the argument runs, union leaders made deals with ministers during the 1970s which did not reflect the views of their members, let alone the mass of voters. This is a variant of the 'elite rule' critique that democracy is controlled by a small, out-of-touch group in charge of the system.

PARTY GOVERNMENT MODEL

This analysis sees political parties as the wellsprings of policy, formulating them in opposition and implementing them in government. This is closer to the traditional Westminster model.

WHITEHALL MODEL

This argues that it is the able, well briefed, experienced and permanent senior civil servants who in practice subtly dominate the inexperienced and temporary elected ministers of distinctly varying abilities. This is very much the satirical *Yes Minister* view, which, many ex-ministers attest, has some basis in fact.

RATIONAL DECISION-MAKING

This line of argument sees decision-makers acting rationally, considering options presented by their civil servants and then opting for the optimum course. Critics question whether external factors do not distort this process, for example whether politicians' emotional attraction to an idea might not predispose them to adopt it; for example, Tony Blair seemed not to question the idea of supporting Bush's Iraq policy, so keen was he to write a 'blank cheque' of support to the US president.

INCREMENTALISM

Charles Lindblom is the guru behind this approach, which doubts the rationality of decision-makers but sees them as 'muddling through' using precedent and a range of less rational strategies. This approach owes something to the notion that things often happen through blunders and miscalculations rather than by design.

POLICY COMMUNITIES AND NETWORKS

Some political scientists – for example Jordan, Richardson, Rhodes – perceive policy 'communities', comprising a range of inter-communicating groups and individuals. Membership of the community will depend upon conformity to the accepted 'rules of the game', as well as a measured confidentiality regarding the progress of consultations. Rhodes additionally discerned a less organised community of networks, outside the inner core and subject to frequent change of membership.

POLITICAL MARKETING

Lees-Marshment's (2001) book suggests that parties need to learn lessons more generally from marketing. She suggests Labour was 'product based' in the early 1980s – offering up something only the activists wanted and failing badly as a result in 1983. She sees the party then trying a 'sales oriented' approach, based on much improved campaigning and advertising. But the message was still poorly conceived and a second failure arrived with Thatcher's 1987 victory, followed by Major's surprise victory in 1992. She argues that once the party learnt how to listen to what the 'market' really wanted, under the banner of 'New Labour', then finally success came, in the form of the 1997 landslide. The logic of such an approach, however, suggests that politicians should merely reflect the results of opinion polls and focus groups, and abandon any attempt to refine a philosophy and lead, rather than follow, public views, however populist they might be.

THE POLICY CYCLE

Policy studies is quite a crowded field but most of the scholars in it recognise a three-stage policy cycle: *initiation, formulation* and *implementation*, with the consequences of the measure, in the jargon, feeding back to influence future inputs.

POLICY INITIATION

Figure 16.2 indicates the various sources of policy ideas, using the metaphor of 'distance' of initiators from 'core' decision-makers. The source could be a letter to *The Times*, the mind of an incoming minister, a creative civil servant, a whim of a prime minister, or the product of a think-tank, bursting with brilliant intellectuals. But the idea on its own is useless unless the means and the will exist to advocate it, push it up the political agenda and then make it happen.

GENERAL PUBLIC

The influence of the public, perhaps paradoxically in a democracy, is, most of the time, furthest away from the centre of decision-making. But on election days, it can be argued, the public exercise briefly the sovereign power, though the degree of choice involved is only between broad party prospectuses. Sometimes the public rouses itself to demonstrate, as over Iraq in February 2003, but to no effect:

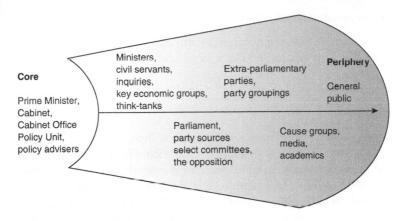

Figure 16.2 Policy-making initiators

Source: Jones, B. and Norton, P. (2013) *Politics UK* (8th edition), Routledge: p. 469.

their protest was ignored. Politicians often feel the general public's views, uninformed and swayed by prejudice and self-interest, should be resisted. Douglas Hurd, former British foreign secretary, wrote, revealingly, in 1993 that 'if we had followed the polls, we would have been in and out of the EU several times in the last 20 years. On matters of principle, like the monarchy and membership of the European Community, the job of the politician is to persuade, not automatically to follow' (quoted by Ben Page, *Guardian*, 25 March 2013).

CAUSE GROUPS, MEDIA, ACADEMICS

Cause groups are the democratic means of representing opinion groups and are a constant feature of political life. They can batter away at the doors of ministers for years with no success, but, like Charter 88 in the late 1990s, suddenly find doors fly open and their views adopted virtually as government policy. Media campaigns can often be part of such activity, while academics can find that suddenly their work expresses the zeitgeist and, in similar fashion, are adopted. Economist John Maynard Keynes's ideas were initially resisted in the 1930s but had become government orthodoxies by 1945.

These can be influential when a particular party is in government; ministers turn up to their meetings and direct influence can be applied.

PARLIAMENT

Groups of MPs constantly seek to impress their views on their leaderships, occasionally with success – for example, Labour MPs urging more funding for public services during the 1990s – on other occasions failing – for example, MPs from the same party seeking to persuade their leaders to support the unilateral abolition of nuclear weapons. On still other occasions an active group can succeed in merely blocking progress on a range of issues, like John Major's rebels over the European Union (EU) during the 1990s.

MINISTERS, DEPARTMENTS, INQUIRIES AND THINK-TANKS

Ministers will seek to push through their favourite policy ideas in order to attract praise and recognition. For example, Michael Foot as employment secretary felt that his health and safety legislation represented his most worthwhile achievement. Departments also devise policies of their own every week and month of the political year but there will always be politicians waiting to walk away with the credit for themselves. 'Think-tanks' tend to be more a feature of US policy-making but Thatcher, frustrated by a civil service she felt was still immersed in the consensus views of the 1960s, reached out to right-wing think-tanks like the Adam Smith Institute for ideas which chimed in more closely with her own instinctive beliefs. This is how the 'community charge' or 'poll tax' idea came into being (though perhaps this is not the best advertisement for the success of think-tank ideas).

CORE EXECUTIVE

This is the term (see Chapter 14) now commonly used to describe the phalanx of people who take the major decisions in British politics. It comprises the prime minister, of course, plus cabinet colleagues, principal aides like the press secretary, members of the Policy Unit and other close advisers on foreign affairs, the EU and so forth, the cabinet secretary, the permanent secretaries of the departments of state and members of cabinet committees. These people, it should be noted, are not all elected, but in the mix of policy-making such distinctions do not necessarily apply when knowledge and force of argument are just as important as rank or status. These are the people who are involved in dealing with the biggest, most intractable problems facing the state: whether to join the euro, how to cope with government debt, how to stimulate the economy, how to handle emergencies, whether to go to war.

POLICY FORMULATION

This occurs once the initiative has been absorbed by the government machine and enters a period of consultation and refinement. This stage can take hours, days or months, depending on its complexity and the time available; with international crises there may be only minutes to take decisions.

EMERGENCIES

Prime ministers inevitably have all the most unsolvable problems ending up on their desk. On many of them, they have precedents to guide them and an able staff to advise. But on some issues, a hijack, or a kidnapping, a plane crash or a terrorist outrage, there might be no files in the cupboard to guide responses: vital decisions have to be made in a very short timescale upon which life and death may depend. This is when a premier's leadership qualities are truly tested.

CONSULTATION, EVOLUTION AND AMENDMENT

Some ideas are mulled over and refined while others might be rejected once their down sides are fully realised. David Evans, MP for Luton, for example, suggested an identity card system for football supporters to Thatcher which was initially welcomed by his prime minister, but after a long period of silence it was assumed, correctly, that number 10 had looked at the idea carefully and thought it best not to pursue it.

LEGISLATIVE HURDLES

If there are bureaucratic obstacles to the acceptance of policy, there are of course also legislative hurdles – the not necessarily easy passage through the Houses of Commons and Lords (see Figure 16.3). Mostly the Commons majority, which supports the government of the day, will ensure measures get voted through, but sometimes they fail. The Sunday Opening Bill in 1986, for example, was voted down through an accumulation of dissident pressure group activity. Other measures can be extensively amended, like the top-up fees (for university education) initiative in 2004. Opposition to this bill succeeded in passing several amendments that substantially changed the

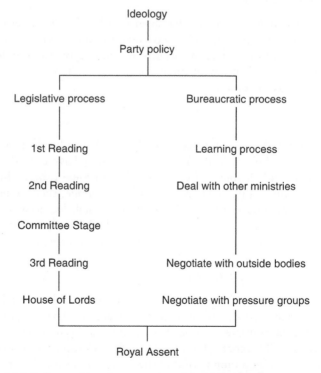

Figure 16.3 Policy-making: bureaucratic and legislative hurdles

Source: Jones et al. (2004) *Politics UK* (5th edition), Pearson: Figure 24.4.

detail of the final act. The Lords, too, seldom manage to end the life of something the government seriously wants to pass into law, but for example, the Hunting Act, hugely contentious to Conservative MPs and supporters in the country, was delayed for quite some time and it took the invoking of the Parliament Act 1949 to finally pass it onto the statute books.

POLICY IMPLEMENTATION

Jordan and Richardson (1987) observe that implementation can never be taken for granted and, to be successful, requires a number of conditions to be fulfilled. There must be: no conflict of authority to weaken control; uniform norms and rules in the control system; perfect obedience or perfect control; perfect information, communication and coordination; and sufficient time for the necessary resources to be mobilised. In other words, merely passing an act does not change reality unless some or all of these requirements are met. The above two students of policy in practice might also have added that another requirement is 'acceptance' by the voters.

For example, in 1988 the poll tax (a uniform per capita local tax replacing the historical 'rates' levied on property) was passed into law and the act was implemented for a while but there was much dissension among British people: many refused to pay a levy which taxed the poor as much as the rich; many had refused to register their vote, disenfranchising themselves to disguise their liability for payment. Still others took to the streets – there were serious riots on 31 March 1990 in Trafalgar Square. This failure of acceptance was a decisive element in the fall of Thatcher in the autumn of that year, and one of the first actions of John Major's successor government was to abolish the hated tax and replace it with the council tax.

CONSTRAINTS UPON POLICY-MAKERS

Clearly, as the poll tax example demonstrates, the democratic system imposes rather more constraints upon policy-makers than an autocratic one might. However, there are many other factors which are common to all, whatever the system.

FINANCE

Governments must have the means to fulfil their policy objectives. Harold Wilson's Labour government in the 1960s was stronger on stating objectives than achieving them, simply because the economy was in decline, with balance-of-payments deficits and devaluation of the pound arising from a manufacturing base which was atrophied and uncompetitive. Cameron's 2010 coalition government was virtually excluded from new spending initiatives by its need to focus on reducing the deficit on government spending.

TIME

Passing new measures can take many months and legislative time is always severely limited, so much so that MPs who win ballots to float private members' bills are often assailed by government departments seeking to persuade them to adopt one of their bills. New measures also often need to time to settle in and some are 'piloted' in different parts of the country before being rolled out nationwide.

POLITICAL SUPPORT

This is required for a measure to be initiated, naturally, but is also necessary for it to pass through what may be a tortuous process of sniping and lobbyists seeking to amend it in certain ways or even out of existence. The identity card project, for example, has attracted varying degrees of support throughout its history. The Conservatives considered it and rejected it in the 1990s, but when Labour brought it back after terrorist outrages, support was seldom unanimous, with the Conservatives and Lib Dems opposing, and, in the spring of 2008, large sections of the Labour Party becoming sceptical. No objections ensued when Cameron's government killed the idea in August 2010.

COMPETENCE OF KEY PERSONNEL

The crucial element in this equation is the quality of the minister. An able, ambitious minister is likely to have the energy to push plans through to completion, while a weak 'time-server' will be happy to let the issue lie when civil servants also less than enthusiastic about the measure might be happy to let it die a death. It can also happen that a measure's chances of being passed depend on a minister staying in post in the ministry. By the same token, key civil servants who have absorbed expertise in a complex area might be 'poached' by the private sector. This happened during privatisation transitions in the 1980s, when newly privatised businesses looked to those who had helped create them to go on and help run them.

COORDINATION

Some measures straddle a variety of departmental responsibilities – poverty, crime, infrastructure projects – and coordinating them can prove difficult. New Labour came to power offering 'joined up government' to remedy such problems, but few would claim the problem has been solved, or anything near. One approach by Blair was to set up units in the Cabinet Office, like the Exclusion Unit, to provide a more comprehensive attack on problems caused by poverty.

PERSONALITY FACTORS

Most large departments have a team of ministers and sometimes their personalities clash. Some evidence of this was provided in May 1997, when Ann Widdecombe (former Home Office minister of state) criticised her former boss, Michael Howard, as having 'something of the night about him'. The comment is thought to have done much to torpedo the former home secretary's then current bid for his party's leadership. The most notorious clash of personalities, however, was provided by the Labour Party in the form of Tony Blair and Gordon Brown. These two former firm friends in opposition feuded, when prime minister and chancellor respectively, over whether Blair had promised Brown he would step down and allow his chancellor to contest and take over the leadership after a given period of time. The constant warring between the party's two major figures had implications for several policy areas, including possible membership of the euro, the reform of public services and, not least, top-up fees for universities.

INFLUENCE OF THE EU

Membership of the European Union (EU) remains a contentious
matter within both major parties, mostly on the grounds that it
reduces UK sovereignty and threatens a 'federal' European encroach-
ment into all spheres of policy. While such claims are probably highly
exaggerated, it is true that the scope of EU concerns have spread from
the narrowly economic to extend into social affairs as well as defence
and foreign policy. Any minister now has to consider the implications
of EU membership whenever a new policy initiative is raised.

INTERNATIONAL EVENTS

One of the most famous quotations regarding the work of a prime
minister was made by Harold Macmillan when he responded to a
question on what, as prime minister, kept him awake at night with a
shaking of the head and 'Events, dear boy, events'. Hijackings, revolutions, natural disasters or terrorist atrocities can steamroll their way
onto the best-laid agenda for ordered progress and demand instant
action. So 9–11 precipitated major losses on the stock exchanges and
catalysed security policies the world over. In January 2008 another
run on the stock exchanges – this time the result of foolish lending
in the form of 'sub-prime' mortgages in the USA – caused the loss of
several trillions of dollars and posed questions which, at the time of
writing, Western finance ministers are still trying to solve.

EXAMPLE: MANAGING THE ECONOMY

As Chapter 4 on the social and economic context emphasised, much
of politics is about the economy. This should not be surprising in a
democracy, as most people's primary concern is with material things
like their job, income, housing: Bill Clinton's slogan in his successful
1992 presidential campaign was 'It's the economy, stupid', designed
to exploit the fact that stewardship of the economy under George
Bush Senior had produced a recession. Ensuring that prosperity is
delivered to the people is the *sine qua non* of most democratic government. Policy has to overcome the disadvantages Britain suffers
economically.

- *Geography.* As a small island, Britain lacks good land communications with Europe and any substantial natural resources, apart from coal.
- *History.* As the first industrial power, Britain was able to establish a position of hegemony in the nineteenth century which was reinforced by its imperial role. But competitors soon caught up and were able to utilise modern equipment to narrow the gap with the 'workshop of the world'. During the two world wars Britain had to sell and realise huge assets to survive and ended up in 1945 virtually bankrupt. Moreover, once the Empire imploded after World War II a valuable cushion for the economy was removed.
- *Culture.* Britain's dominant class, even when its wealth has been founded in manufacturing or trade, has tended to disdain such activity and to value the arts as a profession or the countryside as a place to live.
- *Politics.* After World War II, Labour produced a massive public sector which disadvantaged private enterprise. Furthermore, successive governments changed approaches to economic management.
- *Economics.* Britain suffered from poor industrial relations after the war, poor productivity and poor design compared with competitors like Germany, Japan, Sweden and Italy. There was also a tendency for investment in future industrial activity to be inadequate.

TWO APPROACHES TO MANAGING THE ECONOMY

Since 1945 there have been two major approaches to managing the economy: Keynesianism and monetarism.

KEYNESIANISM

Maynard Keynes, in his *General Theory of Employment, Interest and Money* (1936), argued that the best way to deal with recessions was, counter-intuitively, to spend and not save. He argued that the government could stimulate economic activity in this way, thereby creating demand and employment. He argued that interest rates (monetary policy) and taxation (fiscal policy) could be used to manage the economy, to control demand and stave off the slumps which had traditionally followed booms. This approach was initially regarded as heresy by traditional economists and Treasury mandarins but the war seemed to legitimise it and by 1945 it had become the orthodoxy followed by both major parties. However, when growth began to slow in an economy failing to stand up to the competition, government spending seemed to coincide with galloping inflation rather than the desired growth. This presaged the emergence of a new approach.

MONETARISM

This analysis, formulated most famously by the Chicago economist Professor Milton Friedman, argued that inflation was the product of too much money circulating in the economy. The theory is that if business people and workers know the money is there, the former will push up prices for their products while the latter will demand more for their labour. The antidote to inflation therefore is to increase interest rates, to make money more expensive to borrow and thus less present in the economy: reducing 'money supply' therefore reduces inflation. After the runaway inflation of the mid-1970s, Labour chancellor Dennis Healey came to accept this equation but less enthusiastically than Conservative converts like Enoch Powell, Sir Keith Joseph, Margaret Thatcher and her chancellor, Nigel Lawson.

When the Conservatives came to power in 1979, this approach was applied more fully than under Healey. Monetarism combined with cutting back or restricting public spending caused widespread bankruptcies and unemployment but it did eventually make the British economy more efficient and, by the early 1990s, Labour dropped its vehement opposition and came to accept the Thatcherite approach to the economy, while still rejecting totally the concomitant attitudes towards public spending. So important was the control of interest rates in curbing inflation for Brown that, immediately on coming into power in 1997, he gave this responsibility to an independent Bank of England, advised by an expert, non-political committee called the Monetary Policy Committee.

THE INSTRUMENTS OF MANAGEMENT

Governments do their best to control the economy to make it perform more effectively. Available to them are a number of instruments (see also Table 16.1):

Table 16.1 Economic measures that governments can adjust

	Up	**Down**
Exchange rates	Reduces inflation. But makes exports more expensive	Makes exports cheaper. But increases inflation
Interest rates	Makes borrowing money more expensive so reduces amount of money in economy. This reduces inflation. But it makes survival for some companies harder, resulting in bankruptcies and unemployment	Makes it cheaper for businesses to borrow and thus improves investment. But can cause inflation
Taxes	More revenue into Treasury; anti-inflationary; selective use can discourage undesirable spending e.g. on smoking. But upsets voters	Pleases voters. But reduces revenue, can be inflationary and increases consumer spending
Public spending	Increases employment, improves public services, pleases voters. But increases taxation which displeases voters, worries overseas investors	Reduces taxation, which pleases voters. But increases unemployment, public services suffer, voters unhappy
Employment laws ('up' = favour workers; 'down' = favour business)	Unions happy. But business costs increase, loss of competitiveness	Business happy, unions not, costs decrease, competitiveness improves

- *Fiscal measures.* They can adjust direct or indirect taxation to achieve objectives like raising revenue or discouraging certain activities like those causing pollution.
- *Monetary measures.* Controlling interest rates is the key instrument, as they determine the amount of money available through lending, the major means whereby business is financed and sustained.
- *Stimulating trade.* Governments can encourage economic activity by encouraging trade deals with foreign countries.

- *Support and subsidies.* These can be handed out to sections of the economy which either are in trouble or require assistance to develop.
- *National infrastructure.* Improving this in terms of, for example, transport or IT capacity can stimulate economic activity and produce efficiency savings.

WHO MAKES ECONOMIC POLICY?

Clearly, as the most important area of the policy-making 'community', this will involve the prime minister, the chancellor, members of the core executive like the top officials in the Treasury, close economic advisers (Brown relied much on Ed Balls for such advice when chancellor) and the governor of the Bank of England. Inputs will also be received from connections with the European Union, Washington and other international bodies, like the World Bank

Relations between prime minister and chancellor are always crucial. Thatcher treated Geoffrey Howe disrespectfully, for example, and paid for it by alienating him in November 1990 when her sources of support had begun to ebb. Blair endured 10 years of constant tension with Gordon Brown, who was intent on taking his place in number 10. As part of this tension they disagreed over joining the euro; Blair was generally in favour but Brown so opposed he defined five tests to be met before joining could be contemplated.

QUESTIONS FOR DISCUSSION

1. Which policy-making model seems closest to how policy is really made?
2. Consider, in turn, the contribution made to policy-making by: the media, pressure groups and civil servants.
3. How easily can government direct the development of the economy?

FURTHER READING

Certainly the best contemporary study of policy-making is Dorey (2014). More dated but still useful texts include Parsons (1995), Wildavsky (1979) and Hogwood (1992).

Burch, M. and Wood, B. (1990) *Public Policy in Britain*, Martin Robertson.

Castles, F. (1982) *The Impact of Parties*, Sage.

Dorey, P. (2014) *Policy Making in Britain* (2nd edition), Sage.

Downs, A. (1957) *An Economic Theory of Democracy*, Harper and Row.

Easton, D. (1965) *A Framework for Political Analysis*, Prentice Hall.

Ham, C. and Hill, M. (1998) *The Policy Process of a Modern Capitalist State*, Wheatsheaf.

Hogwood, B. (1992) *Trends in British Public Policy*, Open University Press.

Jordan, G. and Richardson, J. J. (1987) *Governing Under Pressure*, Martin Robertson.

Lees-Marchment, J. (2001) *Political Marketing and British Political Parties*, Manchester University Press.

Lindblom, C. (1959) The science of muddling through, *Public Administration Review*, 19(2): 79–88.

Parsons, W. (1995) *Public Policy*, Elgar.

Schmitter, P. C. (1977) Introduction, *Corporatism and Policy-Making in Western Europe*, special issue of *Contemporary Political Studies*, 10(1): 3–6.

Smith, M. (1993) *Pressure, Power and Policy*, Harvester Wheatsheaf.

Wildavsky, A. (1979) *Speaking the Truth to Power*, Little, Brown.

WEBSITES

Demos (think-tank): http://www.demos.co.uk.

NO2ID (campaigning organisation): http://www.no2id.net.

Prime minister's office: https://www.gov.uk/government/organisations/prime-ministers-office-10-downing-street.

SUB-NATIONAL GOVERNMENT

This level of government is mostly defined as what happens outside London. Accordingly Part VI comprises chapters on devolution, local government and the judiciary.

DEVOLUTION

One fairly obvious reform of a highly centralised state would be to devolve power down to regional or local units. During the years 1997–99 this is precisely what happened in the UK but the motive behind it was not so much governing efficiency but recognising national identity. Acts of Union in 1536, 1707 and 1800 had apparently set in stone the adherence of Wales, Scotland and Ireland to England, within the United Kingdom. But these unions – solid on the surface – in reality were being eroded by the forces of nationalism.

In the thirteenth century Edward I had defeated the armies of the Welsh but not their sense of who they were or their resentment at being a subordinate people. Scotland was never conquered in the same way as Wales and the 1707 union was engineered – some Scots believe they were hoodwinked by the English – for economic and politically strategic reasons. However, Scotland was able to retain its own church, legal and education systems, significantly more than Wales had managed. Ireland's independent history went back centuries, to the days of the *High Kings*, but Henry II's invasion in 1172 made Ireland a vassal state of England, to be characterised by absentee landlords and frequent rebellions harshly suppressed. The mostly calm surface of the United Kingdom in the nineteenth and twentieth centuries concealed, at its peripheries, a history of bloody conquest, imperial domination and seething nationalist resentments.

The feeling that Scotland required more detailed attentions from London had been reflected in 1885 when the Scottish Office was set up. The Welsh office appeared much later, in 1965. Both Offices are headed by a cabinet minister. The Northern Ireland Office was created March 1972, in the wake of the Troubles, when the functions of Stormont were directly administered from London.

NORTHERN IRELAND

Ireland was the first to insist on reinstating its independence. When rebellion proved futile, Ireland was able to use its representation in the House of Commons after 1800 to advance its case for home rule. The Irish MPs caused so much turbulence that Liberal Prime Minister Gladstone became confused and frustrated before finally converting to their cause. The outbreak of war in 1914 destroyed the delivery of what might have proved home rule but the harsh British reaction to the 1916 Easter Rising in Dublin ensured there was instead an armed conflict, although that did eventually bring Britain to the negotiating table. Protestants in Northern Ireland proved so formidable in their own right that a partition was granted in 1920 allowing six northern counties to continue as part of the UK. The Catholics in the new province were outnumbered two to one by the Protestants, who used the power of their majority in the devolved provincial government of Stormont to marginalise the Catholics and advantage their own 'tribe'.

The protests of the Catholics in the late 1960s morphed rapidly into the sectarian violence of 'the Troubles', set to last three decades and cost some 3500 lives. The element of violence made Ireland an especially urgent case of governance but the threat of even more helped delay any settlement until the combined efforts of John Major and Tony Blair produced the Good Friday Agreement, of 10 April 1998. This set up the Northern Ireland Assembly, once again in Stormont Castle, to which 108 members were to be elected according to proportional representation to ensure a higher degree of reflection than in the rest of the UK of the province's differing and volatile elements. In June 1998 the first elections made David Trimble's Ulster Unionists the biggest party and him the 'first minister'. His education secretary was Sinn Fein's Martin McGuinness, formerly closely connected with the Provisional IRA and rumoured to be a major player in the infamous Derry incident in January 1972, later dubbed 'Bloody Sunday'.

Trimble found himself under great pressure as a representative of the Protestant majority from Ian Paisley, leader of the hard-line Democratic Unionist Party (DUP, who maintained too many concessions had been made to the nationalists and that the IRA should disarm fully. The election results in November 2003 reflected a new polarity, with the DUP and Sinn Fein greatly strengthened. Much to the political world's surprise, the implacable foe of Catholicism, the 80-year-old Paisley, and the leaders of Sinn Fein seemed to generate a new understanding from this electoral impasse. On 8 May 2007, Paisley became first minister with McGuinness his deputy; in June the following year, the latter remained in post when Peter Robinson succeeded the retired Paisley.

DEVOLUTION IN THE 1970s

NATIONALIST PARTIES' ORIGINS

John Saunders Lewis established Plaid Cymru (Party of Wales) in 1925. Initially, its prime concern was to promote the Welsh language but during the 1930s home rule was added to the list of the party's objectives. Gwynfor Evans gained the party's first seat in 1966, with two more added in 1974.

The Scottish National Party (SNP) was founded by John MacCormick in 1934, declaring from the outset that Scotland could and should raise its own taxes and pay its own way. The discovery of North Sea oil off the Scottish coast strengthened SNP demands that 'Scottish oil' should benefit the Scots rather than the UK as a whole. The SNP won its first seat in 1967 and then a relative avalanche: 11 more in 1974.

KILBRANDON REPORT

Nationalist stirrings led the Labour government in 1969 to set up the Royal Commission on the Constitution under Lord Kilbrandon. Independence and a federal structure were both rejected as solutions in favour of devolved legislatures with authority over domestic affairs. It was hoped these limited concessions to nationalist feeling would draw its sting, neutralise calls for independence and any threat to the Union's viability. However, the referendum for a Welsh assembly was heavily defeated and the Scottish one, though returning a majority, was below the stipulation – established by opponents during the passing of the relevant bill – that it exceed 40% of the electorate.

Devolution as an issue then took a back seat during the 1980s, though Margaret Thatcher's very uncompromising English style of rule did nothing to reduce nationalists' enthusiasm for their cause. Labour and Liberal Democrats cooperated over the need for devolution and when Blair's landslide arrived in 1997 the necessary referendums and other legislation were quickly passed (Box 17.1).

Box 17.1   Powers of the devolved assemblies

Scottish Parliament

This was established in 1999 at Holyrood. There is a four-year term. Elections use a 'mixed member proportional representation' system, sometimes known as 'amended additional member system', based on the German system; this allocates two votes to each voter. One vote goes to help elect the 73 Members of the Scottish Parliament (MSPs) from geographical constituencies on first past the post (FPTP), while the other helps elect 56 from the 'top-up' pool to achieve the proportionality FPTP seldom delivers. The latter is via party lists with seats going according to the percentages achieved. So voters vote for a person with one vote and a party with the other.

The Scottish Parliament has the right to pass primary legislation on: home affairs and the judiciary, health, housing and local government, farming and fishing, social services and implementing European Union (EU) directives. It also has the option to adjust income tax by plus or minus three pence in the pound.

The powers reserved by London are in the areas of employment law, economic and monetary policy, social security benefits and pensions, passports and immigration, dealings with the EU and foreign policy.

National Assembly for Wales

The 60 Assembly Members (AMs) sit in the Senedd, in Cardiff. Forty AMs are elected from single-member constituencies and 20 from regional lists, on the same basis as in Scotland.

The Welsh Assembly lacks the ability to pass primary legislation but can pass secondary legislation to amend the former. Supporters of the Assembly campaign for the same powers as Scotland. In practice, however, certain important financial adjustments have been made: prescription charges have been abolished; tuition fees for Welsh students studying in Wales have been reduced; and there is more generous provision of nursing care.

The Assembly has powers and responsibilities over: agriculture, fire services, economic development, environment, food, health, transport, local government, sport, town and country planning. The Government of Wales Act 2006 became law on 25 July 2006. It gave the Assembly powers similar to other the devolved legislatures. However, Assembly order-in-council requests – a form of direct government fiat – is subject to veto by the secretary of state for Wales and the House of Commons or the House of Lords.

Northern Ireland Assembly

This was established following the 1998 Good Friday Agreement. It meets at Stormont Castle and has 108 members elected according to the single transferable vote system of proportional representation, chosen for its ability to fully represent all the communities in the province. Members are known as Members of the Legislative Assembly (MLAs). The Assembly has the power of appointing the executive but this has been suspended, with authority handed back to the Northern Ireland Office, on more than one occasion (when this happened in October 2002, full power was not restored until 8 May 2007).

The first and deputy first ministers are elected by a cross-community vote, while the remainder of the ministers are appointed to parties in accordance with their elected strengths. The powers which Westminster retains are divided into 'excepted matters', which are permanently excluded from the Assembly, and 'reserved' matters, which may be transferred at some future date.

Laws which are in conflict with the powers of the Assembly, EU law or the European Convention of Human Rights can be struck down and if the secretary of state for Northern Ireland judges a bill which has passed through the Assembly violates its constitutional powers, he or she can refuse to pass it upwards for royal assent.

Transferred matters are: education, health, agriculture, enterprise, trade and investment, environment, regional development (including transport), employment, finance, social development, and culture, arts and leisure.

'Reserved matters' are: navigation and civil aviation, international trade and financial markets, telecommunications/postage, the foreshore and sea bed, disqualification from Assembly membership, consumer safety and intellectual property.

'Excepted matters' are: royal succession, international relations, defence and armed forces, nationality, immigration and asylum, taxes levied across the United Kingdom as a whole, appointment of senior judges, all elections held in Northern Ireland, currency, and the conferring of honours.

SCOTLAND

The referendum in September 1997 delivered a hefty 3–1 majority in favour of a Scottish Parliament together with a slightly smaller majority endorsing the chamber's competence to vary tax levels by a small degree. The first elections were held in May 1999, after which a Labour–Liberal Democrat coalition emerged and survived the 2003 elections. However, in 2007 the SNP sensationally won 47 seats to Labour's 46 and ruled successfully as a minority government under its able first minister, Alex Salmond. In 2011 the SNP went even further, winning an overall majority of 69 seats and setting the SNP's sights on full Scottish independence from the UK.

WALES

In contrast to Scotland, enthusiasm for Welsh devolution was muted, with only 50.3% in favour of an assembly and 49.7% against. Support for the idea was strongest in the Welsh-speaking north and west and weakest in eastern areas adjoining England. In 1999 Labour took control of the Assembly. A year later Alun Michael, Blair's choice, was forced to resign as first minister, giving way to the popular Rhodri Morgan. After the 2007 election Labour stayed in power by virtue of a coalition made with Plaid Cymru. In 2011 Labour won power again, with 26 seats, though Plaid Cymru moved up, with 15 seats.

DEVOLUTION: RELATED PROBLEMS

- *West Lothian question*. This famous question was posed by Scottish MP Tam Dalyell in 1977 (representing West Lothian at the time): is it fair that English MPs elected to Westminster cannot have a say in the affairs of West Lothian yet possible for MPs elected from Scotland still to have a say in the affairs of West Bromwich? Critics also argue that because Labour was often dependent for its majority in the Commons on Scottish MPs, Scottish MPs are therefore doubly empowered and English MPs reduced to a lower status. Some defenders of devolution point out that this same problem was present when Ulster MPs represented their province at Westminster (voting mostly with the Conservatives) while Stormont exercised domestic jurisdiction. The whole anomaly was generally simply ignored.
- *Cabinet responsibility*. With first ministers in Belfast, Edinburgh and Cardiff, it seems unnecessary to retain secretaries of state in London. Yet these residual titles are allocated often to existing cabinet ministers, frequently with some connection to the countries concerned.
- *Proportional representation (PR)*. The PR voting systems for the devolved assemblies has greatly benefited the smaller parties (and also the Conservatives in Celtic areas) and implicitly posed the question of why Westminster retains the FPTP system. Yet on 6 May 2011, in a UK referendum on changing this system, the nation rejected it by a 2–1 majority.

- *Pressure for equal powers for Wales.* While the Scottish Parliament can pass legislation through three stages and receive the royal assent as well as adjust taxation, the Welsh Assembly can do neither.
- *Independence demands.* Devolution was designed to satisfy demands for autonomy short of independence but, with nationalist parties competing, it was always possible they might one day win power. This has happened in the case of Scotland (discussed below).
- *'Control freak' danger.* Blair's attempt to exclude Rhodri Morgan for being supposedly 'off-message' and favouring the more compliant Alun Michael reveals that devolution has an Achilles' heel: it gives away power from the centre but some leading politicians will still try to exert control over devolved institutions.

ENGLISH NATIONALISM

Often, English people like to delude themselves that they are immune from anything so vulgar as nationalism but the facts suggest otherwise. England's urge to expand was the original motor for imperialism, absorbing the Celtic periphery before looking overseas. Patriotism was encouraged by the Hundred Years War with France and nourished the sense of superiority which so irritated England's UK neighbours. Yet this nationalism has tended to be passive, seldom showing itself until external attack was threatened by the likes of Spain, France or Germany. However, a raucous form of it – flags, painted faces – is readily displayed in crowds at international sporting events.

PUBLIC SPENDING

It can also be seen in the resentment felt at the 'unfair' shares of public spending allocated to Scotland and Wales compared with England. This is a consequence of the Barnett formula, so-called because it originated with Joel Barnett, chief secretary to the Treasury in the late 1970s, who proposed its short-term use for calculating the block grants to the less prosperous regions of the UK. He confessed in 2004 that it was an 'embarrassment' that a device intended to last one year was still in operation. The proportions for 2011–14 were based on the populations relative to England: Scotland, 10.3; Wales 5.79 and Northern Ireland 3.45. The result delivers disproportionate shares of public spending, for example £1300 to Scots, per capita, yet only £1100 to residents of England.

REGIONS OF ENGLAND

John Major set up nine regions in 1994 to provide Euro-constituencies, endowing them with assemblies appointed by county and borough councils. Kilbrandon had advised the establishment of elected regional assemblies and in 1997 Blair's government set up regional development agencies to coordinate regional plans with national ones, so that regional differences would eventually be reduced. However, 'regional consciousness' varied hugely across the country. In 2004 a referendum was held for a regional assembly in the north-east, the area where regional feeling had been shown to be highest. The result was a 3–1 rejection of the idea, a humiliation for its most fervent advocate, John Prescott, the Deputy Prime Minister. However, in the wake of the Scottish referendum in September 2014, enthusiasm for devolution in England was reborn to some extent, with new powers being granted to city regions by the coalition government.

GREATER LONDON GOVERNMENT

The Greater London Council was set up in 1889 but its boundaries soon became outdated through urban overspill. In 1965 the provisions of the 1960 Herbert Commission were implemented, eliminating the old historic counties of London and Middlesex and absorbing parts of Kent, Surrey and Essex. Thirty-two boroughs were designated, plus the unchanged ancient City of London authority. Margaret Thatcher's determination to abolish the 1974 metropolitan counties was fulfilled countrywide in March 1986 and, despite a spirited left-wing rear-guard action by Ken Livingstone, in London too. In 1998, Labour, now in power, published *A Mayor and Assembly for London*, which suggested a US-style elected mayor, elected by a *supplementary vote* system, plus a 25-strong elected assembly with scrutiny powers (Box 17.2). The mayor has responsibility for transport, fire services, police, culture and economic development.

Currently, Greater London covers over 600 square miles and contains nearly 8 million people. The elected mayor represents the person with the biggest constituency in the country. Tony Blair was criticised for seeking to veto the maverick Livingstone as Labour's candidate but in May 2000 Livingstone left the party to stand as an independent and won an easy victory; in 2004, he won again (on second preferences), but this time as the Labour candidate. Livingstone's attempt at a third term was foiled by the even more maverick Conservative, Boris Johnson, who won a first term in May 2008 and a second in May 2012. In August 2014 Johnson declared he wished to stand for parliament in 2015, though he aimed to complete his mayoral term in 2016.

Box 17.2   Elections for the London Assembly and mayor

The London Assembly is led by a directly elected mayor, who serves a four-year term. In addition to the mayor's powers over budgeting, strategic planning, transport and so on further powers were granted in 2006 over planning, waste, culture, sports, climate change and appointments to the functional bodies controlling the police and so forth.

To stand as a candidate in the mayoral election requires a deposit of £10,000 (which is lost if the candidate polls less than 5% of the vote). The 'supplementary vote' system is used, whereby voters mark their first and second preferences. If no candidate receives over half the vote, second preferences are counted until the margin is reached. The mayor's annual salary in 2007 was £140, 000 (though Boris Johnson receives a £250,000 yearly commission from *The Telegraph*). Candidates for the mayoralty tend to be a bit unusual, relative outsiders, maybe, like Johnson's predecessor Ken Livingstone.

In 2000, the Conservatives gambled with another outsider, the novelist Lord (Jeffrey) Archer, but his candidacy was ended when he was tried and convicted of perjury. In 2008, Boris Johnson's victory seemed to reinforce the impression that 'outsiders' do well. The

Assembly, which has 25 members, is also elected for a four-year term, on the same day as the mayoral election, via an amended 'additional member' system (as used in German elections and in Scotland and Wales), whereby each voter has two votes, one for a constituency member and one for a regional party list. The party list seats are allocated on the basis of the percentages of the vote won by each party, with a qualifying limit of 5%. There are 14 constituencies, returning one member each, and 11 members are returned from the party list; it follows that, to be sure of being returned, candidates need to be placed high up on the party list, but the advantage of the system is that it produces a more proportional end result than the first past-the-post method. In 2012, there were 9 Conservative members of the Assembly, 12 Labour, 2 Liberal Democrats and 2 Greens.

SCOTTISH INDEPENDENCE REFERENDUM AND ITS IMPACT

On 17 December 2013, the Scottish Independence Referendum Act received the royal assent; the vote would take place on 18 September 2014. It was much commented on that that year was the 700th anniversary of Bannockburn, Scotland's famous victory over the forces of the English King, Edward II. The question put to voters? 'Should Scotland be an independent country?'

Alex Salmond's push for independence, as leader of the SNP, could not have come at a more propitious time for this, coinciding as it did with: two years of popular governing as Scottish SNP first minister; four years into an unpopular Tory-led government in London; and a policy of austerity which angered many Scots, including previously non-voting working-class Scots in poor areas of the big cities. If the SNP was going to win, they could not have chosen a better platform from which to launch their campaign.

The referendum marked, to a degree, the failure of the Kilbrandon settlement, which embodied hopes the Scots would be happy with extensive control over their domestic politics while still living within the context of a United Kingdom. Salmond had led an astute campaign, embodying independence explicitly in both his 2007 and

2011 election campaigns, governing with a high degree of public satisfaction and in consequence winning an overall majority of 69 seats out of 129 in the latter election.

On 15 November 2013, *Scotland's Future* appeared, a 670-page white paper explaining the case for independence and charting the route it might take. Salmond hailed it as the 'most comprehensive blueprint for an independent country ever published'. He maintained it showed his government sought not 'independence as an end in itself, but rather as a means to changing Scotland for the better'. The leader of the three main UK parties' 'Better Together' campaign, former Labour chancellor Alistair Darling, dismissed the astonishingly thick document as 'thick with false promises and meaningless assertions'. He spoke for all three of the Westminster-based mainstream UK parties in asserting that 'Instead of a credible and costed plan, we have a wish-list of political promises without any answers on how Alex Salmond would pay for them'.

Labour was fervently against independence, as Scotland had long been further to the left than England, returning 41 of the 59 seats available for Labour and only one for the Conservatives. Without these Scottish seats, it was felt, Labour would struggle to win a UK election. While independence would deliver an enticing political dividend for Conservatives, David Cameron was extremely keen to avoid being the leader of a government presiding over the break-up of the United Kingdom. He was careful, however, to listen responsively to his right-wing colleagues who called for a reformed House of Commons which would allow only English MPs to vote on English laws, thus disenfranchising Scottish MPs to a degree.

Salmond declared he would be happy to retain the Queen as head of state and also wished to remain part of the sterling area, as well as to keep Scotland a member of the EU. While the first possibility was happily granted, the governor of the Bank of England, as well as chancellor George Osborne, said they could not permit the second; Salmond dismissed the refusal as a bluff. The Scottish first minister's wish to remain a member of NATO while opposing nuclear weapons and the basing of Trident in Scotland was also dismissed as impossible. His similar assumption that membership of the EU would be via some kind of automatic transference was also disabused by several EU leaders. Moreover, weighty opinion formers, including US president Obama, Hillary Clinton and even the Pope, expressed degrees of hope that Scotland would not separate from the UK.

POLLS

When it came to opinion polls, the 'yes' supporters had traditionally been in a minority. Well respected psephologist Professor John Curtice estimated the 'yes' campaign's support at between 32% and 38% in January 2012. He saw the polls as stable during 2013, with the 'no' camp leading by 50% to 33% in the latter part of that year.

However, the polls narrowed in the months after the release of the Scottish government white paper on independence, with an average of five polls in December 2013 and January 2014 giving 39% support for 'yes'. It seemed that Scottish voters reacted to London-based attacks on the pro-independence arguments by warming to the 'yes' cause. Appearing to vindicate this analysis, polls again tightened after Osborne stated in February his government's opposition to a currency union, with the average 'yes' support increasing to 43%. An ICM poll, conducted for *Scotland on Sunday*, 15 June 2014, revealed 38% believing divisions would remain whatever the outcome of the poll on 18 September, compared with 36% who disagreed when asked if Scotland would be left 'badly divided'.

It also found that 42% of families were split over independence, with one-fifth of those questioned admitting that discussions with family and friends about the forthcoming referendum had degenerated into rows. On 5 August 2014 Salmond engaged in a televised debate with Alastair Darling, Scottish former Labour chancellor under Gordon Brown and leader of the 'Better Together' campaign. Most expected the wily and nimble Salmond to win easily but Darling's destructive questioning on how Salmond would react if an independent Scotland was unable to join the sterling currency area helped him win a 56–44% victory according to a post-debate ICM poll. However, Salmond came back hard in the second debate and, according to the polls, won an even bigger counter-victory.

On 7 September a YouGov poll in the *Sunday Times* put the 'yes' campaign in the lead. This suddenly galvanised the pro-Union forces. Perhaps too late in the day, the 'no' camp, guessing their case had been too rational, now repackaged it as emotional pleas to Scotland not to destroy a Union which had worked so well since 1707, but such appeals seemed to fall on deaf ears as 18 September approached. Having shunned the tripartite 'Better Together' campaign led by Darling (Cameron wisely gave Labour the leading role), Brown came out of his post-2010 purdah to barnstorm around his country, passionately extolling the benefits of the Union, delivering the best speech of the campaign on 17 September; it concluded with 'What we have built together, by sacrificing and sharing, let no narrow nationalism split asunder ever'.

If anyone could firm up the fragmenting Labour vote, he could. He promised a full devolution of extra powers if the 'no' side won, plus retention of the much-criticised Barnett formula: 'devo max', in effect.

RESULTS, 19 SEPTEMBER

On a turnout of 85%, the 'yes' vote was 44.70% (1.6 million), the 'no' vote 55.30% (2.0 million).

Cameron ignored the advice phoned through by Darling at 5.00 am on the day after polling to avoid partisan politics and announced progress towards Scotland's new devolved state would be accompanied by plans to devolve powers to achieve 'English votes on English laws': a flagrantly partisan response, likely to delay the promised Scottish deal indefinitely. Salmond cried betrayal and, warming to his theme, the SNP's membership grew rapidly to just under 100,000 by the end of the year. What is more, polls showed the party would be likely to take over 20 of the 41 Labour Scottish seats in the 2015 general election (in the event, it took 40).

A House of Commons Library Analysis, 23 September 2014, confirmed that the key correlations in voting support for the 'yes' campaign, identified in prior polling surveys, were: the poorest; those previously supporting the SNP (though with some exceptions, like the local authority area of Eilean Siar, highest SNP vote share in the 2014 Euro-elections but a 7% win for 'no' in the referendum); those over 65; and those born elsewhere in the UK.

Even with three days to go to the vote, 'don't knows' still numbered some 15%, so there was still much to play for right down to the wire. The results of the referendum began to feed in after midnight. The first results revealed a small lead for the 'no's and experts were predicting a likely 'no' victory, but then 'yes' won North Lanarkshire and Dundee to warm nationalist hearts and there were huge cheers in their headquarters when Glasgow voted decisively 'yes'. But apart from West Dunbartonshire, the 'no's began to take district after district until deputy first minister Nicola Sturgeon had to concede defeat around 5.20 am, followed shortly afterwards by Alex Salmond himself. Maybe Brown's intervention, plus that catalysing rogue *Sunday Times* poll, had been crucial in those final days but the margin in the event was substantial rather than the predicted whisker.

THE SIGNIFICANCE OF THE 'NO' RESULT

1. The 'no' victory at 55–45% was decisive, much bigger – by 7% – than the later polls had indicated, suggesting intending 'no' voters were shy of admitting it to pollsters. The Scots and the UK as a whole clearly wanted to stay united; the 'no' camp hoped this vote had stilled the noise for a decade; Salmond initially suggested there would not be another attempt for a 'generation'. However, as SNP membership burgeoned and great enthusiasm was maintained, the possibility returned of another referendum in the near future; polls at the end of 2014 suggested the SNP would win such a vote.
2. The 'yes' vote, at 1.6 million, was still substantial, indicating a great deal of dissatisfaction with current constitutional arrangements and the way political parties operate.
3. The huge turnout – 85% – was so much bigger than any previous one that it put to shame the general election turnouts in the UK as a whole; it was 21 points higher than the 2010 election and 35 higher than the 2011 Scottish Parliament one. As the energy of the 'yes' campaign flowed south of the border, it seemed clear a major rearrangement of the UK, involving much devolution, was required. But the chances of this happening should not be overestimated: the status quo is very resilient on Britain – look at how the banking meltdown of 2008–09 has not really caused any major changes.

4.   Voices in England – mainly Tory MPs on the right – demanded equal powers for England in the wake of the result, linking the delivery of the two. But while the Scottish part was scheduled for January 2015, the English part was seen as a bigger problem, as Labour sees 'English votes on English issues' as ceding hegemony to the Conservatives for the indefinite future.

5.   The vigour of the referendum campaign was transferred into the 2015 general election and helped the SNP win 56 seats, making it the third largest party in the Commons. Nicola Sturgeon felt able in early September 2015 to warn Cameron, playing on his fear the United Kingdom might break up on his watch, that if his policies were too objectionable to Scottish voters, the SNP might call for another referendum. Cameron may have freed himself of the constraints of his former coalition partner, but the SNP was keen to flag up its own ability to constrain.

QUESTIONS FOR DISCUSSION

1.   Is there a strong argument for a federal structure for the UK?
2.   Is Scottish independence inevitable?
3.   Should all the English regions be given extensive devolved powers?

FURTHER READING

For an interesting take on devolution see Bulpitt (1983); for a more up-to-date analysis see Deacon (2006, 2012). On referendums see Quotrup (2005). An outstanding article by Simon Jenkins on devolution to Manchester and its region brokered by George Osborne and the city chief executive, Howard Bernstein, appeared in *The Guardian* on 12 February 2015.

Bradbury, J. (2009) *Devolution, Regionalism and Regional Development*, Routledge.
Bulpitt, J. (1983) *Territory and Power in the United Kingdom*, Manchester University Press.
Deacon, R. (2006) *Devolution in Britain Today*, Manchester University Press.
Deacon, R. (2012) *Devolution in the United Kingdom* (Politics Study Guides), Edinburgh University Press.
Lodge, G. and Schmuecker, K. (2010) *Devolution in Practice: Policy Differences in the UK*, IPPR.

Mitchell, J. (2011) *Devolution in the United Kingdom*, Manchester University Press.

Quotrup, M. (2005) *A Comparative Study of Referendums*, Manchester University Press.

Smith, A. (2014) *Devolution and the Scottish Conservatives* (New Ethnographies), Manchester University Press.

WEBSITES

Northern Ireland Assembly: http://www.niassembly.gov.uk.
Scottish Parliament: http://www.scottish.parliament.uk.
Welsh Assembly: http://gov.wales.

18

LOCAL GOVERNMENT: PROVENANCE AND DECLINE

PROVENANCE

Local government in feudal times could virtually be defined as how lords of the manor chose to run their estates. Administrative units of 'county', 'borough' and 'parish' date back to Norman times, when justice – an important element of local governance – was dispensed via the county assizes, which also raised militias or defensive forces. From the late seventeenth century 'improvement commissioners' were appointed to attend to paving and lighting, financed by local rates. From 1600 the Poor Law obliged parishes to look after the poor and indigent via an 'overseer for the poor'; from 1723 'work-houses' were set up to accommodate those unable to care for them-selves, though the 'care' provided was scarcely worth the name by modern standards.

Local government burgeoned during the nineteenth century, in response to the Industrial Revolution; this created acute problems of poverty, health, sanitation, law and order and transport. Hundreds of thousands had moved into the cities from the countryside, often crammed into appalling damp and inadequate accommoda-tion, several families together. Inevitably it had to be central gov-ernment which took the structural initiative. The 1834 Poor Law

Amendment Act set up boards of guardians to run a new kind of workhouse, though arguably no less harsh in its regime. In 1835 the Municipal Corporations Act required members of town councils – many of which had become self-perpetuating oligarchies – to be elected by ratepayers and for annual accounts to be published. A third of councillors were to be up for re-election each year and aldermen elected from within the council for a six-year term. Later councils formed ad hoc boards to run services like health, highways, transport and education.

The 1888 Local Government Act set up 62 new elected councils plus 61 county boroughs (these last being 'unitary', administering all functions) in England and Wales. In 1894 further complexity was added with 535 urban district and 472 rural district councils, plus 270 non-county borough councils (with fewer powers).

After these measures and the 1929 measure transferring Poor Law guardian powers to local government, the next four decades were virtually free from structural change. This allowed local government to develop its functions and acquire new roles and responsibilities; this is reputed to be local government's 'golden age', when it antici-pated much of what later became the 'welfare state': hospital care, child health, road provision, gas electricity and public libraries. However, the time came when population overspill across local authority bor-ders reached the point when more structural reform was needed.

The complexity of the ageing system, moreover, with 1400 sepa-rate authorities, was such that a complete overhaul was overdue. Redcliffe-Maud's 1969 report recommended a nationwide pattern of unitary authorities. However, Heath's Conservative government feared this would play into the hands of Labour, which dominated urban areas. Consequently, a 'two tier' system was introduced with different (and more important) functions performed at the 'shire county' level than at the 'district' ones.

The Local Government Act 1972 was a huge rationalisation of the patchwork pattern of local government. County councils were reduced to 47, with 334 constituent district ones. A new kind of urban form of local government was also established: six metropoli-tan counties and their constituent 36 district councils. Bigger units would create efficiencies of scale and clarify the system for voters, who tended to ignore their councils and neglect to vote in their elections. However, many voters were bewildered by the removal of what little they had understood about the old system and bigger units meant town halls were further away rather than nearer. See Figure 18.1 for the structure of local government after the 1972 Act, and for its functions Table 18.1.

POST-WAR DECLINE

If the early and mid-twentieth century was local government's golden age, its history since World War II has largely been one of decline.

Firstly, funding: as the range of services expanded, standards were raised, but the yield of local taxes fell away, and local government was forced to look to central government for the extra cash. By the end of the twentieth century funding which originated at the centre – including business rates set in Whitehall – was over three-quarters of the whole. The 'council tax' now provides only 20% of

Table 18.1 Funtion of local authorities

Function	County	District	Unitary
Education	★		★
Housing		★	★
Social Services	★		★
Highways	★	★	★
Transport	★		
Museums and art galleries	★	★	★
Libraries	★		★
Planning		★	★
Strategic planning	★		★
Economic development	★	★	★
Recreation, parks, sports facilities	★	★	★
Weights and measures	★		★
Food and health inspection	★		★
Cemeteries		★	★
Markets		★	★

Source: Jones, B. and Kavanagh, D. (1994) *British Politics Today* (5th edition), Manchester University Press (p. 201).

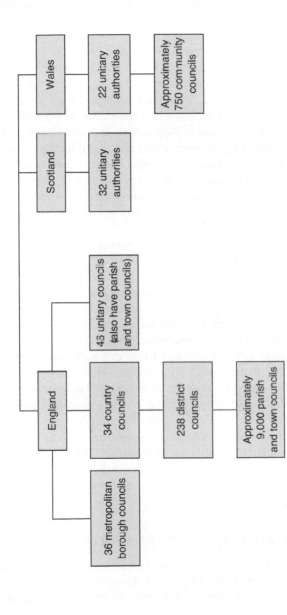

Figure 18.1 Structure of local government

Source: Jones, B. and Kavanagh, D. (1994) *British Politics Today* (5th edition), Manchester University Press (p. 200).

the whole, leaving local government very much in the supplicant role regarding its dealings with the centre.

Secondly, the loss of function: local government has seen a wide raft of its functions stripped away since 1945. Provision of gas and electricity disappeared at that time as well as hospitals, as the National Health Service (NHS) came into being. Then senior criminal courts were lost (1973), water and sewage (1974), ambulances (1974) and elements of education like the polytechnics (1989) and colleges of further education (1993), not to mention police and fire services (1986 onwards), airports (1987) and the million plus council houses, sold to tenants during the 1980s. Local government retains responsibility for education but its control is limited; for example, the national curriculum now determines what has to be taught in schools and school budgets have been handed over, in many cases, to the schools themselves.

Thirdly, fragmentation: as central government became impatient with local government, it began to intervene, establishing agencies more independent of the existing structures, like urban development corporations to stimulate urban renewal or the variety of government-appointed quangos (see glossary) to take care of functions once performed by local government, like local training.

Finally, 'contracting out': this began with the Thatcher government in the early 1980s. Convinced that privately owned business was more efficient than the public sector, Thatcher insisted local councils put an ever-growing list of functions out to private tender so that they could be contracted out at lower cost to private concerns. Many disputed that greater efficiency was the result and former municipal employees found their new private employers paid less and on less generous terms of employment. This shift tended to remove front-line activities from the control of local government and make them more into 'enabling authorities', issuing contracts and monitoring progress.

THATCHER AND LOCAL GOVERNMENT

Margaret Thatcher's period in power saw a virtual war being waged against local government. The Local Government Planning and Land Act 1980 was the one which ordered the contracting out of functions; urban development corporations facilitated redevelopment free of the shackles of local government controls. The Local Government Finance Act 1982 set up the Audit Commission, tasked usefully with monitoring expenditure in a wide range of public agencies. The Rates Act 1984 introduced 'rate-capping'. Over half of local authorities' funding came from central government, so local government had tried to raise rates to compensate for government cuts. Controlling the legal framework as well as funding, central government was able to squeeze local government with impunity.

With the 1985 Local Government Act, Thatcher was able to abolish the Labour-dominated metropolitan county councils and later Ken Livingstone led the Greater London Council (GLC). Labour hoped for a backlash against such arbitrary dismantling of the constitution but the fact was, apart from the GLC, few missed the loss of the metropolitan counties. Perhaps buoyed up by her astonishing success, electorally and militarily, Thatcher over-reached herself with her next attack on local government, the 'poll tax'.

The Local Government Act 1988 installed the 'community charge', or, as it was popularly known, the 'poll tax'. Thatcher had long hated the way the property-based 'rates' were paid disproportionately by the better-off while poorer people received discounts or exemptions. Politically this meant that Conservative voters – who favoured low rates – tended also to be the biggest payers of them, while Labour – which advocated high rates to fund high levels of service – was supported by people who often paid no rates at all. This was 'power without responsibility' argued the Tories and the community charge was designed to distribute responsibility to every voter in the country. It was a flat charge payable by everyone, though discounts were available to students and others. The theory was that once voters realised they had responsibility for charge levels, they would vote to keep it low and that all parties would compete to keep it low as well; thus would Tory policy be served.

Theory was one thing, practice another. The tax was expensive to collect, many avoided registering for it in the first place, and some well publicised rebels refused to pay. The basic problem was the regressive nature of the charge; it required the char lady to pay as much as the Duke of Westminster and this was widely seen as plainly unfair. In the spring of 1990 demonstrations against the tax spilled over into riots and this further weakened a premier whose imperious style had thoroughly tested the patience of her party. The European Union was the immediate cause of her departure but few failed to recognise the major role played by her stubborn insistence that the poll tax was both a fair and an efficient means of raising local revenue.

THE PROFESSIONAL IN LOCAL GOVERNMENT

At Westminster, the tradition has been for elected ministers to be advised by civil servants who are *generalist* in their talents and outlook (see Chapter 15): the theory is that someone educated to a high level, whether it be classics or history, is as well able to advise a chancellor as any economist. Such an approach was criticised in the Fulton report and to some extent ameliorated in practice, but the theory still has its supporters. In local government, on the other hand, such an approach has never been dominant. Councils are concerned with sewers and roads and buildings and have never had any doubts about employing appropriately qualified architects, lawyers, engineers or town planners. Councillors are advised not by 'Sir Humphrey' types but by hard-bitten professionals with long years of experience in local government. This means that management of local government tends to be conducted by elites, comprising senior elected members in close alliance with their professionalised chief officers. Some claim that local government is more efficient than central government, citing its ability to maintain good front-line services after 2010, even after suffering budget cuts of over 40%.

FURTHER REFORMS

The Local Government Finance Act 1992, conceived by Thatcher's partial nemesis, Michael Heseltine, shifted the basis of local government taxation back to property. Houses were categorised and payments made basically according to house values. As richer people tended to live in bigger houses, this seemed much fairer and instantly removed a huge public animus against the government of the day.

The two tier system of allocating functions had proved confusing and less efficient than the 'unitary' (all purpose) county authorities.

Labour had always favoured Redcliffe-Maud's unitary authorities, as its strength lay in urban centres. The Conservatives, with strength in the shires, went for the two-tier approach, with the top tier controlling the bigger spending functions. However, this preference was reversed by the mid 1990s, with the Major government coming around to the view that unitary authorities were the clearer, more efficient and accountable option. Major's Local Government Commission was tasked with reviewing local government structures, under its chair, Sir John Banham. However, Banham refused to impose the unitary solution uniformly, preferring retention of the two-tier approach in some localities. His successor proved more compliant but by 1998 only 46 unitary authorities had been formed: some way short of uniformity.

Reforms in Scotland and Wales emphatically adopted the unitary model. County and districts in Wales were replaced in 1994 by 22 unitaries, while Scotland's regional and district councils gave way to 32 unitaries (Table 18.2). The Local Government Act (Northern Ireland), back in 1972, had set up 26 district councils, replacing the

Table 18.2 Summary of local government structure

Type of authority	Number of bodies
Two-tier structure	
County councils	27
District councils	201
All-purpose authorities	
English unitary authorities	55
Metropolitan districts	36
London boroughs	32
Scottish unitary authorities	32
Welsh unitary authorities	22
City of London	1
Isles of Scilly	1
Total	179
England Wales and Scotland total	407
Northern Ireland district councils	26
Grand total	433

tiered system bestowed upon the whole of Ireland (when it was part of the UK) back in 1898. Naturally, local government in these areas comes under the control of the relevant elected assembly and not central, Westminster government in London.

PARISH COUNCILS

There are about 8700 of these, the smallest units of local government; they are related to original church parishes but are civil, not religious. They are more common in rural rather than urban areas but since 1997 150 new councils have been established. The councils are served by some 70,000 councillors, 80% of them serving populations of less than 2500. Their funding is often only a few thousand pounds, gathered via a precept on the council tax. Functions performed include things like youth activities, transport for the elderly, burial activities, play schemes, footpaths and litter collection. Surprisingly, perhaps, parish councils employ 25,000 people and spend £400 million per annum. Often these small units group together to provide services – like transport – over a wider area; many also share the services of the same parish council clerk. On 15 February 2008 the government announced that from that day local councils would be able to create town and parish councils without seeking permission from the government. Town and parish councils vary in size and function considerably, serving populations from 100 right up to 70,000. A 'town council' is a council representing a parish but which chooses to call itself a town council. The idea of the initiative is to give councils the chance to create smaller units, closer to the public, which can operate more quickly and efficiently than normal councils.

ABOLITION OF THE AUDIT COMMISSION

The Audit Commission, a Thatcher-inspired innovation, was held to be too expensive by the coalition government formed in May 2010, though the decision to abolish it was much criticised as many judged it to be a useful guarantor of efficient practice. It was announced that the Commission's functions would be transferred to the voluntary, not-for-profit or private sector. Despite this early announcement, closure did not occur until 1 April 2015.

ELECTED MAYORS

This has probably been the major new political life-form introduced in local government over the past decade. The idea originated most obviously in the US, where it is common for an elected mayor to be granted substantial powers to run a town or city efficiently and peacefully, using leadership skills and energies. The New York mayoralty is probably the best-known example to British people and it offered a striking contrast to the largely ceremonial role this office has represented in the past on this side of the Atlantic.

It was first taken up by the Conservative, Michael Heseltine, when he was at the Department for the Environment; it was an idea that appealed to someone who personally believed a strong leader could transform a situation if given the authority to do so. New Labour took up the idea, Tony Blair possibly being of the same mind and personality as the Conservative cabinet minister. The fact was that executive structures in local government were not especially effective. Functions used to be run by large committees with the chairperson wielding a great deal of power. A report by Sir John Bains in 1972 urged the reduction in the number of committees running things and recommended that a central committee be formed to coordinate activities, which would include committee chairs. This was not unlike a cabinet for local government and many councils adopted the model during succeeding decades.

The 2000 Local Government Act sought to change decision-making structures in local government by obliging all councils with over 85,000 population to choose from three alternatives:

1. a directly elected mayor
2. a mayor and a council manager
3. an indirectly elected leader and cabinet.

It may seem surprising that the third option proved the most popular, but the fact is that it came closest to existing structures, influenced by Bains several decades earlier. The idea here was for the ruling group in a council to elect its leader as leader of the council, who thereupon would select up to nine colleagues to form a cabinet (in the event of a 'no overall control' council, the make-up of the cabinet would change). This was more or less what happened before, so many councillors felt comfortable with it and distrusted the directly elected mayor, whose provenance seemed to bestow an over-mighty legitimacy, and, by comparison, reduced their own importance. Copus questions the rationality of this attitude as the powers of both the elected mayor and the indirectly elected leader are nearly identical (Copus, 2014: p. 577).

The elected mayor was to be chosen via the supplementary vote, the system used to elect the London mayor, ensuring that the winner receives a majority of votes cast. The cause of the councillors' caution at such a proposal can be appreciated by the role such a publicly elected official would perform. As the highly visible 'first citizen', elected mayors would have a mandate to lead, to form a policy framework, prepare the budget and drive ideas through the council. Moreover, the directly elected mayor would have a legal status as the head of the executive, with councillors relegated to a 'legislative' checking role. Given that the 'leader and cabinet' model requires councillors to provide a separate 'legislative' form of opposition, it will be made more difficult, in that the majority group will have produced the council's leader and their support is likely to blunt any 'opposition' they might deliver.

The 2000 Act required councils to consult with voters via referendums but voters have not been especially excited by the idea. Of the 51 referendums up to May 2013 only 16 have said yes: Watford, Doncaster, Liverpool, Leicester, Copeland, Bristol, London, Tower Hamlets, North Tyneside, Middlesbrough, Newham, Bedford, Hackney, Mansfield, Salford and Torbay. Referendums are initiated by a resolution in council, by a local petition or intervention by central government. The average 'yes' vote has been 45%, with turnout around 30%. There have been four referendums on removing the post of elected mayor: in consequence two have been abolished and two retained.

Elections took place in May and October 2002 and produced some surprising results, in that of the 11 mayors elected, four were independents. The mayor of Hartlepool, Stuart Drummond, was the local football team's monkey-suit mascot; in office he proved to be a committed and, by all accounts, competent official, being re-elected in 2009; in 2012 the Labour group on the council called a referendum on style of governance and subsequently a council leader plus cabinet system being installed May 2013.

After the second round of elections for mayors, Labour ended up with 7 out of the 12 (including London), suggesting that old party patterns are beginning to re-emerge. The 2008 London contest, featuring Ken Livingstone, ex-policeman Brian Paddick and the eccentric blond-haired old Etonian Boris Johnson sparked much interest, with David Cameron championing his old school chum Boris to be the eventual winner, and who gained 53% of the vote. The contest was rerun in 2012 with Johnson triumphing, again 51.53% to Livingstone's 48.47%.

'REVOLUTIONARY' DEVOLUTION OF POWERS TO LOCAL GOVERNMENT IN 2014–15

Even though the September 2014 Scottish independence referendum was lost, there were calls from local government leaders, especially Manchester's Sir Richard Leese, for matching devolution for English regions. Regional devolution had been explored via a referendum in 2004 in the north-east and it was roundly rejected 4–1.

Now, however, the idea seemed to have absorbed some of the super-charged energy of the Scottish 'yes' campaign. Coincidentally, both major parties had in any case been formulating new devolution policies based on giving wide-ranging new powers to cities and their hinterlands. This was quite a step, as the UK is the most fiscally centralised of the major OECD nations, with 95% of all taxation in the hands of the Treasury, while the remaining 5% (council tax) was (in 2014) frozen and capped. Manchester had already formed a collective body for all the council leaders of the 10 boroughs of Greater Manchester but new powers were announced by George Osborne on 3 November 2014 to an elected mayor for the whole of that region. That new mayor's powers were to be 'most of the powers of the mayor of London' plus responsibility for skills and further education. Elections will use the supplementary vote as used in London and other mayoral elections.

Almost inevitably, this renewal of interest in devolution of increased powers to the regions will have a knock-on effect with other city regions – Leeds, Birmingham, Bristol, Newcastle – eager to negotiate and enjoy the same privileges. Simon Jenkins, in an outstanding article in *The Guardian*, 12 February 2015, analysed the November 'deal' between Osborne and the Manchester chief executive Howard Bernstein, and quoted Michael Heseltine's speech to Manchester University on 3 November 2014: 'English devolution is now unstoppable'. Tony Travers, of the London School of Economics, was quoted as saying that the powers allowed by Osborne would be subject to some controls from the centre but remarked that 'in a country as centralised as England, any offer of greater devolution has to be encouraged'.

Later in the month, an even more spectacular devolution measure was implemented. Again in *The Guardian*, Jenkins commented on 26 February 2015: 'George Osborne's Manchester Devolution deal last November – so-called devo-Manc – began a process that is clearly unstoppable'. That measure gave the city region control of some £2 billion in the areas of housing, transport, planning and skills. But the new proposal, in February 2015, was worth as much as £6 billion, 'devolving nationalised hospitals and GPs to merge with local clinics, homes and home care services. NHS "in crisis" has become a national cliche. Big has not worked. Now is the turn of small.'

If Jenkins is right and the 'Manchester template' is adopted nationwide in England, a revolution will have occurred. Granted such dramatic change was created by a direct 'deal' which short-circuited democratic procedures and involved George Osborne, the leader of Manchester Labour-led council, Sir Richard Leese and its chief executive, Howard Bernstein.

LOCAL GOVERNMENT ASSOCIATION (LGA)

This body acts as an advocacy body for local government in its dealings with government. The LGA is subject to partisan control but its network of committees and sub-committees has been an effective intervening element in central–local relations ever since it was set up in 1997.

POLITICS AND LOCAL GOVERNMENT

In the earlier incarnations of local government, local property-owners tended to exercise more power and influence than political parties. Joseph Chamberlain, a one-time Birmingham city councillor and then mayor, was influential in applying Liberal ideas through an efficient local party. After he became a Liberal MP and cabinet minister the importance was emphasised of establishing a local government foundation to one's political career, together with the advantages of party support in the localities. During the twentieth century Labour entered the picture and, for the most part, made big cities its own. By the middle of the twentieth century, all parties looked to their local councils and elections became partisan, as they remain today (Box 18.1).

Box 18.1   Local government: election and function

- *Eligibility to vote.* People aged 18 years or more can vote if they are citizens of Britain, Ireland or the Commonwealth; live in the locality; and are registered to vote.
- *Candidates.* Since 1969 can be as young as 18 years; they have to live locally and have the support of 10 local people.
- *Electoral system.* Elections in England and Wales are via first past the post but in Ireland and Scotland the single transferable vote system is used, producing more coalition control.
- *Timing of elections.* Local elections take place every year on the first Thursday in May. County councils are elected in their entirety every four years but district councils have a choice of having elections for the whole council every four years – at the mid-term point for the counties – or via one-third of councillors standing for re-election in each non-county year.
- *The May 2014 elections.* Conservatives won 2121 seats (down 236); Labour 1364 (up 324); Liberal Democrats 427 (down 310); UKIP 163 (up 161); Greens 38 (up 18). The outcome saw Conservatives controlling 41 councils, Labour 82, Liberal Democrats 6, and councils with no overall control 32.

- *Functions.* In metropolitan counties it was the district tier which exercised the most expensive functions, like education, housing and social services, while the county level had more regional functions, like transport and planning, functions which disappeared when these councils were abolished in 1986. In shire counties, it is the county councils which have the major functions, while the districts are limited to housing, planning, environmental health.

WESTMINSTER RESPONSIBILITY FOR LOCAL GOVERNMENT

The department dealing with local government has varied over the years, from Housing and Local Government in the 1960s, to Environment during the 1970s, then Transport, Local Government and the Regions, then the Office of the Deputy Prime Minister before coming under the Department of Community and Local Government in 2006. Gordon Brown appointed Hazel Blears to this post in June 2007. The department has nine regional offices to assist its work throughout the country.

QUESTIONS FOR DISCUSSION

1. Do you think British local government is 'local' enough?
2. Do you consider local government is given sufficient powers to fulfil its functions?
3. Do you think a local income tax offers the best way of funding local government?

FURTHER READING

Really up-to-date texts on UK local government are in short supply but I would recommend: Chandler (2009), plus the excellent short chapter (chapter 20) by Colin Copus in Jones and Norton (2014). See also Copus (2013).

Chandler, J. A. (2009) *Local Government Today*, Manchester University Press.

Copus, C. (2013) *Leading the Localities: Executive Mayors in English Local Governance*, Manchester University Press.

Copus, C. (2014) Local government, in B. Jones and P. Norton (eds), *Politics UK*, Routledge.

Jenkins, S. (2008) Instead of elected local leaders, we have the police, *Guardian*, 27 February.

Miliband, E. (2014) The future is local, *Guardian*, 7 July.

Rallings, C. and Thrasher, M. (1997) *Local Elections in Britain*, Routledge.

Stoker, G. (2003) *Transforming Local Governance in the UK*, Palgrave.

Wilson, D. and Game, C. (2002) *Local Government in the United Kingdom*, Palgrave.

WEBSITES

Guide to local government: http://www.gwydir.demon.co.uk/uklocalgov/structure.htm.

Local Government Association: http://www.lga.gov.uk.

Local Government Information Unit: http://www.lgiu.org.uk.

New Local Government Network: http://www.nlgn.org.uk.

19

THE JUDICIARY AND POLITICS

OVERLOOKED?

Maintaining the law is something all governments seek to do efficiently and, in most countries, fairly. Back in Britain's early history, Henry II (1133–89), for example, saw it as his duty to reform England's legal system and establish a national circuit of county courts. So it is perhaps surprising that such an important function tends to be overlooked in analyses of British government. Perhaps this is because courts are 'subordinate' to parliament, which has supreme legal authority, and because they are 'autonomous' or detached, in that they interpret rules made elsewhere. But in the present day it would be a mistake to view the judiciary – the judges and the courts nationwide – as merely of secondary importance to the nation's politics. This chapter considers how the judiciary fits into and serves the political system and provides a thumbnail sketch of the highly complex British system of judges and courts.

SUBORDINATE?

The courts cannot strike down a piece of statute law – laws passed by a legislature – as only parliament can do this. Yet, once, the monarch could always override statute via the common law using the judicial machinery; the Glorious Revolution (1688–89) put an end to this, as from then onwards statute law became superior to any other form of law. However, 'judicial activism' (see below) has made the courts less subordinate. Courts have the power to interpret the precise wording of a law in practice in a way that subtly changes its effect and they can 'review' the actions of ministers to assess whether they are within the law as written or beyond it, or, in the widely used Latin term, *ultra vires*.

AUTONOMOUS?

Judges have autonomy in that they have virtual security of tenure: it takes both Houses of parliament to sack one and they receive their salaries on a permanent, not renewable, basis. The Commons is not allowed to discuss court cases in process or *sub judice*; ministers and civil servants do the same. Judges are supposed to avoid any partisan activity or, indeed, any kind of comment on current issues, following the Kilmuir guidelines of 1955, which forbade it. However, the dividing lines between the spheres of government are tenuous; membership of the legislature, executive and judiciary are not mutually exclusive in Britain (see Figure 19.1).

JUDICIAL POSTS

THE LORD CHANCELLOR

At one time, this officer was a member of all three branches of governments: legislature (presiding in the House of Lords); judiciary (appointing judges, hearing appeals) and executive (member of cabinet). In the past, this position was filled by a senior heavyweight politician, for example Tory Lord Hailsham (1979–87) or Labour's Lord Irvine (1997–2003). The post used to be effectively head of the judiciary plus speaker of House of Lords and head of the Chancery Division of the High Court. The Constitutional Reform Act (CRA) 2005 transferred these functions respectively to: the lord chief justice (LCJ), the Lord speaker; and the chancellor of the High Court. The office still exists as an adjunct to the secretary of state for justice – the

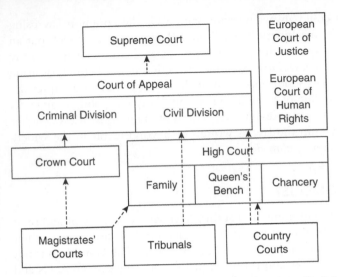

Figure 19.1 The three spheres of government and location of judiciary

incumbent at the time of writing was Michael Gove – but the power of the office has been greatly attenuated (for example, the requirement for the holder to be a qualified lawyer has been dropped). It looks as if the post of lord chancellor is steadily making its way constitutionally from the 'efficient' part towards the 'dignified'.

THE ATTORNEY-GENERAL (AG) AND THE SOLICITOR-GENERAL (DEPUTY)

Both these posts also have a judicial and executive role. The AG represents the government in the courts and gives advice to the government on the legality of its actions, the best recent example being the legality of the Iraq War.

THE LORDS

This used to be the highest court in the land, in that its Appellate Committee used to sit as the highest court of appeal. However, this function was invested into a new Supreme Court in October 2009 (discussed below).

JUDGES

Judges occasionally say controversial things but their autonomy is limited: a Supreme Court judge can be dismissed only by a resolution of both Houses of parliament, though judges can be rebuked by the lord chief justice (LCJ). Some claim judges were allowed more freedom to debate public issues when Lord Woolf was LCJ (2000–05).

HOME SECRETARY

This senior minister (the equivalent of what elsewhere in Europe would be called 'minister for the interior') has quasi-judicial powers, including the right to influence terms of imprisonment for prisoners. Such 'crossings' of the boundaries between the three branches of government means the judiciary cannot truly be said to be either truly subordinate or truly autonomous.

THE COURTS AND THEIR PERSONNEL

The court system has two major branches: one dealing with criminal law; the other with civil law (although the lowest-level courts, staffed by lay magistrates, deal with either type of legal case). Before these two branches are explained, a short section looks at the Supreme Court, which spans both.

SUPREME COURT OF THE UNITED KINGDOM

This replaced a section of the House of Lords as the highest court in the land following the CRA 2005. It is the highest court in all matters of English and Welsh law, as well as law in Northern Ireland and Scotland. It is at the same time the highest court of appeal, apart from the High Court of Judiciary, which retains the right of appeal for criminal cases in Scotland. It also has the power to resolve disputes over devolution in the UK and over the legal powers of the devolved assemblies. Figure 19.1 shows the hierarchy of courts in the UK.

CRIMINAL LAW

This body of law is the one with which most people are better acquainted, dealing with offences against society: motoring offences, robbery, murder and so on.

CROWN PROSECUTION SERVICE (CPS)

This office is headed by the director of public prosecutions. The police used to decide whether to prosecute a case but this was deemed unfair and in 1986 the new structure was set up, vesting the decision to prosecute in a separate body. The CPS has 42 areas, each headed by a chief crown prosecutor and each staffed by experienced lawyers.

MAGISTRATES' COURTS

These are comparatively unusual in that few other countries allow non-lawyers to sit in judgement over their fellow citizens; this has been a practice in England since the enabling law of 1327 allowed 'good and lawful men' to guard the peace in every county. Around 98% of criminal cases are tried in magistrates' courts, about 2 million cases a year. Many fines are now fixed penalty, and this has reduced the burden on magistrates to a degree. They can also levy fines and imprison those convicted, but only for up to six months. Mostly they deal with motoring offences but can also deal with cruelty to children and animals.

There is generally a period of about 100 days between the offence taking place and it being tried. Often the business takes only seconds where a guilty plea is offered. Professional magistrates are now called district judges; they are full time and tend to serve in cities. 'Lay' magistrates mostly operate in rural areas. Usually white, middle class and middle aged, their uniformity of background is often criticised but their contribution to the judiciary, mostly free of charge apart from expenses, is immense. Those who disagree with their conviction at this level can appeal to the higher crown court for a review of their case.

CROWN COURTS

These are presided over by a judge and are concerned mostly with more serious, so-called 'indictable' offences, with verdicts decided by a jury; lengthy sentences can be delivered to those found guilty.

Crown courts deal with around 10,000 cases every year. They operate via six 'circuits', with a High Court judge presiding over the most serious cases and a circuit judge or 'recorder' hearing the rest. Recorders are part time but are trained lawyers (solicitors or barristers).

COURT OF APPEAL

Around 10% of those convicted in a crown court appeal against their sentence. The Court of Appeal may quash the conviction, uphold it or change the sentence imposed. Sentences may be appealed against, too, with the permission of the Court of Appeal. The attorney-general may intervene if the sentence is thought too lenient and may increase the sentence. The court is served by (currently) 38 lord justices of appeal; it has two divisions to hear, respectively, appeals of a criminal or civil nature. The Civil Division is headed by the master of the rolls – originally the keeper of the lord chancellor's scrolls, he became a judge in 1881 and has responsibility for solicitors – and the Criminal Division by the lord chief justice, who replaced the lord chancellor as the overall head of the judiciary by the CRA 2005.

PRIVY COUNCIL JUDICIAL COMMITTEE

This is a legacy of Britain's colonial history: it acts as a final court of appeal for a number of former colonies, comprising law lords plus several ex officio members. It also hears legal challenges to devolved assemblies, acting as a kind of 'constitutional court' at this level of government.

CIVIL LAW

This branch of the law is that concerned with disputes between people, for example a tenant with a landlord, a seller with a customer, or parties to a contract. Most of these cases are heard in county courts before a circuit judge or, for more important cases, the High Court.

THE HIGH COURT

The High Court is divided into three divisions: Queen's Bench; Equity (Chancery); and domestic cases (Family). The three divisions are headed by judges, assisted by a total of 80 other judges.

The Queen's Bench Division sits to hear writs of habeas corpus (this orders the addressee to deliver a person in custody to a court – usually to restore the person's liberty). It may require a public body to fulfil a duty (mandamus), to desist from an action (prohibition) or to quash a decision already taken (certiorari). It also hears appeals from magistrates' courts on points of law. From the High Court appeals go to the Civil Division of the Court of Appeal.

The Chancery Division deals with business – trusts, probate and land law for the most part.

The Family Division deals with divorce, children and medical treatment (for example, the court gave authority to a hospital to separate conjoined twins).

TRIBUNALS

These quasi-judicial bodies now cover: unfair dismissal, rents, social security, benefits, immigration, mental health, and compensation for compulsory purchase. Those appearing can call witnesses and cross-examine on most occasions. A tribunal usually comprises three people – often a mix between professional and lay. Industrial tribunals have an independent chair plus two representatives of both sides of industry. These tribunals are cheap and quick and less formal than court proceedings. In 1996 an employment tribunal told the Labour Party that all-women short-lists were in breach of sex discrimination law. Labour withdrew such regulations but later changed the law when in power.

THE RECRUITMENT OF JUDGES

J. A. G. Griffiths, a professor at the London School of Economics, won some support for the argument that judges were drawn from a narrow and exclusive stratum of society: white, elderly and middle class. On top of this they do not have to retire until they are over 70; only just over a fifth are female; three-quarters are privately educated; and senior judgeships mostly go to former barristers (though increasingly now solicitors are also selected). Critics claimed judges were out of touch with the rest of society, notoriously unable to understand, for example, the feelings of women in rape cases. It is also asserted that the background of most judges tends to inject a bias towards the government of the day, especially when it is Conservative. Partly for these reasons, selection of judges was invested in a new and independent body.

THE JUDICIAL APPOINTMENTS COMMISSION

This is an independent body set up in 2006 under the CRA. Previously, judges were appointed by the lord chancellor on the basis of a complex process of information feedback, which, despite the assurances of Lord Irvine (a former lord chancellor) to the contrary, was perceived as a glorified part of the 'old boys' network. In October 2006 the new Commission set about looking for candidates to fill 10 High Court judgeship vacancies and 15 for a reserve list. Candidates were to submit an application form, and short-listed candidates were then interviewed. All candidates were judged by five core criteria including: intellectual capacity; fairness; ability to communicate; and ability to work efficiently.

'JUDICIAL ACTIVISM'

This is the term used for the power judges have to strike down acts by government which they judge to be *ultra vires* or at variance with statute law or which violated 'natural justice' (i.e. fair in the mind of most people). As the courts before the 1960s were largely deferential towards the government, there were few examples of review, but during that decade judges began to worry that civil liberties were being eroded and judicial review came into frequent use. One famous example was the abolition of grammar schools in Tameside in 1976, when the Labour government's action was overturned. During the 1980s it was the Conservatives' turn for its actions to be reviewed and reversed.

From 500 reviews in the early 1980s, the figure increased to 1000 by 1985, 1500 by 1987 and 2000 by 1990. Since 2000 there have been 4000–5000 a year. During the 1990s Michael Howard as home secretary had his decisions overturned on several occasions: a criminal injuries scheme; the referral of parole applications by lifers; and a petition demanding a minimum sentence for the killers of Liverpool toddler Jamie Bulger. As home secretary (1997–2001) Jack Straw did not escape similar experiences. Moreover, judges have been able to interpret laws when terms are unclear, to change their effect significantly.

Lord Denning in particular was able to insert 'his own policy judgements into the loopholes left in legislation' (Oliver and Drewry, 1998). But judicial review should not be exaggerated: most applications concern local authorities and not ministers; only a quarter are allowed to go forward; and only 10% against the government manage to win. But when ministers' actions are negated they look bad; the judiciary have indeed come to play a role not just in the implementation of the law but in its interpretation as well.

ENFORCING EUROPEAN LAW

The UK became a member of the European Community on 1 January 1972 and on that day all Community law became 'UK law'; all future European law became British law in addition. Parliamentary assent is not required for such legislation: it is automatic. Questions of law are decided by European Court of Justice (ECJ). Lower courts in the UK may ask the ECJ for a ruling on questions of law relating to the treaties of the European Union (EU). Domestic law is *always subordinate* to EU law, a point which infuriates the Euro-sceptics, who resent parliament losing its historic, exclusive powers.

The Factortame case in 1990 demonstrated the superiority of EU law. This case concerned Spanish trawler owners, who challenged a ruling against them made under the UK Merchant Shipping Act 1988; the ECJ eventually found for their plea that EU law overruled UK domestic law.

The ex parte Equal Opportunities Commission 1999 case concerned a dispute over part-time workers who were not allowed to claim under a 1978 Act for unfair dismissal or redundancy; it was ruled this was unlawful in terms of EU law. Philip Norton comments that 'Although the Factortame case attracted considerable publicity, it was the EOC case that was the more fundamental in its implications. The courts were invalidating the provisions of an Act of Parliament' (in Jones and Norton, 2013: p. 448).

All this has placed so much of a burden on the ECJ that it has had to invent an extra court: the Court of First Instance. The greater the integration of nations within the EU, then the greater the significance of the courts has tended to be in applying European law. The Maastricht Treaty also gave the ECJ the power to fine nations which do not obey European law. The body of case law built up in consequence is now huge.

'Parliamentary sovereignty' is believed to remain intact in that Britain can leave the EU, although some say this is a fiction and that the power of the EU has intruded too deeply inside the political system. The courts now therefore have a precautionary role in interpreting law to see if it is congruent with EU law, thus strengthening their role.

ENFORCING THE EUROPEAN CONVENTION ON HUMAN RIGHTS

This further strengthens judges, as it adds a new dimension to the law: human rights. Judges now can decide if human rights have been violated. This role used to be performed only in the Strasbourg court, which heard cases till 1998, when the Human Rights Act (HRA) was passed. Some of those earlier cases were controversial. For instance, the killing of three members of the IRA members in Gibraltar was ruled a violation of the right to life. The HRA makes it illegal for local authorities to act in a way inconsistent with Convention rights. If a law is inconsistent, then the courts can leave it up to parliament to do something about it. This role makes the judges much more political and increases the tension between executive and the judiciary. Already the ECHR, via the HRA, has had a major effect on many cases (see Box 19.1). However, the Conservative Party returned to government in May 2015 pledged to repeal the HRA, for the difficulties it posed for British courts to administer justice without external constraint. However, robust internal opposition led Cameron not to include the repeal in his government's first Queen's Speech, 27 May 2015.

Box 19.1   European Convention on Human Rights (ECHR)

The Human Rights Act 1998 came into force on 2 October 2000. For the first time, individuals have a range of civil rights which are enforceable in British courts as embodied in the ECHR:

- Article 2. Right to life
- Article 3. Prohibition of torture
- Article 6. Right to a fair trial
- Article 8. Right to respect for private and family life
- Article 9. Freedom of thought, conscience and religion
- Article 10. Freedom of expression
- Article 11. Freedom of assembly and association
- Article 12. Right to marry
- Article 14. Prohibition of discrimination
- The sixth protocol, article 1. Abolition of the death penalty

QUESTIONS FOR DISCUSSION

1. To what extent is the judiciary 'subordinate to' and 'autonomous from' parliament?
2. What is the difference between criminal and civil law?
3. Should judges be drawn from a wider social base than at present?

FURTHER READING

A more detailed introduction can be found by Philip Norton, Chapter 21 in Jones and Norton (2014). Full-length book introductions to the law are Golden (2000) and Mansfield (2003). For a fascinating discussion of the law see Sadnel (2009).

Adler, J. (2005) *Constitutional and Administrative Law*, Palgrave.
Banner, C. and Deane, A. (2003) *Off With Their Heads: Judicial Revolution in Modern Britain*, Imprint Academic.
Bradley, A. W. and Ewing, K. D. (1997) *Constitutional and Administrative Law*, Longman.

Jones, B. and Norton, P. (2013) *Politics UK* (8th edition), Routledge.

Nolan, Lord and Sedley, Sir S. (1997) *The Making and Remaking of the British Constitution,* Blackstone.

Oliver, D. and Drewry, G. (1998) *The Law and Parliament*, Cambridge University Press.

Windlesham, Lord (2006) 'The Constitutional Reform Act 2005: ministers, judges and constitutional change', *Public Law*, winter.

WEBSITES

European Court of Human Rights: http://www.echr.coe.int.

Court Service: http://www.hmcourts-service.gov.uk.

Judiciary of England and Wales: http://www.judiciary.gov.uk/index.htm.

Magistrates Association: http://www.judiciary.gov.uk/index.htm.

20

BRITAIN AND THE WORLD

HISTORICAL PERSPECTIVE

Britain has always been substantially beholden, and still is, to people and forces outside its borders. The very early settlers travelled from northern and eastern Europe, often in search of good agricultural land or in retreat from hostile invasion. Several Celtic tribes occupied the islands when the Romans arrived with intent to conquer, unsuccessfully, in 55 BC, and then more permanently in 43 AD. They stayed for four centuries and established several towns plus cities as well as building a network of roads, viaducts, aqueducts and the 80-mile Hadrian's Wall as a northern bulwark of their empire. When this empire began to implode and its power fade, other tribes began to make the journey from elsewhere in Europe with a view to settling in this damp, cool, but unusually fertile set of islands.

From central Germany, in the fifth century, came the Angles, Saxons and Jutes; seven 'Anglo-Saxon' kingdoms were established in south, east and central England. From north-east Ireland the Scots traversed the Irish Sea to settle in Argyll. Then in the late ninth century the Vikings invited themselves, initiating an extended war with the Saxons, adding further to the racial mix and helping to create the present-day British. Even more formative was the 1066 Norman invasion, which effectively colonised the country, expunged the Anglo-Saxon ruling elite and replaced it with a French one, albeit of a variety originally Viking.

By the end of the first millennium British connections had been established with the outside world via successive waves of invading European tribal groups. As the second millennium got under way, more groups of immigrants arrived – for example Huguenots, Jews in seventeenth century – and the country began to acquire a character and a consciousness of its own as it set about defending and promoting what its rulers saw as its national interests. Such interests were heavily influenced by the country's lack of natural resources, apart from coal, and its close relationship with the sea.

FRONTIERS

For any state, defence of its frontiers is a fundamental interest. The 150-mile English Channel, formed 200,000 years ago, has provided, since the Norman invasion, a vital barrier to those who wished to threaten the British state. Spain, France and more recently Hitler were seen off partly because this trench of water, only 21 miles wide at its narrowest point, together with its varying weather conditions, has proved such a formidable barrier.

PRIMACY OF TRADE

From early on, Britain has been a trading nation, exporting metals – mostly tin and later iron – and raw materials like wool and timber (now largely exhausted). As the home of the Industrial Revolution, Britain manufactured an immense range of goods, especially cotton but also steel and engineered artefacts. To facilitate such trade required peace, making Britain broadly an advocate of rules whereby international relations could be peacefully conducted.

EUROPEAN BALANCE OF POWER

Despite the fact that only the invasion by the Normans was truly successful, fear of invasion has underlain much of the history of British foreign policy. It was thought that a dominant European power might well decide to set its sights on the country beyond the Channel and so Britain has tended to join or form coalitions to counter or pre-empt the emergence of such dominant powers, whether they have been Spain, France or Germany. These three themes – protection of its frontiers, defence of trade and maintaining the European balance of power – have been constants in British relations with the outside world, with the latter interest reducing in importance by the late twentieth century. As long-serving British foreign secretary, Viscount Palmerston, famously observed, 'Nations have no permanent friends or allies; they only have permanent interests'.

THE EMPIRE AND DECLINE

Over time, Britain's navy proved superior to those of Spain, Holland and France: by the mid-eighteenth century, the British Empire was a relative 'superpower'. Even after the loss of the American colonies the Empire continued to grow in Asia and Africa, eventually occupying a quarter of the world's landmass and containing 500 million people. However, Britain's period of dominance did not last long; events in the twentieth century shrank Britain's relative strength and its worldwide reach.

Firstly, Britain held no patent on the Industrial Revolution it had invented and other economies, especially those of Germany and the USA, soon caught up, and, by virtue of their superior resources and more modern machinery, were able to overtake Britain.

Secondly, the depredations of two world wars – 1914–18 and 1939–45 – left the country bankrupt by 1945; many of the country's overseas assets accumulated during the glory days of Empire were sacrificed in order to defeat Hitler. Contrastingly, the USA, relatively unscathed economically by World War II, emerged as the dominant power in the world, both economically and militarily. The Soviet Union, under Joseph Stalin, sought to match the USA in military terms, as the Cold War ensued, but was never in the same league economically. Britain tried to act as if it was still one of the Big Three but few believed this fiction (except possibly certain politicians on the right).

Thirdly, Britain's economy after 1945 was not best placed to maintain anything like its earlier strength. Building on its 2% share of world economic output in 1750, Britain soared to 23% by

1880 – at that time the USA commanded a mere 14.7%. During the mid-nineteenth century Britain produced two-fifths of the world's manufactured goods, including over half of its iron and coal. From 1870–75 an average of £75 million – then a huge sum – was invested abroad annually. But already by 1914 Britain's percentage of world trade had declined to 14.1% as other industrialised nations made up ground. The impact of World War I was immense in terms of finance and lost manpower but the weakening effects of World War II were yet greater, as assets had to be realised in order to prosecute the conflict against Germany and huge loans taken out from America in order to sustain it.

In his book, *Empire*, historian Niall Ferguson controversially argues that the effects of Empire were for the most part beneficent and that Churchill, despite his love of the British Empire, decided to sacrifice it in order to defeat Hitler. However, Britain's relative economic decline for the two to three decades after 1945 was not a topic for debate: it was a fact which any British visitor to European countries, especially Germany, could see with their own eyes. Paul Kennedy's book *The Rise and Fall of Great Powers* argues that it is the available resources to powers which determine their degree of dominance and that relative economic decline almost always heralds a scaling down in the international pecking order. The UK still has the ninth largest economy in the world but its share of world trade is now a fraction of what it once was.

Facing the post-war world, Attlee was forced to recognise that defending such a vast Empire with such depleted armed forces was not viable. The Empire was based upon a myth of omnipotence which events in the war – especially, for Asian possessions, the fall of Singapore – had subverted totally. India was promptly – perhaps too promptly, given the civil strife which erupted in the north-west of the subcontinent – given its independence. The Conservatives, however, found it harder to reconcile themselves to the fading away of Empire and were prepared to defend its eroding frontiers. Their fatal error occurred in 1956, when Anthony Eden's government collaborated with the French and the Israelis to seize back the Suez Canal after Egypt's Colonel Nasser claimed possession of it. This reckless act brought them face to face with an unpalatable reality regarding lost power. Eden was forced to retreat humiliatingly in the face of America's refusal to support what was seen as an 'imperialist' adventure. It was now crystal clear that Britain had neither the money nor the support of its major ally to maintain its Empire.

In September 1960 British Prime Minister Harold Macmillan addressed the South African Parliament and stated:

> The wind of change is blowing through this continent. Whether we like it or not, this growth of national consciousness is a political fact.

The apartheid government received the speech in appalled silence: it would take several more decades before it, too, came to terms with the new realities. Independence for the African colonies quickly followed until, by the end of the 1960s, there were a mere few stale crumbs of Empire left, scattered around the oceans. The residual diplomatic dividend from the Empire, the Commonwealth, was a free association of former colonies – now independent nations – representing substantial populations but with negligible political clout. Ireland chose to stay out, while India, perhaps surprisingly, opted in. The record of the organisation, which boasts a secretariat in London and regular conferences, is one of difficulty in keeping its own house in order, on matters such as apartheid and various other civil rights violations by members, plus vacuous statements on wider global issues.

THE SPHERES OF FOREIGN POLICY

In his perceptive book *Between Europe and America* (2003: pp. 30–34) Andrew Gamble recalls Churchill's 1946 invocation of Britain being at the touching point of three circles: the British Empire; Anglo-America; and Europe. Gamble suggests that 'Britain' should now be seen as a 'union' of its now devolved constituent parts. There were at least three areas in which post-war UK foreign policy could invest its emphasis, often represented by three spheres: Europe, America, the Empire/Commonwealth. In practical terms, as the above paragraph suggests, the choice is these days limited to two, Europe or America, though the Empire should not be discounted totally, as it established a tradition for Britain of striding on the world's stage, seeking to influence the direction in which events develop. This tendency has not been totally expunged; doubters are advised to visit the Foreign Office and judge from its still splendid interior whether ministerial incumbents can escape the legacy of Britain's worldwide imperial past. Perhaps the loss of Empire has been a factor in the nourishing of nationalist sentiment in Scotland, Ireland and Wales.

THE EUROPEAN UNION AS A FOCUS OF FOREIGN POLICY

Britain has always been ambivalent about Europe. For centuries it was the source of danger, bloody entanglements and the need for endless diplomacy. During the twentieth century it was the stage on which the bloodiest dramas in history – two world wars – were played out. There was much to recoil from some 20 miles across the Channel. Yet while advocating a sense of togetherness and the virtues of political unity, Britain could never quite accept the latter's reality. Both Churchill and Bevan praised the idea in the wake of World War II but in time it seemed they saw it as good for the rest of Europe but not for Britain, which had its 'proper' place at a much bigger table, along with the USA and the USSR. So it was that Britain declined to join the movement towards a united Europe which culminated with the signing of the Treaty of Rome in 1957 and the birth of the European Economic Community (EEC), or the Common Market as it was more popularly known in those years. Labour, too, was not enthusiastic; Clement Attlee once expressed his rather dismissively mordant view on European integration thus:

> The so-called Common Market of six nations. Know them all well. Very recently, this country spent a great deal of blood and treasure rescuing four of 'em from attacks by the other two.

However, ironically perhaps in terms of their present attitude, the Conservatives, under Harold Macmillan, decided that the ailing British economy, the surging new 'Common Market' one, the fading of Empire and the Suez-related slump in Anglo-US relations made an application to join the EEC now a viable option. It took three applications, a decade and the death of the veto-wielding French president De Gaulle for Britain to squeeze its way into the EEC in 1973. A substantial minority of both major parties were opposed to the idea of joining a club of nations whose laws over-ruled those of its members: domestic law bending the knee to Community law sounded too much like unacceptable loss of sovereignty to many in the UK. Socialists suspected the 'capitalist club' of the EEC would erode the 'socialist' achievements of Labour governments. And both sets of sceptics feared national identity would be sacrificed to a faceless unelected bureaucracy in Brussels.

Only the Liberals agreed that Ted Heath's achievement of winning membership was an unalloyed success. By the 1980s a 'Euro-sceptic' faction in the ruling Conservative Party had developed, which grew as successive treaties strengthened what, with the Maastricht Treaty in 1992, became the European Union (EU). The split over this issue among the Tories made them virtually ungovernable in the 1990s. Labour also had its doubters but they were less numerous and not prepared to create so many problems for their leadership. Tony Blair was keen to place Britain 'at the heart of Europe' and showed willing by addressing the French National Assembly in French, a risk few other British politicians would take.

His enthusiasm for joining the single European currency, the euro, however, was not shared by chancellor Gordon Brown, who insisted on five conditions for doing so, which somehow, perhaps fortunately, never came near to being met. This meant that Britain was never quite at the 'heart' of Europe and became less so as Blair seemed to be far too close to US presidents Bill Clinton and George Bush, especially when he committed to the ill-fated adventure in Iraq.

THE ANGLO-AMERICAN BOND – A SPECIAL RELATIONSHIP?

The founding of the USA was won through violent revolution against the British crown in the late eighteenth century, followed by the 1812–15 war between the same countries, which entailed the British burning of Washington DC in 1814: not the best of foundations on which to build any kind of relationship. But during the nineteenth century the two countries developed, for the most part, a good trading relationship, reinforced by common cultural and kin connections, so that someone from America was not really seen as a 'foreigner' when they visited Britain. Indeed, impecunious British aristocrats eagerly wooed rich American heiresses to help maintain their mansions and high standard of living. By the early twentieth century, the USA, not without reluctance, joined the fight against the Kaiser but then, repelled by Europe's perennial squabbles, relapsed into isolationism.

It took the subtle political skills of Roosevelt plus the aggression of the Japanese (Pearl Harbor, 7 December 1941) to bring the GIs flooding back over the Atlantic. World War II cemented a collaboration that united the two countries as never before. American troops and popular culture – the films, the music – were hugely popular too and many GIs married British girls. But this high point of togetherness masked differences at the top between Churchill and Roosevelt over the conduct of the war and the determination of the US to receive tangible returns for its loans to the UK of cash and equipment. Despite British receipt of Marshall aid and the warmth between Churchill and Eisenhower, the Suez adventure alienated the USA and brought home to the UK the stern lesson that it had lost the ability to do anything much abroad without US support. Adding some insult to injury a few years later, US secretary of state Dean Acheson said in speech at West Point, 1962, that 'Great Britain has lost an Empire yet not yet found a role'.

The story since then has been one of Britain seeking to remind the US of the ties that once bound the two countries and the White House keeping the British politely at arm's length. In between there was the refusal of Harold Wilson to send troops to Vietnam, as Lyndon Johnson would have liked; Margaret Thatcher appreciating US help during the Falklands War and bonding with Ronald Reagan – though balking at his 1983 invasion of Grenada; and John Major helping George Bush Senior in the Gulf War of 1991.

Then came Tony Blair, eager to pursue an 'ethical foreign policy' and to use American power by association and proxy to further some of his own visions for the future of the world. He succeeded in taking Clinton along with him in the Balkans, where the killing in Kosovo was curtailed and Milosevic effectively toppled.

Emboldened, perhaps, by such success, he sought to articulate a philosophy of humanitarian intervention, roughly translated as 'where evil exists in the world, it is the duty of moral states to fight it'. In a speech in Chicago in 1999, he spelt out the framework of his ideas on 'international community'. Praising America's role as de facto world policeman, Blair argued that other countries had a moral duty to contribute towards such interventions. How are we to decide if such action is justified? Firstly, we must be sure of our case that action is necessary; secondly all diplomatic options must have been exhausted; thirdly military operations must be judged whether they can be 'sensibly and prudently' undertaken; fourthly, intervention must be taken with the long term in view; and finally one has to ask are there 'national interests involved'?

Shortly after this speech, on 11 September 2001, a traumatic shock was administered to the Western world when two commercial aircraft, hijacked by terrorist group Al-Qaeda, were deliberately crashed into the twin towers of the New York's World Trade Center. In the wake of this event, Blair promised that Britain would stand 'shoulder to shoulder' with its ally. Despite their differences of belief, Blair and Bush forged a very close relationship, far too close in the view of many of Blair's fellow Labour Party members. Many could accept that Britain was closely involved in the war against Afghanistan in pursuit of the Al-Qaeda leader Osama bin Laden, but the war against Iraq's Saddam Hussein was different.

Nobody questioned that he was the worst kind of psychopathic dictator, but he was not directly connected to Al-Qaeda and Blair's assertion that he had 'weapons of mass destruction' which he was prepared to use had first to be proven. It never was. In retrospect, Tony Blair has not expressed any regret at the outcome of the Iraq War; nor has his closest policy adviser, Jonathan Powell. Maybe history will support the decision but from the perspective of over a decade from invasion day, it seems difficult to imagine how the events of the war can ever be placed into a favourable context, nor made congruent with Blair's own Chicago guidelines.

It has to be said, further, that the extended war in Afghanistan cannot be viewed as successful. Reviewing the 13 years of the war, Will Hutton commented, quite fairly, that over a period of eight years, none of the objectives of three prime ministers and six defence

secretaries had been met in Helmand province. The price had been
£40 billion, 453 British deaths, 247 amputations and over 2600
wounded. And all this is before the thousands of Afghans killed are
counted. After all this effort and cost, government in the province
had not improved, the economy was weaker, heroin production was
higher and the security situation was worse than before:

> Helmand is more of a recruiting sergeant for terrorism and jihadism
> than it was. . . . The central government in Kabul is more rather than less
> threatened. If one aim was to make the British homeland safer by victory
> in southern Afghanistan – a fantastical claim of last resort – Britain is
> now less safe.

The election of Barack Obama as president in 2008 perhaps slightly
cooled the relationship – Obama tended to pay more attention to
Asia than Europe and Cameron's distancing of Britain from the EU
tended to encourage Obama to deal more closely with Europe's
undoubted strongest leader, Angela Merkel of Germany.

THE GROWTH OF EURO-SCEPTICISM

British ambivalence over Europe has already been noted but the
rapid progress of Euro-sceptic views from the 1980s onwards
requires some explanation. There are rather obvious explanations in
terms of Britain's island status; this has perhaps encouraged a sense
of being different, apart from the 'continent', together with a more
outgoing seaward mind-set, as well as a (well founded) suspicion that
certain nations on the French side of the Channel might look across
it with predatory intent.

One historical legacy of Empire has perhaps been a misplaced
sense of superiority to European nations, which has occasionally come close to racism: Cecil Rhodes once opined of his own
race that: 'We happen to be the best people in the world, with
the highest ideals of decency and justice and liberty and peace'. A
close companion of this kind of view was the idea that Britain was a
'world' rather than merely a regional 'European' power. Moreover,
the British state had survived World War II intact; those which had
been invaded and occupied – France, Belgium, Italy, Holland and

finally Germany – maybe had less trust left to invest in the state as an institution and were willing to contemplate new supra-national alternatives.

All these factors underlay negative attitudes to Europe within the two major parties: Conservatives reluctant to abandon the imperial role; Labour suspicious of the 'capitalist club'; and both with sections wary of surrendering any of parliament's precious 'sovereignty' to any supra-national body, especially the unelected European Commission, which apparently wielded so much power within it. Yet substantial parts of both parties were enthusiastic that Britain should participate in this exciting experiment aimed at ending Europe's blood-soaked experiences during the twentieth century while facilitating greater economic growth and prosperity throughout the continent of Europe. Edward Heath led the Conservatives into the EEC in 1972, supported by most of his cabinet colleagues, including Margaret Thatcher at that time.

Enoch Powell was a prominent and maverick dissenter who attracted some support though not decisively so during the 1970s. It was during the 1980s that Thatcher, having accepted the pivotal 1986 Single European Act, which established the integrated single market, began to object when Commission president Jacques Delors sought vigorously to advance towards the 'ever closer union' envisaged by the Treaty of Rome. Her objections – sustained energetically behind the scenes throughout her years of retirement during the 1990s – helped nourish a powerful tendency on the British right to view the European Union (as it became known after the 1992 Maastricht Treaty) as wasteful, corrupt, undemocratic and injurious to the potential prosperity Britain would enjoy if it withdrew from the EU.

The United Kingdom Independence Party (UKIP) did not initially attract much support but sections of the right-wing press, most notably the Murdoch papers (*The Sun, The Times, Sunday Times*), helped fan the flames of opposition. In 2004 UKIP won 16% of the vote in the European Parliament elections, its leader, Nigel Farage, UKIP's leader after 2006, quickly establishing himself as a charismatic national political figure. The euro-zone crisis, beginning in 2009, seemed to destroy the EU's image of facilitating prosperity and replace it with that of perpetual crisis and poverty. This helped propel UKIP to even greater electoral heights: it picked up scores of councillors in the 2014 local elections and topped the poll in the European elections in May of the same year. In April of that year Nigel Farage had the confidence to take on Nick Clegg in a televised debate on the EU. Surveys of the public showed that he won both easily.

UKIP's opposition to immigration levels – attracting the accusation that it is a 'closet racist' party – strengthens its appeal to right-wing Conservative voters and caused Conservative leader David Cameron to be pulled far to the right to pre-empt an appeal which might, as it then seemed, deny the party several seats in the 2015 election. He consequently toughened up policy on immigrants, making it more difficult for them to draw benefits and seeking to limit their overall numbers. He also promised an 'in–out' referendum in 2017 providing he won an overall majority in 2015. With that majority, albeit a small one, intact, Cameron could implement his plan and in May 2015 began a series of meetings with EU heads of government designed to win back powers surrendered to the EU over the years. At the time of writing, he intends, having renegotiated Britain's relationship with the EU, to hold the in–out referendum.

QUESTIONS FOR DISCUSSION

1. Do you think Britain's national interests have essentially changed since the nineteenth century?
2. Given its relative decline in the twentieth century, can Britain realistically play a major role in world politics?
3. Should Britain commit its future to being part of the EU?

FURTHER READING

Many of the arguments for and against UK's membership of the EU are aired in daily newspapers and the weekly journals. However, there are a few books available too. The *Financial Times* (2015) is a good short summary and can be downloaded to Kindle free of charge. Also useful is Bootle (2015) and Cohen (2015).

Blair, A. L. (1999) The Blair doctrine, at http://www.pbs.org/newshour/bb/international-jan-june99-blair_doctrine4-23.
Bootle, R. (2015) *The Trouble With Europe: Why the EU Isn't Working, How It Can Be Reformed, What Could Take Its Place?*, Nicholas Brealey.

Byrd, P. (1988) *British Foreign Policy Under Thatcher*, Manchester University Press.

Cohen, Y. (2015) *The British Reverence Towards Nationality*, Priests Publishing.

Cooper, R. (2006) War and democracy, *Prospect Magazine*, June.

Ferguson, N. (2004) *Empire*, Allen Lane.

Financial Times (2015) *Britain and the EU – In or Out?*, Financial Times.

Gamble, A. (2003) *Between Europe and America: The Future of British Politics*, Palgrave.

Hutton, W. (2014) Right of centre ideology has lost us the war in Afghanistan and much else besides, *Observer*, 28 December.

Kennedy, P. (1989) *The Rise and Fall of Great Powers*, Random House.

Smith, M., Smith, S. and White, B. (1988) *British Foreign Policy*, Routledge.

WEBSITE

Foreign and Commonwealth Office: https://www.gov.uk/government/organi sations/foreign-commonwealth-office.

21

CONCLUSION: BRITISH POLITICS IN FLUX?

This short final chapter seeks to draw together some of the 'change' themes which readers will have noticed throughout the foregoing text. Indeed, it seems that so many factors are subverting the status quo that it is legitimate to ask whether British politics, in common with other European polities, is undergoing a state of flux in which the eventual direction of change is as yet impossible to predict.

COLLAPSE OF THE CENTRE GROUND – A EUROPEAN PERSPECTIVE

For years, Europe has been dominated by centrist parties of left and right and electoral victory has consequently been associated with those parties which sat squarely in that part of the spectrum. Not anymore. The collapse of the centre ground has been caused by the impact of such factors as: perceptions of the trans-national super-rich; mass migration of workers from poorer to richer countries; the remoteness of the political elites; and, especially, the long-standing failures of European governments to solve the 2009 economic crisis caused by the bankers in any way except the imposition of auster-ity. In consequence we see the traditional power holders all over

Europe forced on the defensive by an insurgent group of left- and especially right-wing extremists. The results of the 2014 European elections, with UKIP winning in the UK, saw the latter making huge inroads. Ian Traynor, writing in *The Observer*, 16 November 2014, said that the shift to parliaments with party systems involving five, six or seven parties, rather than just two or three, 'has been a long time in the gestation', but that the process was accelerated by the economic crisis from 2007–08 onwards:

> What started as a financial and currency emergency has morphed into a broader political, social and economic crisis, with Europe mired in stagnation and deflation, no growth, no jobs and the mainstream elites struggling to come up with answers.

In Italy Beppe Grillo, a former stand-up comedian, has led his Five Star Movement to 20% of seats in the Italian parliament. We see in Austria, Ireland and Germany a drastic weakening of the centrist parties: Austria's centre left and centre right in permanent coalition to exclude the far right; Germany's Merkel forming a 'grand coalition' with Social Democrats for five of her nine years in power; and in Ireland Fine Gael and Fianna Fail combining to contain a resurgent Sinn Fein. In Sweden and Denmark, the reaction to the emergence of right-wing insurgent parties has been to persevere with minority governments. Cameron must have hidden a grim smile when he observed how the man he opposed as president of the European Commission, Jean-Claude Juncker, was being pilloried for turning his native Luxembourg into a tax haven beloved of multinational companies. Fortunately for Juncker, when being questioned in the European Parliament, the ranks of centre-left and centre-right members came to his rescue.

THE 'HOLLOWING OUT' OF THE UK POLITICAL SYSTEM

DECLINE OF SUPPORT FOR MAIN PARTIES

In the 1950 general election the Conservative and Labour parties won 97% of the vote and shares over 90% continued into the 1960s.

But the Liberal Party then began to improve its vote, so that in 1974 it polled 19.3%; together with the rise of the nationalist vote, this reduced the two main parties' share to 75.1%. The formation of the Liberal–Social Democratic Alliance in the 1980s saw the 'third party' share rise to 25.4% in 1983 and the two main parties reduced to 70% of the total. The Alliance morphed into the Liberal Democrats in 1988 but its share still neared one-fifth of all voters, with the nationalist vote steadily climbing. In 2010 Labour and Tories' joint share was 65.1%, with Lib Dems on 23% and 'others', including the nationalists, 11.9%.

When both main parties collectively struggle to command two-thirds of the vote, it is so much harder for them to muster the required 50% of seats for an overall majority. So we saw in 2010 that government was possible only via the joining of the Lib Dems' 23% to the Tories' 36.1% in the first post-war peacetime coalition. Many believed that this development was so entrenched that Tories and Labour could never again win an overall majority. Certainly, the polls leading up to the 2015 election, showing a dead-heat between the two big parties, reinforced this belief. But, as so often in politics, real life confounded solid consensus when the Conservatives won a shock victory in 2015, winning an overall majority of 12. In June of the same year, a last-minute Labour leadership candidate, Jeremy Corbyn, whose 32 years on the back benches had scarcely altered his hard-left beliefs, was the recipient of a tidal wave of support which carried him to a 59% first-round victory. The left-wing surge already witnessed in Greece and Spain seemed to have arrived belatedly in the UK but with no less devastating effect.

PARTY MEMBERSHIP

In the 1950s party membership totalled close to 3 million; by 1981 it had halved and more recently both big parties have mustered under 200,000 (see Table 21.1). However, there was a surge in Labour's membership (including affiliates and 'supporters') in 2015, fuelled by enthusiasm for Corbyn, and the figure rose to over 500,000.

Meanwhile, the membership of the Scottish National Party (SNP) leapt to over 100,000 at the end of 2014 and membership of the UK Independence Party (UKIP) doubled from 2013 to over 40,000; even

Table 21.1 Party membership, 1951–2011

Year	Conservatives	Labour	Liberal Democrats
1951	2,900,000	876,000	
1971	1,300,000	700,000	
1981	1,200,000	277,000	
1991	1,000,000 to 500,000	261,000	91,000
2001	311,000	272,000	73,000
2011	177,000	190,000	66,000

Source: Estimates based on party reports and House of Commons Library.

more surprising, Green Party membership actually exceeded that of UKIP in early 2015. Given the 'Corbyn effect' on Labour, the referendum effect on the SNP, not to mention burgeoning membership for the Greens and, paradoxically, the pulverised Liberal Democrats, the hollowing-out process in terms of party membership seemed to have been at least partially reversed during 2014–15.

As detailed in Chapter 7, on political parties, there has been, over the past five or six decades, a dramatic decline in people who identify strongly with their political party, as shown in Figure 21.1.

TURNOUT

A further sign of UK democracy in decline has been falling levels of participation in elections. In 1950 turnout was 85%; it remained in the 70s until 1997, when it sank to 71% and then plunged to 59% in 2001. From then it has partially recovered, to 65% in 2010, but the old days of high turnout seem to have gone. But if voters are asked a question which really matters to them they will still come out to vote, as the 85% turnout in the Scottish independence referendum demonstrated. The loss of female votes is especially marked. Between 1992 and 2010 the number of women voting in general elections fell by 18% and in 2010 more than 9.1 million women failed to vote; worryingly, only 39% of women in the 18–24 age cohort voted, compared with 50% for men. Leading up to the 2015 election, efforts were made to encourage the over a million citizens not registered to vote, with some limited success. Turnout in this

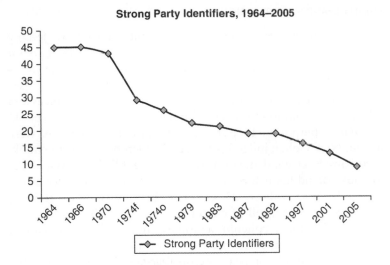

Figure 21.1 Decline of strong party allegiance

Source: P. Dunleavy and C. Gilson, Is the UK electorate disengaged?, LSE Blog, 6 May 2010.

election worked out on average at 66.1%, nowhere near the levels of 20 years previously, but at least a slight increase on 2010. However, this average masked big differences: over-55s registered a turnout of over 75% while the youngest age group, 18–24, the voters of the future, managed only 44%.

TRUST

This quality, indicating the degree of belief voters have in their leaders, has plummeted over the last 10–20 years. In 2009, the year of the MPs' expenses scandal, Sir Robert Worcester, founder of MORI, commented (*Observer*, 27 September 2014):

> Politicians talk about 'restoring trust in politicians'. [But] for the last four or five years only about one person in four has said they trust politicians to tell the truth. This year, following the expenses scandal, politicians hit a 25-year low, with just 13% of the public saying they have faith in what politicians say.

RUSSELL BRAND'S INTERVENTION

On 23 October 2013, the comedian, interviewed by Jeremy Paxman on *Newsnight*, excoriated political elites as totally ignorant of the society in which they live and as controlled by the moneyed minority who were responsible for the 2008 economic crisis. He claimed it was not worth voting in present circumstances and called for a revolution to reverse this state of affairs. His 2014 book, *Revolution*, purported to elaborate his ideas but reviewers were mixed. Nick Cohen judged (*Observer*, 26 October 2014) the book: 'atrocious: long-winded, confused and smug; filled with references to books Brand has half read and thinkers he has half understood'. Owen Jones (*Guardian*, 23 October 2014) was more positive: '*Revolution* is funny, full of charm, and engaging. Is it a thorough textbook detailing a coherent alternative new society? No, and let me know when someone strings that together.' My own impression, gained from his appearance on *Question Time* (11 December 2014), was that Brand is certainly sincere but that his thinking is patently muddled; however, by expressing what so many people, particularly the young, are strongly feeling, he helped to initiate an important debate.

DEMOCRACY FAILING, SAY BISHOPS

On 18 February 2015, *The Guardian* led with an attack by the Church of England on Britain's political culture. Its open letter warned that 'our democracy is failing', one symptom being the 'growing appetite to exploit grievances and find scapegoats in society'; the letter called for ' fresh moral vision of the kind of country we want to be'. In an attack aimed at the coalition government it argued, 'There is a deep contradiction in the attitudes of a society which celebrates equality in principle yet treats some people, especially the poor and vulnerable, as unwanted, unvalued and unnoticed'. Referring to Brand's intervention, the Reverend Graham Jones, Bishop of Norwich, said 'Russell Brand telling people that they should not bother to vote has had a profound effect, while the bishops don't have the sex appeal of Brand, we think that we should counter it'.

FRAGMENTATION OF POLITICAL PARTIES

May 2010 saw the drawing into government of Britain's traditional 'third party' but in the present day we have seen the strengthening of nationalist parties, plus, on the right, UKIP, and, on the left, the Greens. In 1950 Tories and Labour took 90% of the votes but in 2010 this had reduced to 65%, meaning that the ability of either to win half of the Commons seats is hugely reduced and making coalitions increasingly likely.

DEVOLUTION

This is something which has been catalysed by the referendum on Scottish independence, 18 September 2014. That cause was defeated 55–45 but two aspects will maybe prove legacies of the campaign and the energies thereby generated. Firstly, the extra devolution measures promised by UK party leaders as voting day approached prompted a demand from UK MPs, especially on the right of the Conservative Party, especially John Redwood. He insisted on 'English votes for English laws' (EVEL), which had a powerful political motive of rendering Scottish Labour MPs powerless to rule the UK as a whole. Secondly, there were calls from local government leaders, especially Sir Richard Leese, for matching devolution for English regions. Regional devolution had been explored via a referendum in 2004 in the north-east and it was roundly rejected, 4–1.

Now, however, the idea seemed to have absorbed some of the super-charged energy of the Scottish 'yes' campaign. Coincidentally both major parties had been formulating new devolution policies based on giving wide-ranging new powers to cities and their hinterlands. This was quite a step, as the UK is the most fiscally centralised of the major OECD nations, with 95% of all taxation in the hands of the Treasury, while the remaining 5% (council tax) is frozen and capped. Manchester had already formed a collective body for all the council leaders of the 10 boroughs of Greater Manchester but new powers were to be given to an elected mayor for the whole of that region. That mayor's powers were to be 'most of the powers of the mayor of London' plus responsibility for skills and further education. Elections will use the supplementary vote as used in London and other mayoral elections.

Almost inevitably this renewal of interest in devolution of increased powers to the regions will have a knock-on effect with other city regions – Leeds, Birmingham, Bristol, Newcastle – eager to negotiate and enjoy the same privileges. Tony Travers noted that the powers allowed by Osborne will be subject to some controls from the centre but remarked that 'in a country as centralised as England, any offer of greater devolution has to be encouraged' (LSE Blog, 7 November 2014).

UKIP

An aspect of the above fragmentation has been the rapid emergence of the UK Independence Party. An authoritative academic study on UKIP's membership (Ford and Goodwin, 2015) revealed that UKIP disproportionately attracts voters who are older, poorly educated and paid, white and *angry*! This is a group of voters, often formerly employed in defunct traditional industries, who felt ignored and left behind and resented the growth of immigrant groups in their communities. Initially, support was seen to shift in southern constituencies held by the Conservatives, but, as Ford and Goodwin warned, this group crucially belong to Labour's core vote; in the Middleton and Heywood by-election on 9 October 2014, UKIP accordingly nearly destroyed a massive 2010 Labour majority by coming within a few hundred votes of winning.

On 21 November 2014 Tory MP Mark Reckless, who had defected to UKIP, won his by-election in Rochester and Strood by a huge majority, in the process reducing Labour's share from 29% to 16% in a constituency which until 2010 it had held. In his victory speech Reckless bizarrely claimed continuity with the Radical traditions of the Diggers and the Levellers, an association more usually claimed by Keir Hardie or the late Tony Benn. That he felt he could make such a statement is further evidence of UKIP's confidence it can win over the Labour vote, despite its mostly right-wing policies.

UKIP's phenomenal rise since 2010 has been on the back of immigration as an issue: from registering low down in that year it has more recently come a narrow second only to the economy in voter concerns. Andrew Rawnsley (*Observer*, 16 November 2014) cites a study done by the left-of-centre think-tank British Future. This found that the 'rejectionist minority' – those who 'would close all borders, or even send all migrants back' – is no more than 25% of all voters. The majority of voters are not 'desperate' to put an end to all immigration, but neither necessarily wanting more of it. Rather,

> they are worried about the impacts on jobs, public services and on the 'Britishness' of our culture; but aware of the benefits to our economy. Nigel Farage likes to claim that he speaks for 'the silent majority'. He is actually the megaphone of a noisy minority.

WILL UKIP REAP RICH REWARDS?

In 1983 it seemed the new Social Democratic Party (SDP), having garnered 26% of the vote, might sweep all before it in the next election. Enoch Powell predicted that 'like the snow in springtime, its support will melt away'. And it did, not entirely of course, but certainly as a serious challenge to the existing order of the time. Labour's Dick Taverne, when threatened with de-selection, stood down and re-fought his constituency, winning by a margin of 12,000 in March 1973. He held the seat in February 1974 but lost in October 1974 to Margaret Beckett. Thus do general elections offer different options to voters compared with by-elections, where protest votes or just the novelty of the event can cause voters to change their normal voting behaviour.

There is some evidence that UKIP voters and supporters are unaware of what their party believes in. For example, the party supports re-nationalisation of the railways, something wholly at odds with its otherwise far-right economic policies. Few members seem to be aware their party is funded by right-wing billionaires or even that their leader is a public-school-educated former banker. The party's performance in the 2015 election, however, was impressive – it won 12.6% of the vote (4 million in total) – yet pathetic in winning only one seat, that of Carswell, Mark Reckless's seat having gone the way of Taverne's back in 1974.

LABOUR'S PROBLEMS:

As with the Tories after their 2005 defeat, some pundits are forecasting the ending of Labour as an election winning organisation in

British politics. Certainly its collapse in Scotland (see Chapter 12), its failure in winning key marginal seats in England and the large bites into its support taken by UKIP and the Greens suggest it has an acutely uphill struggle. Ed Miliband resigned after his defeat in the 2015 general election and opened up an astonishing contest. Labour was unsure which way to turn: going back to 'New Labour' by embracing business and eschewing left-wing policies risked alienating the support of its core and potential converts from the Greens, and possibly even UKIP, while a further shift to the left suggested another likely rejection by voters in 2020. The party maybe needed a leader with the charisma and persuasive power of Tony Blair, without his apparent tendencies both to over-reach himself and to embrace material wealth. What they received, however, as noted above, was the triumphal progress of a little-known back-bencher through a long campaign in all parts of the country, to the highest throne of Labour's leadership. The energy injected into Labour by thousands of new and rejoined members might well revive a party still in the shadow of the massive May 2015 defeat. However, if Corbyn survives until the 2020 election, some predict he will preside over a defeat as sweeping as that suffered by Nick Clegg's party in 2015.

THE LIBERAL DEMOCRATS' PROBLEMS

The Lib Dems arguably took a brave step in joining a coalition in which they were the junior partner. They hoped they would gain credit for their 'responsible' actions and 'success' in government. Unfortunately for them, this did not at all work out as hoped. They were initially badly hit by the fact that so many senior figures had publicly signed a pledge not to increase tuition fees for university students. When they supported a tripling of such fees they lost much credibility with both students and the general public. The referendum on the alternative vote (AV) was supposed to be their 'payback' from Cameron for supporting the coalition but soon after the campaign started Cameron reversed his alleged promise to take a back seat and campaigned at the front of the anti-AV cause: it won 2–1. Clegg won back a modicum of respect by refusing to endorse a redrawing of constituency boundaries when Tory MPs refused to support his plans for reforming the Lords. On the evening of 7 May,

2015 Liberal Democrats could not believe the BBC exit poll which predicted a loss over 40 seats but as events unfolded they were forced to accept a defeat of humiliating proportions, ending up with just eight MPs. In July Tim Farron was elected as new leader of this much-diminished band of MPs but at their September conference he took heart that with an all-Tory government and a far-left new Labour regime, the centre ground was wide open to be filled by his own moderate, financially responsible progressive party.

GENERATIONAL DIVIDE

Few would deny that the so-called 'baby boomer' generation – those born immediately after World War II – have led charmed lives. They have benefited from: free higher education, plentiful work opportunities during the 1960s and 1970s, the decline of sexual taboos, access to affordable housing and the improvement in longevity assisted by improved medical provision. During the coalition's time in government after 2010, favoured treatment continued, with maintenance of senior citizen privileges like free prescriptions, free local bus transport, annual winter fuel allowances and increased pensions. A report from the Institute for Fiscal Studies (IFS) in early March 2015 revealed how younger strata have suffered by comparison: hugely increased university tuition fees; 15–20 years of saving required for a deposit for a flat or house as prices have soared, leading to a halving of home ownership for 25-year-olds; plus an overall salary loss of 8% for those in their 20s. During the election campaign neither of the big parties offered much to younger cohorts, but chose instead to continue the cosseting of senior citizens whose voting behaviour has proved so regularly way above the average.

CONSERVATIVE PARTY

The Conservative Party have led a difficult path from May 2010, accepting coalition and pursuing an unpopular deficit reduction policy which seems not to be working, in that a deficit which we were initially told would be cleared by now is still substantially there.

Cameron led the coalition with some aplomb and showed elements of great political skill plus arguably some incompetence. Some in his party have still not forgiven him for not winning the election he 'should have won' in 2010 when an unpopular prime minister led a discredited party. Often such critics condemn his acceptance of the television debates which allowed Clegg to shine, if briefly (in retrospect this was possibly the high point of Clegg's political career). These same critics could never truly accept the 'compassionate Conservatism plus big society' version of their party, even though very little ever came of this mostly rhetorical foray into alien territory and that it was largely abandoned after a few months in power.

Europe, once again, has been the bane of the Conservative Party, with perhaps 100 Tory MPs in favour of withdrawal while Cameron, of necessity close to the business community, wants to stay within but only, says he, after reforms have been made. His time as prime minister has been characterised by assiduous wooing of and careful obedience to his Euro-sceptic right wing. So he vetoed the EU's plan to solve the euro-zone crisis; he vetoed the appointment of Jean-Claude Juncker as president of the Commission – to no avail; he shadowed UKIP's line on immigration throughout the autumn of 2014 to counter UKIP's by-election challenges; and, most important, he promised an in–out referendum on the EU by 2017.

In December 2014, Osborne announced in his 'autumn statement' that further deep cuts to public expenditure were necessary. The Office of Budget Responsibility, set up by Osborne himself, announced such cuts would be likely to return public spending back to the pre-welfare state levels of the 1930s. Liberal Democrats like David Laws condemned the proposed cuts as 'a political suicide note'. Osborne's cabinet colleague Vince Cable weighed in by telling Andrew Marr:

> There is a table in the documentation behind the autumn statement which suggests that if the plans were realised we would roughly halve the total spending on the Home Office, i.e. the police, on the defence services, and our armed forces would, arguably, become almost ceremonial.

COALITION GOVERNMENT

The United Kingdom experienced five years of coalition government. Many doubted the May 2010 coalition would survive for more than a few months, but in practice it proved to be as strong as many one-party governments in the past. The level of cooperation and cordiality between the Lib Dems and the Conservatives varied over time, encountering difficult obstacles, especially concerning reform of the voting system, House of Lords reform as well as the redrawing of constituency boundaries. But it survived the whole five years and set a precedent of sorts for the future.

Steve Richards in *The Independent* in December 2014, argued that all these apparent major changes in British politics might be a mirage: 'We are on an anti-politics helter-skelter ride, but after the trip is over, the broad political landscape might look more or less the same as it did when we began'. Richards deserves some credit for anticipating the shock result of an overall majority and maybe even Labour's return to a once-rejected philosophy, but many of the changes identified above are of long standing and will continue to influence British politics for the foreseeable future.

One possible legacy of the 2015 election results might just be a renewed emphasis on electoral reform. Andrew Rawnsley in *The Observer*, 31 May, 2015, pointed out the absurdity of the outcome. The Conservatives received 36.9% of the vote yet won over 50% of the seats; nearly two-thirds of voters did not vote for them. Half of Scotland's voters did not want the SNP yet this party won 56 of the 59 available seats and all this on only 4.7% of the UK vote. At the other end of the spectrum the Greens won 3.8% of the vote (1.16 million in total) yet won only one seat; even more absurd, UKIP won 3.88 million votes yet also came away with only one seat. If the Lib Dems' 2.4 million votes had won seats proportionately, they would have ended up with a respectable 51. Rawnsley notes that in the wake of the election a petition bearing the names of half a million people was handed in to Number 10 Downing Street, the address described by him as the 'least likely to be interested in changing the way we elect governments':

> David Cameron . . . has just converted a minority of the vote into all the spoils of power. When he looks at first past the post, far from seeing a broken system, he sees one that has just worked perfectly for him.

QUESTIONS FOR DISCUSSION

1. How correct is it to say Britain now has a multi-party political system?
2. Did the 2015 election result provide a damning verdict on the 'first past the post' electoral system?
3. What is required to restore British voters' faith in their politicians?
4. How receptive are UK voters to Jeremy Corbyn's ideas?

FURTHER READING

There are several journalistic analyses worth reading but possibly the best on why Labour lost as it did is by Patrick Wintour (2015). Other pieces worth reading include Dunleavy and Gilson (2010); McVeigh and Helm (2015), Rawnsley (2015), and, for a provocative wide angle perspective see, Richards (2014).

Dunleavy, P. and Gilson, C. (2010) Is the UK electorate disengaged?, *LSE Blog*, 6 May.

Ford, R. and Goodwin, M. (2015) *Revolt on the Right: Explaining Support for the Radical Right in Britain*, Routledge.

McVeigh, T. and Helm, T. (2015) Female candidates are on the rise – but why aren't women voting?, *Observer*, 8 March.

Rawnsley, A. (2015) The real reason David Cameron is sitting on a Commons majority, *Observer*, 31 May.

Richards, S. (2014) Our political landscape is not changing anywhere near as much as we assume it is, *Independent*, 24 November.

Wintour, P. (2015) The undoing of Ed Miliband, *Guardian*, 4 June.

GLOSSARY

Accountable: the requirement to take responsibility for one's actions and make redress when appropriate.

Anarchism: an approach to politics which rejects the need for the state and its coercive institutions.

Ancien régime: the monarchic, aristocratic, social and political system established in the Kingdom of France from the fifteenth century until the later eighteenth century under the late Valois and Bourbon dynasties.

Authoritarianism: a highly directive system of government where rulers make decisions without the explicit consent of the population.

Autocratic: a domineering style which takes no account of other people's wishes or interests.

Bill: name given to a legislative proposal before it has passed through the parliamentary procedures.

Bourgeoisie: name given by Karl Marx to the property-owning middle classes.

Broadsheets: name given to 'quality' newspapers aimed at a more educated audience and which traditionally came in this larger size.

By-election: single-constituency election held when a vacancy arises in the House of Commons.

Cabinet: the supreme committee of government chaired by the prime minister.

Canvassing: practice used by political activists of making contact with voters in their homes.

Capitalism: term used by Karl Marx for an economic system comprising an unregulated market, private property, investment in projects and a workforce who produce profit for the owner in return for wages.

Centrist: someone whose political beliefs are in the middle of the accepted left–right continuum.

Coalition: when two or more political parties combine to form a joint government.

Communism: a system of government in which all property is held in common and, in theory at least, all people are free and are treated equally and fairly.

Constituency: the name given to electoral registration and voting districts in the UK (there were 650 in all in 2015).

Constitutional monarch: a monarch constrained by the terms of a constitution. In the case of Britain, this leaves virtually no political power but a good deal of ceremony plus public acclaim and affection.

Core executive: political science term for the apex of decision-makers, including prime minister and cabinet plus top civil servants and political aides.

Cultural revolution: term used for the overthrow of cultural values and practices during the 1960s.

Democracy: system of government in which all the people are involved, if only through the act of voting.

Devolution: the transfer of governmental authority from the centre to the regions.

Direct democracy: system of democracy – possible only for small communities – which directly involves all members of a social group.

Divine right: the idea that a monarch had a holy right to succeed to the throne.

Electorate: all people in a country with the right to vote.

Énarques: graduates of the elite French École nationale d'administration.

Euro-sceptic: those opposing the European Union, even to the point of advocating national withdrawal.

Executive: the function of running government on a day-to-day basis.

Executive agency: a generic term for any government body but given a specific sense by the recommendations of the 1988 Ibbs report, which led to the establishment of the 'Next Steps' agencies.

Fabian: member of the Fabian Society, established 1884 and dedicated to progress towards socialism through gradual change.

False consciousness: Marxist idea that most people are 'brainwashed' in capitalist society into supporting its dominant values.

Fascist: right-wing ideology based on authoritarian nationalism.

First past the post: voting system whereby the candidate receiving the most votes wins the contest however many failed to give their support. Used famously in the UK and the USA.

Franchise: right or eligibility to vote.

Free speech: the freedom to express one's views, even if they are unpopular.

Gini coefficient: the measure of income distribution across a country's citizens.

Hereditary: titles in House of Lords used to be passed down by inheritance before 1998.

Human rights: entitlements everyone is believed to be born with, such as the rights to life and free speech.

Hung parliament: situation after an election, as in May 2010, where no party has an overall majority.

Judiciary: the legal system, including law courts, judges and courts of appeal.

King's court: in medieval times this was the 1000 or so people who surrounded the king, advising, serving, entertaining, helping him and his family in whatever ways were required

Legislature: the law-making assembly of a political system.

Legitimation: to give legal force to; make legal in appearance and substance.

Levellers: radical group who argued for democracy in wake of the English Civil War.

Manifesto: document issued by a political party during an election campaign containing policy pledges it claims it will implement if it wins the election.

Marginal: a constituency where a swing in voting behaviour of a few percentage points will change the party which controls it.

Poll: a survey of attitudes applied to a sample of people representative of society as a whole and thus likely to have predictive value for how people will vote in elections.

Pressure group: a body comprising people who perceive common interests who seek to influence specific government policies.

Quasi-autonomous non-governmental organisations (quangos): public bodies which advise or administer government activities and which carry out their work at arm's length from government control, although they still ultimately operate under ministerial control.

Referendum: a ballot in which voters usually have a 'yes/no' choice, in British cases usually on a constitutional issue (as in the Scottish independence referendum in 2014) or a major political question (as in the planned one on membership of the European Union by 2017).

Representative democracy: government whereby decisions are taken by people who are (normally) elected by popular vote to represent substantial groups of fellow citizens.

Sectarian: concerning members of sects, denominations, or other (usually religious) groups.

Sovereignty: autonomy over national decision-making or the ultimate legal authority within a state.

Spin doctor: a politically appointed official specialising in the management of a senior politician's media activities.

Westminster: the area of London containing the Houses of Parliament and therefore used to denote central UK government.

Whip: a party official appointed to manage the activities of that party's members of a legislature, especially voting according to party policy.

Whitehall: a street in London on which is located much of the government bureaucracy and therefore used generically to denote the departments of state run by civil servants.

BIBLIOGRAPHY

Adler, J. (2005) *Constitutional and Administrative Law*, Palgrave.

Adonis, A. and Pollard, S. (1997) *A Class Act: The Myth of Britain's Classless Society*, Penguin.

Almond, G. and Verba, S. (1965) *The Civic Culture*, Little, Brown.

Altrincham, Lord, *et al.* (1958) *Is the Monarchy Perfect?*, John Calder.

Ashford, N. and Timms, D. (1992) *What Europe Thinks: A Study of Western European Values*, Dartmouth.

Atkinson, A. B. (2015) *Inequality*, Harvard University Press.

Bagehot, W. (2001) *The English Constitution*, Oxford University Press.

Baldwin, N. D. J. (2005) *Parliament in the twenty-first Century*, Politicos.

Bale, T. (2011) *The Conservative Party from Thatcher to Cameron*, Polity.

Banner, C. and Deane, A. (2003) *Off With Their Heads: Judicial Revolution in Modern Britain*, Imprint Academic.

Barberis, P. (ed.) (1997) *The Civil Service in an Era of Change*, Dartmouth.

Barnett, A. (1997) *This Time: Our Constitutional Revolution*, Vintage.

Barnett, J. (1982) *Inside the Treasury*, Deutsch.

Beech, M. and Lee, S. (eds) (2011) *The Cameron–Clegg Government*, Palgrave.

Beer, S. (1982) *Britain Against Itself: Political Contradictions of Collectivism*, Faber.

Beer, S. (1982) *Modern British Politics*, Faber.

Black, J. (2000) *Modern British History Since 1900*, Macmillan.

Blair, A. L. (1999) The Blair doctrine, at http://www.pbs.org/newshour/bb/international-jan-june99-blair_doctrine4-23.

Blunkett, D. (2006) *The Blunkett Tapes*, Bloomsbury.

Bogdanor, V. (1995) *The Monarchy and the Constitution*, Oxford University Press.

Bogdanor, V. (2009) *The New British Constitution*, Hart.

Bond, J. (2012) *The Diamond Queen*, Carlton Publishing.

Bootle, R. (2015) *The Trouble With Europe: Why the EU Isn't Working, How It Can Be Reformed, What Could Take Its Place?*, Nicholas Brealey.

Bradbury, J. (2009) *Devolution, Regionalism and Regional Development*, Routledge.

Bradley, A. W. and Ewing, K. D. (1997) *Constitutional and Administrative Law*, Longman.

Brazier, R. (1994) *Constitutional Practice*, Oxford University Press.

Brazier, R. (1997) *Ministers of the Crown*, Clarendon Press.

Browne, J. (2014) *Liberal Democracy*, Biteback.

Bulpitt, J. (1983) *Territory and Power in the United Kingdom*, Manchester University Press.

Burch, M. and Wood, B. (1990) *Public Policy in Britain*, Martin Robertson.

Burnham, J. and Pyper, R. (2008) *The Modernised British Civil Service*, Palgrave.

Butler, D. E. and Stokes, D. (1974) *Political Change in Britain* (2nd edition), Macmillan.

Byrd, P. (1988) *British Foreign Policy Under Thatcher*, Manchester University Press.

Byrne, L. (2015) How Labour rebuilds the radical centre, *Sunday Times*, 14 June.

Cabinet Office (2010) *The Ministerial Code*, Cabinet Office.

Cadwalladr, C. (2008) It's the clever way to power, *Observer*, 16 March.

Carrell, S., Watt, N. and Wintour, P. (2014) The real story of the Scottish referendum, *Guardian*, 16 and 17 December.

Carswell, D. (2012) *The End of Politics and the Birth of iDemocracy*, Biteback.

Castles, F. (1982) *The Impact of Parties*, Sage.

Chandler, J. A. (2009) *Local Government Today*, Manchester University Press.

Chippendale, P. and Orrie, C. (1992) *Stick It Up Your Punter*, Mandarin.

Clark, T. (2014) *Hard Times: The Divisive Toll of the Economic Slump*, Yale University Press.

Clarke, A. (2012) *Political Parties in the UK*, Palgrave.

Clarke, C. (ed.) (2014) *The Too Difficult Box: The Big Issues Politicians Can't Crack*, Biteback.

Clarke, H., Sanders, D., Stewart, D. and Whiteley, P. (2009) *Performance Politics and the British Voter*, Cambridge University Press.

Cohen, Y. (2015) *The British Reverence Towards Nationality*, Priests Publishing.

Constitution Unit (1996) *Reform of the House of Lords*, University College London.

Cooper, R. (2006) War and democracy, *Prospect Magazine*, June.

Copus, C. (2013) *Leading the Localities: Executive Mayors in English Local Governance*, Manchester University Press.

Copus, C. (2014) Local government, in B. Jones and P. Norton (eds), *Politics UK*, Routledge.

Crick, B. (2000) *In Defence of Politics*, Continuum.

Criddle, B. and Norton, P. (2005) The make-up of Parliament, in P. Giggings (ed.), *The Future of Parliament*, Palgrave.

Crump, T. (2010) *How the Industrial Revolution Changed the World*, Robinson.

Deacon, R. (2006) *Devolution in Britain Today*, Manchester University Press.

Deacon, R. (2012) *Devolution in the United Kingdom* (Politics Study Guides), Edinburgh University Press.

Denver, D. (2012) *Elections and Voting in Britain*, Palgrave.

Denver, D. and Garnett, M. (2014) *British General Elections Since 1964*, Palgrave.

Dorey, P. (2014) *Policy Making in Britain* (2nd edition), Sage.

Dorling, D. (2014) *Inequality and the 1%*, Verso.

Downs, A. (1957) *An Economic Theory of Democracy*, Harper and Row.

Driver, S. (2011) *Understanding Party Politics*, Polity.

Dunleavy, P. and Gilson, C. (2010) Is the UK electorate disengaged?, *LSE Blog*, 6 May.

Eagleton, T. (2011) *Why Marx Was Right*, Yale University Press.

Easton, D. (1965) *A Framework for Political Analysis*, Prentice Hall.

Elliot, L. (2015) The regions cannot thrive with Whitehall in charge, *Guardian*, 19 January.

Evans, S. (2014) *UKIP*, Biteback.

Farrell, D. (2011) *Electoral Systems: A Comparative Study*, Palgrave.

Ferguson, N. (2004) *Empire*, Allen Lane.

Financial Times (2015) *Britain and the EU – In or Out?*, Financial Times.

Fitzpatrick, A. (2011) *The End of the Peer Show?*, Constitution Society/Centre Forum.

Foley, M. (1999) *The Politics of the British Constitution*, Manchester University Press.

Ford, R. and Goodwin, M. (2015) *Revolt on the Right: Explaining Support for the Radical Right in Britain*, Routledge.

Frank, R. (2007) *Richistan*, Piatkus.

Gamble, A. (2003) *Between Europe and America: The Future of British Politics*, Palgrave.

Golden, A. (2000) *Everyday Law*, Dealerfield.

Grant, W. (1989) *Pressure Groups, Politics and Democracy in Britain*, Phillip Allan.

Grant, W. (2000) *Pressure Groups and Politics*, Macmillan.

Griffiths, J. A. G. (2010) *Politics of the Judiciary* (5th edition), Fontana.

Hall, P. (1999) Social capital in Britain, *British Journal of Political Science*, 29(3): 417–461.

Halsey, A. and Webb, J. (eds) (2000) *Twentieth Century Social Trends*, Macmillan.

Ham, C. and Hill, M. (1998) *The Policy Process of a Modern Capitalist State*, Wheatsheaf.

Hardie, F. (1970) *The Political Influence of the British Monarchy 1868–1952*, Batsford.

Haseler, S. (2012) *The Grand Delusion*, I. B. Tauris.

Hennessy, P. (1986) *Cabinet*, Blackwell.

Hennessy, P. (1992) *Never Again*, Jonathan Cape.

Hennessy, P. (2001) *Whitehall*, Pimlico.

Hennessy, P. (2006) *Having It So Good*, Allen Lane.

Herbert, N. (2014) *Conservatives*, Biteback.

Heywood, A. (1998) *Political Ideologies*, Macmillan.

Hills, J. (2014) *Good Times, Bad Times: The Welfare Myth of Them and Us*, Policy Press.

Hilton, S. (2015) *More Human*, W. H. Allen.

Hoffman, J. and Graham, P. (2006) *Introduction to Political Theory*, Pearson.

Hogwood, B. (1992) *Trends in British Public Policy*, Open University Press.

House of Commons Library (2013) *Members of Parliament 1979–2010* (House of Commons Library Document), House of Commons.

Hutton, W. (2014) Right of centre ideology has lost us the war in Afghanistan and much else besides, *Observer*, 28 December.

Institute for Public Policy Research (1992) *A New Constitution for the United Kingdom*, Mansell.

James, L. (2006) *The Middle Class: A History*, Abacus.

James, S. (1999) *British Cabinet Government*, Routledge.

Jarvis, D. (2014) *Labour*, Biteback.

Jenkins, S. (2008) Instead of elected local leaders, we have the police, *Guardian*, 27 February.

Jenkins, S. (2012) *A Short History of England*, Profile.

Jenkins, S. (2015) The secret negotiations to restore Manchester to greatness, *Guardian*, 12 February.

Jones, B. (2004) *Dictionary of British Politics*, Manchester University Press.

Jones, B. and Kavanagh, D. (1994) *British Politics Today* (5th edition), Manchester University Press.

Jones, B. and Norton, P. (2013) *Politics UK* (8th edition), Routledge.

Jones, N. (1995) *Sound-Bites and Spin Doctors*, Indigo.

Jones, N. (1999) *Sultans of Spin: The Media and the New Labour Government*, Orion.

Jones, O. (2012) *Chavs: The Demonisation of the Working Class*, Verso.

Jones, O. (2014) *The Establishment*, Allen Lane.

Jordan, G. and Richardson, J. J. (1987) *Governing Under Pressure*, Martin Robertson.

Kampner, J. (2014) *The Rich: From Slaves to Super-Yachts – A 200 Year History*, Little, Brown.

Kaufman, G. (1997) *How To Be a Minister*, Faber.

Kavanagh, D. (1972) *Political Culture*, Oxford University Press.

Kavanagh, D. and Seldon, A. (1999) *The Powers Behind the Prime Minister*, Harper Collins.

Kennedy, P. (1989) *The Rise and Fall of Great Powers*, Random House.

King, A. (ed.) (1985) *The British Prime Minister*, Macmillan.

King, A. (2015) *Who Governs Britain?*, Pelican.

Kingdom, J. (2014) *Government and Politics in Britain*, Polity.

Kureishi, H. (2011) *Collected Essays*, Faber.

Kynaston, D. (2007) *Austerity Britain, 1945–51*, Bloomsbury.

Kynaston, D. (2008) The road to meritocracy is blocked by private schools, *Guardian*, 22 February.

Lansley, S. (2012) *The Cost of Inequality*, Gibson Square.

Lansley, S. and Mack, J. (2015) *Breadline Britain*, Oneworld.

Lasswell, H. (1936) *Who Gets What, Where, When and How?*, McGraw-Hill.

Lawson, N. (1992) *The View From Number 11*, Bantam.

Lee, C. and Dorling, D. (2011) The geography of poverty, *Socialist Review*, October.

Lees-Marchment, J. (2001) *Political Marketing and British Political Parties*, Manchester University Press.

Lindblom, C. (1959) The science of muddling through, *Public Administration Review*, 19(2): 79–88.

Lloyd, J. (2004) *What the Media Are Doing to Our Politics*, Constable.

Lodge, G. and Schmuecker, K. (2010) *Devolution in Practice: Policy Differences in the UK*, IPPR.

Lynne, J. and Jay, A. (1982) *Yes Minister: The Diaries of a Cabinet Minister by the Rt Hon James Hacker MP*, BBC.

Mackenzie, R. and Silver, S. (1968) *Angels in Marble*, Heinemann.

Mackintosh, J. M. (1962) *Cabinet Government*, Stevens.

Mackintosh, J. P. (1962) *The British Cabinet*, Toronto University Press.

Maclean, I. (1996) *Dictionary of Politics*, Oxford University Press.

Mansfield, M. (2003) *The Home Lawyer*, BCA.

Marquand, D. and Seldon, A. (1996) *The Ideas That Shaped Post-War Britain*, Fontana.

Marr, A. (2007) *A History of Modern Britain*, BBC.

Marshall, O. and Laws, D. (2004) *The Orange Book: Reclaiming Liberalism*, Profile Books.

McQuail, D. (1983) *Mass Communication Theory: An Introduction*, Sage.

McVeigh, T. and Helm, T. (2015) Female candidates are on the rise – but why aren't women voting?, *Observer*, 8 March.

Miles, D. (2005) *The Tribes of Britain. Who Are We? And Where Do We Come From?*, Phoenix.

Miliband, E. (2014) The future is local, *Guardian*, 7 July.

Mitchell, J. (2011) *Devolution in the United Kingdom*, Manchester University Press.

Moon, N. (1999) *Opinion Polls: History, Theory and Practice*, Manchester University Press.

Moran, M. (2005) *Politics and Governance in the UK* (1st edition), Palgrave.

Moran, M. (2011) *Politics and Governance in the UK* (2nd edition), Palgrave.

Nolan, Lord and Sedley, Sir S. (1997) *The Making and Remaking of the British Constitution,* Blackstone.

Norton, P. (2011) *A Century of Constitutional Reform in the UK*, Oxford University Press.

Norton, P. (2013) *Parliament in British Politics* (2nd edition), Palgrave Macmillan.

Oborne, P. (2007) *The Triumph of the Political Class*, Simon Schuster.

Oliver, D. and Drewry, G. (1998) *The Law and Parliament*, Cambridge University Press.

Owen, D. (2007) *The Hubris Syndrome: Bush, Blair and the Intoxication of Power*, Methuen.

Parsons, W. (1995) *Public Policy*, Elgar.

Pattie, C., Seyd, P. and Whiteley, P. (2004) *Citizenship in Britain: Values, Participation and Democracy*, Cambridge University Press.

Paxman, J. (2002) *The Political Animal*, Penguin.

Paxman, J. (2007) *On Royalty*, Penguin.

Peston, R. (2008) *Who Runs Britain?*, Hodder.

Piketty, T. (2014) *Capital in the Twenty-First Century*, Harvard University Press.

Pimlott, B. (1996) *The Queen*, Harper Collins.

Prins, G. and Salisbury, R. (2008) Risk, threat and security: the case of the United Kingdom, *RUSI*, 15(1): 22–27.

Pulzer, P. (1967) *Political Representation and Elections in Britain*, George Allen Unwin.

Putnam, R. D. (2000) *Bowling Alone: The Collapse and Revival of American Community*, Simon & Schuster.

Quotrup, M. (2005) *A Comparative Study of Referendums*, Manchester University Press.

Rallings, C. and Thrasher, M. (1997) *Local Elections in Britain*, Routledge.

Rawls, J. (1971) *A Theory of Justice*, Oxford University Press.

Rawnsley, A. (2015) The real reason David Cameron is sitting on a Commons majority, *Observer, 31 May*.

Richards, S. (2014) Our political landscape is not changing anywhere near as much as we assume it is, *Independent*, 24 November.

Robinson, N. (2014) *Live From Downing St*, Bantam.

Rose, R. (ed.) (1974) *Studies in British Politics*, Macmillan.

Rose, R. (2001) *The Prime Minister in a Shrinking World*, Polity.

Rush, M. (2005) *Parliament Today*, Manchester University Press.

Russell, M. (2012) Elected second chambers and their powers – an international survey, *Political Quarterly*, 83(1): 117–129.

Russell, M. (2013) *The Contemporary House of Lords*, Oxford University Press.

Sandel, M. J. (2009) *Justice: What's the Right Thing to Do?*, Penguin.

Schama, S. (2002) *A History of Britain, Vol. III*, BBC Publications.

Schmitter, P. C. (1977) Introduction, *Corporatism and Policy-Making in Western Europe*, special issue of *Contemporary Political Studies*, 10(1): 3–6.

Seldon, A. (2005) *Blair*, Little, Brown.

Seldon, A. (2007) *Blair Unbound*, Simon Schuster.

Seymour-Ure, C. (1991) *The British Press and Broadcasting Since 1945*, Blackwell.

Shell, D. (2007) *The House of Lords*, Manchester University Press.

Smith, A. (2014) *Devolution and the Scottish Conservatives* (New Ethnographies), Manchester University Press.

Smith, M. (1993) *Pressure, Power and Policy*, Harvester Wheatsheaf.

Smith, M. (1999) *The Core Executive in Britain*, Palgrave.

Smith, M., Smith, S. and White, B. (1988) *British Foreign Policy*, Routledge.

Stephen D., Tansey, S. and Jackson, N. (2008) *Politics: The Basics* (4th edition), Routledge.

Stoker, G. (2003) *Transforming Local Governance in the UK*, Palgrave.

Street, J. (2011) *Mass Media: Politics and Democracy*. Palgrave.

Toynbee, P. and Walker, D. (2008) *Unjust Rewards*, Granta.

Turner, A. T. (2014) *A Classless Society: Britain in the 1990s*, Aurum Press.

Tyrie, A. (1998) *Reforming the Lords: A Conservative Approach*, Conservative Policy Forum.

Watts, D. (2003) *Understanding US/UK Government and Politics*, Manchester University Press.

Watts, D. (2007) *Pressure Groups* (Politics Study Guides), Edinburgh University Press.

Wildavsky, A. (1979) *Speaking the Truth to Power*, Little, Brown.

Wilkinson, R. and Pickett, K. (2009) *The Spirit Level*, Penguin.

Wilson, D. and Game, C. (2002) *Local Government in the United Kingdom*, Palgrave.

Wilson, R. (2010) *5 Days to Power*, Biteback.

Windlesham, Lord (2006) The Constitutional Reform Act 2005: ministers, judges and constitutional change, *Public Law*, winter.

Wintour, P. (2015) Joseph Rowntree Foundation report on poverty, *Guardian*, 19 January.

Wintour, P. (2015) The undoing of Ed Miliband, *Guardian*, 4 June.

INDEX